# The Art of Nonfiction Movie Making

# The Art of Nonfiction Movie Making

JEFFREY FRIEDMAN, ROBERT EPSTEIN,
AND SHARON WOOD

Foreword by Michael Fox

 PRAEGER

AN IMPRINT OF ABC-CLIO, LLC
Santa Barbara, California • Denver, Colorado • Oxford, England

Library of Congress Cataloging-in-Publication Data

Friedman, Jeffrey, 1951–
   The art of nonfiction movie making / Jeffrey Friedman, Robert Epstein, and Sharon Wood; foreword by Michael Fox.
     p. cm.
   Includes bibliographical references and index.
   ISBN 978–0–275–99225–5 (cloth : alk. paper) — ISBN 978–0–313–08453–9 (e-book)
1. Documentary films—Production and direction—Handbooks, manuals, etc. I. Epstein, Robert P., 1955– II. Wood, Sharon, 1952– III. Title.
PN1995.9.D6F7363   2012
070.1′8—dc23        2012019878

ISBN: 978–0–275–99225–5
EISBN: 978–0–313–08453–9

16  15  14  13  12    1  2  3  4  5

This book is also available on the World Wide Web as an eBook.
Visit www.abc-clio.com for details.

Praeger
An Imprint of ABC-CLIO, LLC

ABC-CLIO, LLC
130 Cremona Drive, P.O. Box 1911
Santa Barbara, California 93116-1911

This book is printed on acid-free paper ∞

Manufactured in the United States of America

Dedicated to Peter Adair
*Mentor, visionary, and friend*

# Contents

# Foreword

*Michael Fox*

Rob Epstein and Jeffrey Friedman long ago entered the pantheon of American moviemakers for their pioneering contributions to gay identity and history. Honored by Sundance, Oscar, Emmy, and Peabody, the San Francisco-based filmmakers have amassed a deeply moral, difference-making body of work. Yet they've never been credited for their influence on contemporary documentaries, surely one of their signal accomplishments.

When the duo began their careers in the 1970s, the popular definition of documentaries was "educational films." A handful of '70s works began to challenge the prevailing assumption that credible nonfiction was dogmatic, impersonal, bland, and boring. Friedman, who cut his chops as a film and television editor in New York, and Epstein, who at age 19 was introduced to documentary by the quietly impassioned San Francisco filmmaker Peter Adair, rejected that dry-bones attitude, and the ghettoization of docs.

In the mid-'80s, they started collaborating, on carefully crafted films with riveting characters, cascading revelations, and momentous breakthroughs. Beginning with *Common Threads: Stories from the Quilt* (1989), their films were intended to move—and move audiences—in the same unforgettable way as fiction films. Note that character-driven, drama-driven films have become the dominant approach in American documentary in the ensuing decades.

"We've always thought of our documentary films as narrative films," Epstein told an interviewer in 2010, when *HOWL* was released. "So when people say this is our first narrative film, we have to hedge a bit because we've considered all our films to be narrative."

By the time I moved to San Francisco in the mid-'80s and began writing about movies, Epstein was a key figure in local film circles, and *The Times of Harvey Milk* (1984) was required viewing for new arrivals—gay and straight—with its page-turning, heart-stopping recitation of recent local history.

I first interviewed Epstein and Friedman in the fall of 1989 upon the release of *Common Threads*, and they both already possessed a stature and serious-ness of purpose. The tone was markedly different when we sat down in June 1992 to talk about *Where Are We? Our Trip through America*, for the *San Francisco Chronicle*'s widely read Sunday arts and entertainment sec-tion. A contemporary road movie, this kaleidoscopic piece was looser than anything they'd done before or have done since and—revealingly—repre-sents the only place in their filmography where they appear on-screen.

Our conversations in the ensuing years have reflected their relentless will to push forward, avoid familiar ground, and explore the limits of their skills and tastes. At the same time, Rob and Jeffrey have an acute understanding of and appreciation for history.

The seeds for their work can be found in the revelatory *Word Is Out* (1977), the first feature doc to give voice to gays and lesbians. Directed by the Mariposa Film Group, comprising Adair, Lucy Massie Phenix, Veronica Selver, Andrew Brown, Nancy Adair, and Epstein (who came aboard as a production assistant and quickly became a full-fledged member), *Word Is Out* allowed 26 well-chosen queer folks to relate their ordinary yet profoundly touching experiences.

A direct line can be drawn to an outspoken camera store owner-cum-San Francisco supervisor named Harvey Milk, who implored gays and lesbians to declare their homosexuality and erase the stigma. Milk's assassination inspired the powerhouse doc *The Times of Harvey Milk* (1984), which won the Academy Award in an era when Hollywood gays and lesbians had little power or visibility. It also pushed Epstein toward a more classical narrative direction in crafting the film.

Friedman and Epstein's first joint foray after forming Telling Pictures in 1987, *Common Threads: Stories from the Quilt*, used the NAMES Project AIDS Memorial Quilt as the entry point for a collection of family profiles that demolished the myth of "deserving" AIDS victims. The film received the Academy Award for Best Documentary, not least for its ability to trans-form the attitudes of mainstream Americans.

Recognized as the country's premier gay filmmakers—a description they understandably bridled against—Friedman and Epstein were the natural choice to adapt Vito Russo's groundbreaking study of gay stereotypes in Hollywood movies, *The Celluloid Closet* (1995). Reaching deeper into history to fill in a missing chapter in the library of Holocaust documentaries, the duo next examined the lives of homosexuals in Germany before and during the Third Reich. An unsettlingly beautiful work, *Paragraph 175* (2000) received the jury prize for Directing at Sundance.

These films transport you with seamless and seemingly inevitable stories. Revealing in this book how these stories were painstakingly constructed, within the context of practical, engaging advice about filmmaking, Friedman, Epstein, and their frequent writing partner, Sharon Wood, continue to speak to the next generation of filmmakers and filmgoers.

I'm pleased to see *HOWL* included in the book. When Allen Ginsberg's estate approached them about marking the 50th anniversary of "Howl," Friedman and Epstein envisioned a nonfiction film. But as they delved into the bizarre obscenity trial that followed the poem's publication by City Lights Books, and inspired by Ginsberg's outspokenness in the buttoned-down '50s, the filmmakers pushed into uncharted realms: animation accompanied the poem's reading and heartthrob James Franco played Ginsberg, partly to make the piece more inviting for next-generation filmgoers.

"We didn't want it to be a film about older people looking back on their younger selves," Friedman recalled when *HOWL* came out. "We really wanted it to be about younger people in the moment of their vibrancy, and for the story to live in the present tense."

Epstein added, "We knew it was an experimental film. . . . That's what we were interested in doing, really sort of transitioning from documentary to scripted narrative and using a lot of documentary techniques with the narrative."

Epstein and Friedman deserve all the recognition they've received for their marvelous films, and the artful, witty, and subtle ways they've spread tolerance and advanced gay rights. But what distinguishes them is their willingness to step out on the skinny branches rather than repeat past successes. That's what real artists do.

*Michael Fox is a San Francisco film journalist, critic, and teacher.*

# Acknowledgments

We'd like to thank our editors at Praeger, Dan Harmon and Jane Messah, who helped us, respectively, to start and finish this book. Thanks as well to the San Francisco Film Society, for giving us access to a recording of our March 2011 presentation about *HOWL*, and to our colleague Michael Palmieri for sharing his experience with do-it-yourself filmmaking. We also want to thank family, friends, and colleagues who have encouraged us throughout the process, and particularly those who have read the book in various drafts and offered invaluable comments: Jason Friedman, Matthew Lasar, Paul Brennan, Ian McClellan, Kris Samuelson, and Veronica Selver. Of course any errors are our own.

# Introduction

How do movies happen? How do you take an idea and turn it into a finished film, one that audiences will want to see?

Once you've been through the process once or twice, it becomes somewhat demystified but still no less amazing. Every completed film feels like a miracle. You start with an idea—it could be a subject area, a situation you've read about, a character you've seen, or a book you've read. You start believing in it and telling other people about it, until gradually the people around you start to think of it as a tangible thing. Some of them encourage you, others offer to help you out. At some point, you find yourself surrounded by dedicated people who are all committed to helping make your little idea into a movie. And then one day after an enormous amount of hard work, you're sitting in a room full of people watching it unfold on a screen.

That is the real magic of filmmaking: the creation of something out of nothing. It's not rocket science, nor is it as simple as making home movies. Ultimately, the only way to learn how to do it is to do it. Many people learn in film schools, but even there, the real learning is in the doing—making movies. We both learned by working on films—on other people's projects and on our own.

Rob began his career at the age of 19 by answering a classified want ad in a local magazine: "No experience necessary, just insane dedication and a co-operative spirit." He soon became one of the six filmmakers in the Mariposa Group, a collective that jointly directed the documentary *Word Is Out*. (This was the '70s!) He completed his next film, *The Times of Harvey*

*Milk*, in 1984. That film was awarded the Oscar for Best Documentary Feature and numerous other honors.

Jeffrey began more traditionally, by hanging out in editing rooms, learning technical skills while observing his cousin, documentary editor Larry Silk, at work. He joined the editor's union and worked his way up from apprentice to assistant. He had the good fortune to assist some of the most talented feature and documentary filmmakers in New York in the 1970s. He got to see firsthand the working methods of such editing masters as Dede Allen and Thelma Schoonmaker, and such directors as Martin Scorsese, Arthur Penn, William Friedkin, and Carroll Ballard. Gradually, he found opportunities to use the knowledge he'd gained to advance to full-fledged editor, first on an NBC prime-time series called *Lifeline* and then on Carroll Ballard's feature *Never Cry Wolf*.

We met in San Francisco and began helping out on each other's projects. Jeffrey got Rob a job in the sound department of *Never Cry Wolf*; Jeffrey volunteered as a consultant on *The Times of Harvey Milk*. Our formal professional collaboration began on a PBS documentary that Rob was hired to produce and that Jeffrey ended up editing. In the course of that experience we discovered that our filmmaking sensibilities clicked, and decided to make a film together.

In 1989 we finished *Common Threads: Stories from the Quilt*, and that film too was honored with an Academy Award. This success put us on the map as a team, and we have worked as a team ever since.

It's hard to say how or why our partnership has worked so well, but it does seem to have worked. Since we created our production company, Telling Pictures, in 1987, we've produced feature films and television programs, executive-produced projects for others, taught, fought, and otherwise bled for filmmaking in almost every way possible. The one thing we have never done is looked back and regretted any of it.

Filmmaking is not an easy business to get into, nor a hobby to indulge in casually. It has to be a consuming passion or else it's not worth the considerable effort. Filmmaking is art, it's craft, and it's business as well. With new digital technologies, the tools of filmmaking, which used to cost tens and hundreds of thousands of dollars, are much more readily available. Suddenly, everyone is a filmmaker. But having a camera and an editing system no more makes one a filmmaker than having a word processor makes one a writer.

We've tried to pass on what we know to young filmmakers who have worked with us as interns or assistants, and then through teaching—Rob in the NYU graduate film program and as a professor in the film program at

California College of the Arts (CCA), Jeffrey in the graduate documentary program at Stanford and at CCA—and now in this book. We have tried to analyze and articulate many of the processes that we've learned by osmosis over the years.

* * *

We conceived this book as a how-to manual for making nonfiction films—but it's not about cameras, microphones, or editing software. A film[1] is a story told in moving images and sounds. That holds true whether it's fiction or nonfiction. Filmmaking is storytelling. The purpose of this book is to give you the tools to craft a compelling story.

We've organized the book to reflect the actual step-by-step process of bringing a film to life, incorporating as many examples from our own work as we could—including some mistakes we hope you can learn from. We've included case studies for each step of the process, using situations we faced in our films to show a range of approaches to the many different challenges documentaries present. We have also included some sample agreements[2] we've found useful over the years as well as excerpts from our proposals and scripts at various stages, to show how and why those aspects of particular films evolved over time. The processes we describe here can be applied by anyone willing to commit to turning a vision into reality. We hope you'll be able to use what you find in this book to go out and make a film of your own.

This is a practical book on an impractical subject. We have tried to put into words an intangible process that is different for everyone. Or to quote from our 2010 movie, *HOWL*, "You can't translate poetry into prose." But you can use prose to write about poetry, and we've tried to do that in this book.

Jeffrey Friedman & Rob Epstein

* * *

I first met Rob and Jeffrey when we were all working in the postproduction department of *Never Cry Wolf*. Jeffrey was assistant editor and sometimes editor, Rob was an assistant sound editor, and I was an apprentice who floated between the picture and sound departments. At that point, Rob had already begun making *The Times of Harvey Milk*. Later I was Jeffrey's assistant editor on a short film, and later still, writer and coproducer of a documentary that Jeffrey edited.

Having now worked with Rob and Jeffrey on three of their films (*Where Are We?*, *The Celluloid Closet*, and *Paragraph 175*), I most appreciate their willingness to take chances during production and their ruthlessness with their material in postproduction. If a scene doesn't work as part of the larger film, no matter how much effort went into shooting and editing it or how strong it is by itself, they eliminate it (though it might reappear later as a

DVD extra). I've also been struck by their willingness to experiment while paradoxically setting rules for how specific film elements are used, an approach that gives their films a quality of aesthetic rigor. Regardless of subject, their work inevitably combines structural elegance with personal warmth. Finally, not only are they truly collaborative filmmakers, but they keep making different kinds of films, which makes working with them both a familiar and a new experience each time.

Cowriting this book has definitely been a new experience. My role has primarily been to build on the substantial foundation Jeffrey created with Rob's assistance, so while I have added various lessons learned from my own experience writing and producing documentaries over the years, please bear in mind that when the book refers to "we," unless otherwise indicated, it means the two of them.

Sharon Wood

*Part One*

# Development

_____ *Chapter 1* _____

# The Idea

Documentaries emerge from the world around us. The ideas for these films can come from anywhere. There have been successful documentaries about subjects as diverse as Bible salesmen, antiwar veterans, tightrope walkers, and tree frogs.

## WHERE DO DOCUMENTARY IDEAS COME FROM?

In 1986 we happened to be in Washington, DC, to witness the first unfolding of the NAMES Project AIDS Memorial Quilt. It was at once monumental and ragtag—awesome in its scope, and heartbreaking in the grief and love so delicately sewn into each of the panels. Our filmmaker friend Peter Adair was there and said, "Someone should make a movie about this." Seeing the Quilt—and hearing Peter's words—inspired us to develop an idea about the Quilt as our first joint filmmaking effort.

We went back to San Francisco and wrote a proposal. It was one and a half pages long, describing the Quilt, the NAMES Project, and the AIDS epidemic. It was full of vague and grandiose promises to create a celluloid equivalent of the Quilt. We attached our bios, pasted a color snapshot of the Quilt at the top of the first page (this was before desktop publishing), and called it "The Quilt: A Patchwork of Lives."

We decided we'd have more credibility if we had a company, so we found cheap office space and installed a phone. With the help of a designer friend and a thesaurus we came up with a name for our company: Telling Pictures. Another designer friend created a logo for us. And suddenly we weren't just a couple of guys with an idea, we were "Telling Pictures, a film and television production company based in San Francisco." A great deal of the movie business is about creating the illusion that some imaginary thing exists, and then willing the actual thing into existence.

## WHAT MAKES A GOOD IDEA FOR A DOCUMENTARY?

Just as our company began with a name and a logo, every movie—fiction or nonfiction—begins with an idea. The job of the filmmaker is to turn that idea, through sheer force of will, into an actual movie.

Movie making is a grueling process. It's worth spending some thought and energy on deciding whether the initial idea is one that you find so compelling that you are willing to commit yourself to it. Given the amount of effort it takes to make and distribute a film, it's better for all concerned—filmmakers and audiences alike—if the initial idea is a good one. So how does one evaluate the merit of an idea for a film?

There are two parts to this question: Will it make a good film? And if so, is it possible to produce?

Not all good ideas make good films. Many great ideas are too complex or abstract for film, and are better communicated by the written word, diagrams, or even mathematical equations. However much you want to make a film, ask yourself honestly, what is the best way to convey your idea? If the idea is one that will come alive when presented visually in conjunction with sound, rather than with language alone, then you're off to a good start.

What you do with your idea may actually be more important than the idea itself, hence the two-part question. If you're planning to make the film on a shoestring, or if you're independently wealthy and plan to self-finance, congratulations! You can skip the next section. But let's assume that you have an ambitious idea that will require some travel, that you want to hire a crew, and that you want to pay them—and yourself—industry-standard wages. You'll need some kind of financing. While we address fundraising in detail in Part II, most documentary filmmakers discover that generating the necessary funds for their films is inextricably linked to the creative process of developing their ideas from the very beginning.

## IS THE IDEA FUNDABLE?

"Who wants to see a bunch of gay men in San Francisco crying about their dead lovers?"

This was the initial response from a TV executive, responding to our pitch for a film about the AIDS Quilt. It seems no less shocking now than it did the first time we heard it. After a moment of stunned silence, one of us on the conference call recovered: "It's not just about gay men in San Francisco, it's about an incredibly diverse bunch of people . . . "

As appalled as we were by the question, we understood where it was coming from. It was another way of asking the question that all funders want to know: "Who's your audience?" And in fact, this challenging question, while crass, actually helped us shape our pitch. The "incredibly diverse" mix of characters we would be presenting became an important selling point—and an integral part of the film itself.

We've said that filmmaking is an art, a craft, and a business—and the business aspect is never more vivid than when you're asking for money. The executive working for a corporate broadcaster will want to be confident of an adequate return on any investment. The government funding agencies will want assurances that the films they support will have a reasonable chance of getting seen and making a difference.

The largest audience potential is generally in television or home video. Serious documentaries, however, rarely reach audiences as large as those of prime-time sitcoms or dramas. Nevertheless, a well-made film on an important subject—especially if it wins some awards—bestows prestige on a broadcaster and enhances its image. Image is important to these people: they may spend far more money on promoting a program and advertising their network than they will on actual programming. So prestige—good reviews, awards, respect in the community—is one of the most important values a social issue documentary can offer a funder or broadcaster. It may be intangible, but it's still a value.

A big part of your job as a filmmaker is convincing people that your idea has value. You're selling something—your idea, as well as your talent and your team. Most of the value of your project at this early stage rests in the strength of your idea—in your conviction that the idea is a good one, and in your ability to communicate that.

Will you be able to convince broadcasters, foundations, or individual donors to support this project? Answering this requires some understanding of what each of these three entities is seeking—and they're often not looking for the same things.

## WHAT ARE FUNDERS LOOKING FOR?

You need to hone your skills as a salesperson long before there's any film to market—when you have only your idea, yourself, and your filmmaking team. Funders—broadcasters, foundations, and individual donors—will be the first market to which you'll try to sell your product.

American broadcasters are almost exclusively interested in American stories. Foreign broadcasters are generally interested in American stories only insofar as they feel their audiences will relate to them. Subjects such as U.S. foreign policy and those featuring familiar pop-culture figures tend to make easier sales abroad than films about U.S. domestic political or social issues.

Only a small number of private foundations fund film production, although some development grants are offered through state humanities councils, and a few foundations offer finishing funds. Both of these stages—development (research and scriptwriting) and finishing (postproduction)—are less risky than the production stage for grantors. The development phase is relatively inexpensive, and the rough-to-fine-cut editing stage has the advantage that the project will most likely get completed. Funders like to know that there will be a finished film to show for the money they've granted.

Generally, foundations are looking for subjects that relate to their mission statements, which you can research online. Start with the website of the non-profit Foundation Center (http://www.foundationcenter.org), the most complete one-stop-shopping site for information on foundations worldwide. The Foundation Center allows you to cross-reference funders based on whether they support media and what their particular areas of philanthropic interest are. You'll be able to link not only to many foundations' grant application guidelines but also to their annual reports, which reveal the kind of projects they have funded and the size of their grants.

Along with private foundations, government funding sources are also listed. Governmental bodies such as state humanities councils are looking for subjects that relate to their respective states; if your project is national or international in scope, consider approaching the federal funding organizations. There too, research makes all the difference. The National Endowment for the Arts (NEA) is not mandated to fund films about artists; it seeks to fund films that are artful. The National Endowment for the Humanities (NEH) offers substantial grants for films relating to history and culture worldwide, while the National Science Foundation (NSF) provides correspondingly sizable grants for films about science. However, grants from NEH and NSF are very hard to get, and the grant-writing process can be a six-month full-time job in itself. Quasi-governmental entities such as the Corporation for Public Broadcasting (CPB) and the Independent Television Service (ITVS) also provide funding.

For all of these funding sources, don't rely exclusively on their application guidelines. It's important to review the films they've funded in the past, as well as the amounts of money granted—all of which information is publicly available.

All funders—from broadcasters to foundations to individuals—are basically looking for good films that will attract audiences. When evaluating an idea for a documentary, any broadcaster or funder will likely ask the same questions you should ask yourself:

Is the subject worthy?
Will it make a good story?
Is it visually interesting?

Finally, as we've indicated, funders will want to be reasonably certain that the film will actually get made, and further, that it will have an impact. These are all concerns to keep in mind when writing funding proposals. But for now, let's deal with the merits of the idea.

## IS IT A WORTHY SUBJECT?

It's possible to make a film about anything. A lot of first-time filmmakers have the odd notion that their family, or a family member, is so interesting that the whole world will want to know about them. This is occasionally—very rarely—the case. If you've had a tormented childhood like Jonathan Caouette, then making an autobiographical film as disturbing as *Tarnation*[1] feels justified. While it is possible to make interesting, engaging films about your family or yourself, it requires great skill in filmmaking and storytelling, and an ability and willingness to look at your own situation with fresh eyes. Some successful examples of this form are *Sherman's March*, *Nobody's Business*, *Complaints of a Dutiful Daughter*, and *Always a Bridesmaid*.[2]

Whether historical or contemporary, the subject should have a sense of urgency that you can translate into enough passion to fuel the grueling demands of making a film. Is this idea worth spending a year (or three or five years) of your life on? And just as important—unless you're self-financing—can you convince other people that this is a film that deserves to be made? The answer to this last question will affect every stage of the project: your ability to attract funding, to recruit enthusiastic crew members, and eventually to get audiences to see it.

Many people become documentary filmmakers at least partly because they care about various issues, want to effect social change, and believe film is an effective means to that end. If this desire resonates with you, consider an approach taken by some socially conscious filmmakers. Instead of developing an idea on your own that you think is important, first approach

## Dead End Case Study: Worthiness and Timing

In 1991, when we drove across the country filming *Where Are We?*, a few of the people and situations we encountered appeared to have enough dramatic potential to be developed into separate, stand-alone films. We decided to focus our effort on Friends Lounge, a gay bar next to a military base in North Carolina. We knew from having featured the cross-dressing bar owner as well as several of his gay and lesbian military patrons in *Where Are We?* that there were more stories to tell. While some of those stories could come from outtakes, we would need to return to do more filming. This was during the George H. W. Bush administration and just after the first Gulf War— almost two years before "Don't Ask, Don't Tell" was instituted. The issue of gays serving openly in the military was receiving some national attention, and we applied to a foundation dedicated to supporting progressive causes.

Interestingly, our proposal was rejected because the funder could not support a project that might somehow be perceived as promilitary. For that funder, antimilitarism trumped gay rights and the class issues that play a role in who volunteers for military service. We might have been ahead of the times by pursuing that story in 1991, though we probably could have raised the needed funds elsewhere. But just as timing may have led to our rejection by one foundation, it also contributed to our abandoning the project. We simply did not feel strongly enough about the Friends Lounge film; we were beginning to tackle *The Celluloid Closet* at the time. At a certain point, you need to dedicate yourself to one film and for us the choice was clear.

nonprofits or social service organizations you respect that address the issues you're drawn to. Ask them what kind of general-audience film would be most helpful in advancing their work or informing the public about their issues. They will know what films exist about their issues, how effective those films are, and what areas are not addressed, that is, where the content holes are. By reverse engineering your film idea, you can develop one that simultaneously guarantees an audience and perhaps even funding. This approach is based on finding a need to fill instead of convincing others there's a need for your bright idea. As the filmmaker, you will retain creative control but you'll know that your film will have a ready-made audience and the potential to make a difference. Even development grantors may ask you to outline your distribution and outreach plan, and this approach gives you one from the start. You still need to make sure the idea is one that creatively inspires you and that you're willing to commit a substantial amount of time and effort to it—as you would with any documentary idea.

Of course, some documentaries accomplish this kind of synergy in connection with issues without doing such market-driven research, simply because the filmmaker's own interests reflect a rising social concern. Deborah Hoffmann's *Complaints of a Dutiful Daughter* was finished just as awareness was growing about how many older Americans have Alzheimer's disease, and the film offered a lifeline for many overwhelmed and exhausted caregivers of relatives with the disease. More recently, *If A Tree Falls: A Story of the Earth Liberation Front* and *Better This World*[3] both raised questions about civil liberties and aggressive police tactics by featuring young activists ensnared by expanded definitions of terrorism.

## IS THE SUBJECT IMPORTANT?

What are the themes and issues the film will address? Why is it important to make this film now? Start by defining the subject and themes.

*The Times of Harvey Milk* was pitched as "a film about American values in conflict" and a story demonstrating how "one man can make a difference."

*Common Threads* was pitched as the most comprehensive documentary that had yet been made about the AIDS epidemic in the United States, as told through personal stories drawn from the Quilt. At the time, no one in the mainstream media or government had dealt with the epidemic in a meaningful way. It was important for people to learn about this disease and to understand that it affects everyone. We would demonstrate that the experiences occasioned by this epidemic—fear, death, and love—are universal.

*The Celluloid Closet* was presented as a film about how we think about sexuality and gender roles, as told through a 100-year history of gay and lesbian images in Hollywood movies, and interviews with the actors, writers, and directors who created them. "Sexuality and gender roles" would appeal to foundations, while "Hollywood movies" and "actors" (read: movie stars!) would appeal to distributors and broadcasters.

*Paragraph 175* would explore one of the least-known stories of Nazi Germany: the persecution of homosexuals, as related by the last surviving victims. This story had never been told before—at least not in a feature documentary. By the 1990s, for the first time a few of these men were willing to talk. We emphasized the urgency that this film be made now, since the only remaining witnesses were old and in poor health. Their stories would offer "a powerful testament to the endurance of the human spirit in the face of relentless persecution."

Not only was Allen Ginsberg's 1955 poem "Howl" a literary classic that presaged the cultural earthquake known as the Sixties; it also sparked a landmark obscenity case that resulted in broader free speech protections. While we were initially approached to create a film based on "Howl" to premiere on the 50th anniversary of the poem's publication, the poem and its story were significant enough not to need an anniversary hook. In addition, the choices we made in making the film led to a much more ambitious work that does honor to the poem in ways that neither of us could have anticipated when we began. Our 25-word-or-less description to the Sundance Film Festival reflects some, though not all, of those choices: "Using documentary interviews, re-enacted obscenity trial testimony, and mind-blowing animation, *HOWL* examines the making of a groundbreaking American poem and its impact on the culture."[4] (At the moment of the deadline for submissions, we were busy editing and had not yet eliminated all of the "documentary interviews" we had shot with Ginsberg's fellow poets.)

## HAS IT BEEN DONE BEFORE?

Before you go too far developing an idea, you should find out if there has already been a film made on the subject. The Internet makes this easy, whether you simply do a search for your subject or roam through the websites of major documentary distributors. If public television is the most likely broadcast destination for your film, you can even find out what films are already being made by visiting the website of *Current* (http://www.current .org), a print and online newspaper for public television and radio. The site's sidebar "Pipeline" lists all the films and series scheduled to air on public television over the next few years, who is making them, and what stage of production they've reached.

If there has been a film on the subject, can you find a fresh angle? Otherwise you'll need to have a compelling argument to justify making another film on the same subject.

## IS IT A GOOD STORY?

Up to now, we've been evaluating the idea in terms of theme—what the film will *mean*. But the essence of filmmaking is storytelling.

A book or an essay can more easily dispense with the imperatives of narrative. An extreme example is a reference book, which can benefit from an alphabetical structure. But a film, because it unfolds in real time, requires a driving narrative engine to keep the viewer engaged. While film is a visual medium, the most striking images ever shot will eventually lose viewers if strung together without some narrative intention.

Just because documentaries deal in real people and real events, the stories they tell are no less constructed than those of narrative fiction. We think of the kind of filmmaking we are concerned with here as *narrative nonfiction*.

"*Common Threads* is a film about the AIDS epidemic in the United States." This describes a subject. "*Common Threads* is about five very different people who have lost someone they've loved to AIDS, starting before anyone had heard of the disease, following them through the difficulties of dealing with disease, dealing with death, and moving on with their lives." This implies a story. The big difference is that a story has *structure* and *characters*.

Humans are storytelling animals, and stories have a basic structure. Does your idea have the potential to tell a good story? Can you imagine your idea as a film with a beginning, a middle, and an end? A good documentary—like any good film or any good book, for that matter—takes us on a journey with unexpected twists and turns, finally landing us somewhere completely different from where we began.

Many of our films have been reconstructions of previously unfolding events, and this is certainly an advantage when you're shaping the idea. By first identifying the key events of the story you're telling, you can start to determine how you will structure the story.

But even if you're considering an observational documentary—a film that follows events in an ongoing story as it is unfolding—it's possible to make an educated guess as to a situation's dramatic potential or which protagonist to follow to some climactic event.

Classic examples of this formula are competition films, like *Pumping Iron*, *Spellbound*, *Wordplay*, and *Mad Hot Ballroom*.[5] These films all follow similar patterns: we meet a number of contestants, watch them as they prepare to compete against one another, and follow them to the big competition, which provides a ready-made climax. It's a formula, and it works.

*Paris Is Burning*[6] follows the lives of some self-proclaimed super-divas of African American drag balls. Here the competitions are background to the stories of the characters, but they provide a structural framework.

*Hoop Dreams*[7] follows two inner-city basketball hopefuls through their high school years. There's no one competition we're building to, but we get to know these kids and their families, and identify with their desire to get out of the projects. We care about whether they fail or succeed.

*Streetwise*[8] follows an assortment of cast-out kids and runaways hustling to get by in the streets of downtown Seattle. *Dark Days*[9] takes us into the world of homeless people living beneath the streets of New York. Both of these films take us into unfamiliar subcultures, using observational footage and interviews to follow a number of characters over a period of time, so that by the end of the films we are invested in what happens to them.

Earlier classic defining examples of this genre include *Salesman*, which takes us into the world of traveling Bible salesmen, and *Welfare*,[10] which impassively observes the painful bureaucracy of a welfare office. These are pure cinéma vérité,[11] with no interviews or narration. These films derive their power through the simple act of observation. The conceit of vérité filmmaking is that the director chooses the situation and the characters, then simply records as the story unfolds. Of course there's much more to it than that. By choosing what to film, where to place the camera, when to turn it on and off, and how to assemble the material in the editing room, the director shapes the material according to her vision.

As cinéma vérité has been refined, it has found its way to prime-time television. We produced several episodes of *Crime & Punishment*, a documentary spin-off of Dick Wolf's *Law & Order* franchise, that ran for two seasons on NBC.[12] The show followed prosecutors in the San Diego district attorney's office as they took cases to trial. Each episode followed a basic formula: a tease, in which the prosecutor presented the facts of the crime and made the case; then five acts leading up to a trial; and finally a verdict. How we got from act 1 to act 5 was largely up to the directors and the editors. We had hundreds of cases to choose from. We looked for those cases that we judged most likely to yield drama and good scenes. Would there be visits to the crime scene with investigators? Would there be meetings with witnesses and with expert witnesses? Would any of these be at locations other than the DA's office, allowing some visual variety? What does the DA do on his or her time off to unwind? With whom do they go to lunch and discuss their work? All these situations offered the potential for scenes with which we would be able to build a story in the editing room.

Ultimately, though, the most exciting thing about making a documentary is *not knowing*. This is especially true of ongoing stories. Michael Apted's *Up* series[13] (starting with *Seven Up*, and continuing with sequels every seven years) began by interviewing a carefully chosen group of English schoolchildren, then returning at set intervals to catch up with the twists and turns of their life stories. What began as an examination of the British class structure has evolved into a meditation on what it means to be alive.

## ARE THERE STRONG, INTERESTING CHARACTERS?

Is there one person—or group of people—whose story you care enough about to spend weeks or months following it? Or, from another perspective, is there someone whose story an audience will care enough about to stick with it for the running time of your film?

It feels a little strange to refer to real people as "characters"—and of course we would never call people "characters" when addressing them. We use terms like "storytellers," "witnesses," or simply "people we're filming." But for the purposes of constructing a story, we think of them as characters.

In conceiving *Common Threads*, we were looking for good stories and storytellers with whom the audience could identify. In one sense, the protagonist of each story is the person who is memorialized in the Quilt panel and whose story we are hearing—that is, someone who has died. In terms of how the film is experienced, though, the living storytellers effectively become the protagonists with whom we can most readily identify. Our goal was to find five to eight interesting and varied life stories, along with engaging and varied storytellers who could recount them. We had over 2,000 letters in the NAMES Project archives to choose from, many of them already selected for use in a coffee-table book about the Quilt—we knew we could find a handful of great personalities in that vast pool.

At the other end of the spectrum, when we were researching *Paragraph 175* we knew that our options would be severely limited. The protagonists we were looking for were homosexual victims of Nazi persecution. It was 50 years after the fact. Many of them had died, some during the war and many more in the decades that followed. Few of those who survived were willing to speak publicly about their persecution as homosexuals, even after all this time. Finally, of the handful of people whose existence we knew about, several were in very poor health. Ultimately, we expanded our definition of our ideal protagonist beyond victims, to include any gay or lesbian person who could recount a variety of experiences under the Nazi regime. This initially felt like a compromise, but it eventually led us to make a film that was less simplistic in its moral equation, more nuanced and complex.

## IS THERE CONFLICT?

A good story needs conflict. A protagonist needs an antagonist or challenge. This could take the form of a person, or something more general, like societal prejudices—whatever it is, it's a good idea to find someone or something that blocks the hero from getting what she needs.

*The Times of Harvey Milk* had a classic antagonist in Dan White, who actually killed the protagonist. In a larger sense, the film is about communities in conflict: the gay community fighting for recognition and rights on one side, and homophobic politicians and citizens trying to limit their rights on the other.

We struggled for a long time to identify the conflict in *Common Threads*. Was it death versus life? People with AIDS versus a government that seemed indifferent or even hostile? Gradually, we began to think of the HIV virus itself as one antagonist, and the homophobic culture—in this case personified by President Ronald Reagan and his administration—as another.

The Nazis always make for easy villains, so we knew we had a strong antagonist in conceiving and developing *Paragraph 175*. Here, our fear was that it would become too simple a story, with innocent gay victims on one side and evil Nazi persecutors on the other. Fortunately for the film, as we began to research our characters and their stories, we found more ambiguities than we expected. These would make the film more difficult to shape, and ultimately more challenging and interesting to watch.

Directors of observational films always have their senses attuned to detect early signs of conflict. Any simmering disagreement between characters, for instance, could erupt into an argument, and arguments can make dynamic scenes. Filmmakers can develop an unseemly appetite for these kinds of unpleasant situations.[14]

We made a film for HBO's *America Undercover* series about extreme sports called *XTREME: Sports to Die For* (not our choice for a title, incidentally, but one learns to pick one's battles). The show profiled athletes in three sports: skysurfing, mountain bike jumping, and street luge. We had careers to follow and a competition to build to, but the real tension in this film was whether the athletes would get themselves killed or brain-damaged in the pursuit of adrenaline. As we got to know and care about the athletes we were filming, we found ourselves in the uncomfortable position of hoping that none of them would be harmed, and at the same time needing some dramatic footage to demonstrate the potential hazards of what they were doing. Our "big break" came when a street luge contestant spun out of control during a race and was rushed off in an ambulance. On the one hand, we knew we had a great scene; on the other, we were horrified that the athlete had been seriously injured (in fact, he did experience some lingering brain damage). This is precisely the kind of situation in which the serious documentary filmmaker can show sensitivity and restraint, and distinguish himself from the stereotypical local-news ghoul sticking microphones in the faces of bereaved people and asking how they feel.

Some film ideas come with clear conflicts built into the concept. The non-fiction TV series *Crime & Punishment* is a good example: a criminal trial in which the prosecution tries to prove the defendant's guilt and the defense attorney tries to prove his innocence.

The competition films cited above likewise have built-in conflict, in this case between the contestants. There might be one competitor the audience is rooting for more than the others (who becomes the primary protagonist) and someone else the viewer hopes will lose (by default, the antagonist).

The antagonist can be as general as a condition: poverty keeping people down, a dehumanizing bureaucracy. The more you can represent these generalities with real people, though, the more convincing you will be able to make your conflict. In *Paragraph 175* we spent some time trying to find a perpetrator—a former Nazi who had participated in the persecution of homosexuals during the war— who would be willing to talk to us. Not surprisingly, we failed. Nevertheless, the search itself led us to pursue lines of inquiry in the filming and editing that we might not have otherwise.

*HOWL* had a ready-made conflict: artistic expression and free speech versus censorship, wrapped up in a courtroom drama. In 1957, U.S. Customs seized all the copies of the second edition of Allen Ginsberg's epic free verse poem, "Howl," when the books arrived in the United States from Great Britain, where they had been printed. Local police in San Francisco also arrested Lawrence Ferlinghetti, the book's publisher, and charged him with selling obscene materials at his bookstore, City Lights. The court case that followed, *The People v. Ferlinghetti*, became a watershed test for freedom of speech. Fortunately for us, the trial itself was as interesting and surprising as the decision was groundbreaking. Recognizing the trial's dramatic potential was just the beginning of a long and sometimes arduous process of weaving the courtroom scenes with other elements we found similarly compelling to create the final film.

## HOW GOOD IS YOUR ACCESS?

Access is crucial, and it's something funders will want to know about. Do you have the unconditional cooperation of some key players in the story? If you will be filming in an institution, such as a school or hospital, do you have the cooperation of the administration allowing you to shoot there? A simple letter on the institution's stationery acknowledging interest and support of the project can be a big help. If you're going into another culture (or even a subculture) that might be mistrustful of you, do you have someone on your team to smooth the way? If you're basing your research on a book, do you have the rights or at least an agreement with the author—in writing!—to participate?

*Paragraph 175* came to us through Dr. Klaus Müller, a young German historian who had been researching homosexual victims of Nazi persecution for the U.S. Holocaust Memorial Museum and had established relationships over the years with some of them. Klaus was understandably very protective of these people, so we agreed that he would mediate all our contact with them. This put us at a disadvantage, since we would not be able to meet our subjects until we actually filmed them; but we also knew that the pool of subjects was sufficiently small that we had to film whomever we could. Despite our own lack of direct access, Klaus had credibility, through his relationship with the Holocaust Museum, and we were able to parlay our access to Klaus into a convincing request for funding.

## Dead End Case Studies: Access Denied

All documentary filmmakers have stories about films they began and had to abandon. It may be for lack of funds, since fundraising is essentially done on a speculative basis (foundations won't give you money to write grants to other foundations). Often it's because access is denied.

We received a small amount of development money to make a documentary about a public high school being established specifically for gay and lesbian teens, who are often bullied at regular high schools. We began some initial filming but soon we were stymied. The school administration understandably felt protective of the students, but the limited access this allowed us convinced us to abandon that project.

Another project was actually in production when access was unexpectedly retracted. We had just finished producing several episodes of *Crime & Punishment*. Inspired by that experience we wanted to develop a documentary series that would rise above the typical reality show fare. We pitched the idea of a series set in a gay community on Fire Island, New York, and HBO said yes. We did our research. We found characters willing to be followed over time and venues that would allow our crews access. And then we started shooting. But the upscale, media-savvy residents of the community were wary of invasive cameras. One Fire Island regular who was an attorney sent a letter to HBO indicating that he and his colleagues would do everything in their power to block the project. That was enough for the folks at HBO, who did not want to be where they were not wanted, and they pulled the plug. It was extremely hard to accept, but sometimes even when you think you've done your due diligence to assure access, it's not enough.

*Crime & Punishment* was all about access at every stage. Executive producer Bill Guttentag and his team met with district attorney offices around the country, assessing where film crews would be most welcome. Once we were settled in San Diego, with the blessing of the district attorney, we still had to gain the trust of the assistant district attorneys—the lawyers in the office who would actually be prosecuting the cases. Then, when we had a group of prosecutors who were willing (some more than others) to work with us, we had to research the other players in their cases: the investigators, the arresting officers, the expert witnesses, and most important, the victims or, in homicide cases, the victims' families. As always, it was easier to make a case for bringing cameras into someone's life when we could convincingly demonstrate that other victims or potential victims might be helped by making their story widely known. Before the first season aired, NBC agreed to let us include relevant hotline phone numbers at the ends of episodes. After one episode about physically abusive relationships, the domestic violence hotline number we displayed reported a huge spike in calls. This was extremely gratifying to us, of course—and it also gave us persuasive evidence to cite when making our case to invade someone else's privacy for another episode on a comparable theme.

A very large part of producing and of making films in general is talking people into things—convincing your subjects, your funders, and your crew that you are trustworthy and that your project is worthwhile. It helps if you believe it yourself—and then prove yourself right.

## ARE THERE STRONG VISUAL ELEMENTS TO TELL THE STORY?

The basic ingredients for a good story are a strong plot and interesting characters. And because film is a visual medium, your idea must have the potential to be visually interesting.

You need to have some idea of what visual elements you will be using to tell the story. Is there an interesting situation you will be filming, or will you be reconstructing past events using archival elements? If the latter, what do you have to work with? Are there TV news reports about the subject that might be useful? Do the people you're filming have home movies or photo albums? Unless you're making a strictly observational film, these are the building blocks that can help you tell your story.

*Common Threads* had the Quilt—a striking visual metaphor in itself. We were able to film the Quilt using several different visual techniques, allowing us to maximize its potential as a visual metaphor. Along with the various other approaches we took, we were fortunate that the climactic scene of the film involved the Quilt being unfolded and slowly revealed in an intensely emotional scene on the Mall in Washington, DC.

We knew there would be news clips—both local and national—that we could count on to tell the story of the public response to the epidemic, how the media reported it, and how the government and the grassroots AIDS activist movement responded.

Finally, because we had thousands of stories to choose from, we knew that many of the families would have photo albums, home movies, and videotapes, which we could use to bring the stories to life. We used all of these elements—as well as some images we imagined of landscapes, towns, cities, houses, and rooms where our stories had taken place—to create our treatment[15] for the film.

## CASE STUDY: *THE TIMES OF HARVEY MILK*

Some ideas take a long time to evolve into a coherent documentary narrative. The structure of *The Times of Harvey Milk* seems obvious in retrospect, but in fact it began as a slide-show presentation about an antigay ballot initiative, and took years to develop into its final form.

In the mid-1970s gay men and lesbians across the country were coming out in droves, and thousands were arriving in San Francisco from across the country and around the world. Many converged on Eureka Valley, an Irish working-class neighborhood that would soon become known as the Castro, after its main shopping street. Rob lived in the neighborhood and knew Harvey Milk casually, as a neighborhood shopkeeper. In 1978 voters elected Milk to the Board of Supervisors, San Francisco's city council. Harvey was the first openly gay politician elected to public office in California.

Such unprecedented cultural and sexual upheavals provoked a reaction, which took the form of a national antigay movement led by a born-again Christian former Miss America and current orange juice jingle singer, Anita Bryant. In California, a little-known state senator named John Briggs also took up the fight. Briggs's antigay campaign would focus on a California ballot proposition, "Prop 6," which would ban openly gay people from working in the public school system.

Rob's initial thought was to make a short film about this campaign and the issues it embodied. He began by putting together a lecture and slide-show presentation as a fundraising tool. As he followed the story, he began to take note of Harvey Milk, who was tirelessly debating the issue across the state with wit and humor, ultimately exposing Briggs as a misinformed bigot. On Election Day 1978, Prop 6 was voted down by a surprisingly wide margin. Milk was a hero. Three weeks later he was assassinated, along with the mayor of San Francisco, George Moscone.

The night of the assassinations, Rob and tens of thousands of San Franciscans marched down Market Street, the city's main thoroughfare, in a massive candlelight procession, gathering in front of San Francisco's City Hall. It became clear to Rob that the story hadn't ended with the Prop 6 campaign, but rather that this was one chapter in a much larger story of American communities and values in conflict. He began to see Harvey Milk's story as emblematic of this struggle. The movie eventually expanded from a short film about Prop 6 to a feature documentary covering the span of Milk's life and his legacy.

## CONCLUSION

In evaluating your idea, consider both artistic and financial criteria. These can be summed up as follows:

> Does it have the potential to be a good film?
> If so, can you afford to make it?

In fact, none of our ideas was an easy sell to U.S. broadcasters. Probably the easiest, after all is said and done, was *Common Threads*, which was fully financed by HBO. In most cases, we have raised money from other sources such as foundations and foreign broadcasters, and used that early support to start filming key scenes that could be used in a sample reel to help with fundraising. Once we had something tangible to show, it became easier to raise the remaining funding.

Not every good idea is equally fundable, so if you believe in your idea's potential and are truly committed to it, you may need to figure out a way to make the film for less money. Unless you absolutely require budget-busting line items (such as helicopters for aerial shots, outrageously expensive archival clips or music, or extensive travel), this is usually possible. It may require some adjustments in the concept: instead of a hard-hitting documentary about a U.S. war overseas, you might focus on the challenges faced by a refugee resettled in the United States, or a returned American veteran who happens to live within driving distance.

Assuming your story is a good one, your success will depend on two key factors: your absolute commitment to making your film, which comes through clearly when you pitch it to funders and potential collaborators, and keeps you going during hard times; and your willingness to adapt your concept to the circumstances in which you find yourself. If it's a good idea and you give it your all, you can find a way to make your film.

## Chapter 2

# Research and Evaluate Your Subject

One of the best things about making documentaries is the access they allow you—and by extension, your audience—into the lives and worlds of people you might otherwise never know. Researching your topic—whether it's a far-off historical event or a situation that's happening right now—is your first means of entry into this world. This is also the only stage in the filmmaking process where everything is still possible—a prospect both exciting and daunting. Each step in the filmmaking process has its own terrors and delights. From the moment you begin research, you're narrowing your focus but also deepening and enriching your understanding of the topic.

Your research will very likely have begun by the time you've settled on an idea. You need to know enough about your subject to come up with fresh angles and to speak about it with authority. As you proceed, you will continue to immerse yourself in your subject, to find out everything you can, while keeping an open mind about how to interpret what you're learning.

## READ EVERYTHING, TALK TO EVERYONE (WITHIN REASON)

Any film is a journey into a new world. The journey can take many forms: it could be exploring an ongoing situation (as in *Dark Days*), observing an institution (*Welfare*), following a competition (*Spellbound*), watching a process (*Company: Original Cast Album*), making an argument (*Fahrenheit 911*), or taking an actual journey (*Sherman's March*).[1]

No matter what type of film you're thinking about, it will require research, and different types of films call for different approaches to research. If you're making a film about a situation, a person, or a group of people, there's no substitute for legwork and schmoozing. You need to get familiar with the world you want to film. If you're making a historical documentary, the Internet and the library[2] are the obvious places to start. In either case, you will need to read at least enough about the subject so that you can talk about it without making a fool of yourself. It's wise to read multiple points of view about your subject. It will not only broaden your perspective but also increase your chances of coming up with your own synthesis or interpretation of the subject. At the same time, be honest about what you don't know, and retain your readiness to learn.

From the moment you begin your research, take note of your first impressions: what strikes you as particularly interesting, insightful, or visually arresting when first encountered, whether it's a passage in a book, a quality in how someone speaks, or striking details of the surrounding city or countryside. Soon enough, familiarity will set in and these ideas and people will no longer feel as exciting. But your first impressions are a good gauge of how others will react when they first encounter those same people and ideas in the film you're about to make.

Whatever the subject and whatever the form, you'll need to find a way to insinuate yourself into the world you want to film, so that you can understand who the key players are and where the good stories are likely to be. You'll need to get to know people on the inside—whether they're living participants in the story you want to observe and film or experts in the history you plan to re-create—and get them excited about your project. You should, however, avoid getting them excited at this early stage by dangling the possibility of a role in your film.

If there's a great deal of information about your subject, narrow your search. Who has done the most research in your subject area? Who has written or is saying the most interesting things about the subject? Who have you heard or read who has made you stop and rethink your assumptions about the issue? Keep track of these people as potential interview subjects or as project advisors. They can also be valuable resources, directing you to lesser-known but reliable sources of information, rare archival material, and even potential characters. This is especially critical if your subject is broad, such as the Cold War or global warming. You want to make a movie, not become a full-time researcher. But before you contact these people, do them the courtesy of reading something they've written, even if it's only the introduction and conclusion of one of their books.

Your first task will be to make these resource people—whether potential characters or advisors—understand the value of turning their story into a film. If they have written or spoken out about the subject, you won't have to convince them of its importance, but you will have to convince them of your understanding of it and your passion to bring it to a wider audience. Beyond that, you have to convey, through your communication and behavior, that you can be trusted—that you understand the delicacies of their situation and that you will respect them. If you can establish yourself as a comfortable presence in your prospective characters' world—part of their everyday landscape—if and when the time comes to introduce your film crew, you'll be asking to be invited in as a friend, an insider, rather than an intruder. A big part of filmmaking, at every stage of the process, consists of making and maintaining relationships. The sooner you begin to do this, the better.

Organize your research and keep track of your sources from the very beginning: contacts, visual resources, written resources. You and the others who will most likely be helping you make your film will need to access this material and contact these people again at some point. This kind of well-organized information is also critical at the end of postproduction when you're fact-checking and compiling your credit list. At that point, you are most likely exhausted and running out of funds. Searching your memory for an obscure source of some key point in your film is the last thing you want to do.

If your film is in any way historical, one of the most basic but useful tools early in your research is a chronology, either one you create or one you find online or in a book and adapt to your needs. Chronologies reveal historical and social contexts and can help you connect the dots between key events in your film's story. And don't forget to write down your sources for dates and numbers.

## RIGHTS AND LICENSES

It's never too early to figure out what rights you will need—and to start thinking about what they will cost. You may want to purchase the rights to a preexisting story—a magazine article, say, or a book. Or you may need to license the use of certain pieces of music or archival film or video clips. Start doing detective work to figure out who owns these rights. If it's a book, write to the publisher, who will probably refer you to the author's agent. If it's music, the rights will probably be controlled by the American Society of Composers, Authors, and Publishers (ASCAP) or Broadcast Music Incorporated (BMI), the two organizations that represent musicians, composers, and music publishers. Be forewarned that music rights can be prohibitively expensive. Books can be costly to option as well, but it is sometimes possible to defer payment on a book option (unfortunately this won't work for music). Knowing from the beginning which rights you must pay for will inform how you develop your film.[3]

## CASE STUDIES

### Researching a Historical Film: *Paragraph 175*

If you find a recognized expert in the field you're dealing with—as we had with Klaus Müller on *Paragraph 175*—and you plan to include interviews in the film, you need to determine whether this person is sufficiently engaging on camera to be one of your interview subjects. If not, you might want to try to convince him to join the project as a paid consultant. These roles— on-camera expert and project advisor—represent very different sorts of relationships, and the difference can be understood in terms of the financial arrangement: consultants are paid for their time and expertise, while interview subjects are not. This is a basic rule of documentary filmmaking—you never want to allow the suspicion that people in your film are saying what they're saying because you've paid them.[4] We defined Klaus's role as director of research, and because we were impressed by the relationships he had developed with the older men in his research, we discussed the possibility of making him a character in the film—the seeker whose quest we would follow. We also agreed to give him an associate producer credit, to acknowledge his matchmaking role in making the film happen (that is, bringing the subject to the filmmakers).

Although Klaus was far more versed in the subject than we were, we were leery at first about relying solely on him for our information. We felt that as Americans—and as Jews—we would inevitably have different perspectives on the Nazi era, even if the differences were subtle. So in addition to Klaus, we were determined to pursue leads of our own. We read everything we could find on experiences of gay people in the Nazi era, we hired Sharon to do in-depth research and write, and we worked with a native German-speaking co-producer, Michael Ehrenzweig, who could not only read those works that hadn't been translated but also help us communicate with our contacts in Germany. Through his European contacts, Michael was able to discover one of our most important storytellers, Heinz F., who had never told his story before.

Finding archival material for *Paragraph 175* was especially challenging. To build our story of gay life before, during, and after the Nazis, we needed stories, photos, and footage. Most of the material relating to gay and lesbian life in Weimar Germany had been systematically destroyed by the Nazis. We made contact with the Schwules Museum, Berlin's gay history museum, which had been collecting private photos and recording life stories since the 1970s. The museum, in turn, led us to new witnesses and victims of Nazi persecution who would eventually become storytellers in the film.

We also looked for generic images of life in Germany before and during the Nazi era. We had seen many of these images so often that we felt they were starting to lose some of their emotional impact. So we made it our goal to find images that we hadn't seen before. We combed through the catalogue of the Library of Congress, commercial archival footage houses, and the Bundesarchiv in Germany, where we hoped to find new images brought to light by the recent post–Cold War opening of East Germany. We gradually found a few images that felt fresh—to us, anyway. We also ended up using a fair number of shots lifted from Nazi propaganda films, finding ways to present them in a new context.[5]

### Researching an Archival Film: *The Celluloid Closet*

*The Celluloid Closet* was based on a book by Vito Russo that was the most comprehensive and authoritative source of information on gay and lesbian images in Hollywood movies available at the time. This was where we started. A great deal of research and theorizing had been sparked by Vito's book, and many films with gay themes or characters had been released since the book was published. We immersed ourselves in the literature and watched a lot of movies, making notes of scenes or characters that we found interesting. We relied on Vito himself, especially for information about movies that had been released since his book was published. We also read everything else we could find on gay images in popular culture, as well as scholarly works on homosexual subtext in the movies. We sought out films, books, and articles about other groups that Hollywood had stereotyped, such as women, African Americans, and Asians.

We formalized our relationship with Vito early on, making him an advisor on the project and legally securing the film rights to his book. Even though he was a dear friend, we wanted to clearly define what our roles would be, to avoid uncomfortable situations down the line. We videotaped an informal preinterview with him, to use for fundraising and in case we needed it later (Vito had AIDS by then, and in fact wouldn't live to see the film finished).[6]

By securing the book rights, we also gained a valuable marketing tool: we had copies of a published book that we could hand to potential funders or broadcasters when presenting the project. When you're asking people to take a leap of faith and part with their money, anything that makes your intangible idea more concrete can make the prospect less scary to them. A physical object—like a book—can lend credibility and authority to a proposal.

Some writers feel they have proprietary rights to a story they have brought to public attention. You have to decide if you agree with this assessment, and if so, come up with a good reason why they would want to participate. What's in it for them? Someone with a recently published book might be happy for the publicity. Some writers are just happy to get the story more widely known, perhaps for altruistic reasons.

Other writers may feel that because you're a filmmaker you are going to exploit the results of their labor to make yourself rich. These people don't understand the economics of documentary filmmaking, and it's up to you to explain it to them. Vito understood perfectly, and he and his agent Jed Mattes agreed to an arrangement whereby we deferred payment of the option fee[7] until we received the first distribution of revenues.[8]

### Researching Storytellers

We made contact with some of the people Vito had interviewed for his book. Writers and directors were fairly easy to reach. A few actors—not movie stars, but people who had appeared in supporting roles over the years—were willing at least to have an initial conversation by phone. We didn't try contacting any of the big movie stars we wanted to interview at this stage. We did start a database of their names, the names of the agents and agencies that represented them, and the films about which we wanted to interview them.

Celebrity sells, and it makes any project more attractive to financers and broadcasters. Even if your film isn't about show business, it pays to keep your ears open for prominent writers, performers, well-known scientists, or other public figures who have some personal interest in the topic you're dealing with. They may be able to help you get the film made by lending credibility to the project. If your film has narration, a well-known narrator can help increase the film's chances of being noticed.

Once you have located potential participants, then comes the delicate dance of seduction as you convince them to be part of your project—*while not making any promises that they will actually make it into the film when you are finished editing*. They might wind up on the infamous cutting room floor.

### Archival Research

In any film that will require archival material, the development period is the time to start identifying possible sources. Which newspapers have relevant headlines? Which film or video archives have relevant footage? Are there small museums or obscure historical societies that might have a rare treasure trove of material about your subject? If so, start working with them sooner rather than later as they're often run by volunteers, have limited hours, and are generally not set up to quickly and efficiently send you high-quality scans from their collections. This caution also applies to individual collectors.

For *The Celluloid Closet*, we began with Vito's ever-growing personal collection—clips from films he had discovered over the years and that he used in a clip-show lecture presentation he delivered to audiences around the world. Vito helped us establish a relationship with the film department of the Museum of Modern Art in New York, where he had worked and where he had discovered many of the rare early examples of queer images. We learned where the archives of old Hollywood scripts and studio memos were stored in Los Angeles; we made friends with a sympathetic archivist and looked for clues there. We collected hundreds of movies on videotape and worked with editor Arnold Glassman to isolate the most telling scenes.

We started another database of movie titles, with fields for other relevant information (for example, writer, director, actors, studio, year of release, and scene descriptions). We cast our net as wide as we could. Besides Vito's vast inventory, we pulled favorite films from our own memories. Arnold was a fount of Hollywood knowledge and contributed a number of titles, as did producer Michael Lumpkin (who was director of programming at the San Francisco Lesbian and Gay International Film Festival) and our assistant editor Jeffrey Schwarz, who knew about an astonishing number of obscure films that none of the rest of us had heard of. Archivists in stock footage libraries would become sources for relevant scenes in little-known early silent films—examples that even Vito had never come across. It's amazing what half a dozen interested minds can accomplish.

We continued collecting titles and film clips as we were writing the treatment with Sharon and working with Arnold to edit many of these clips into sample reels and what would become our first rough cut.

### Researching an Observational Film: *Crime & Punishment*

*Crime & Punishment* was conceived by executive producer Bill Guttentag and pitched to *Law & Order* creator Dick Wolf as a cinéma vérité series that would play like a dramatic TV hour. The series was focused on an institution, the San Diego district attorney's office; the individual episodes were structured around criminal trials, which have a structure of their own. The dramatic form of each episode closely resembles that of a competition film—in this case, the contest is between the defense and the prosecution.

We began our research by sitting and watching trials as they unfolded in the courtrooms, to understand the protocols of the court system and to get a sense of how this world functioned. In the process, we also became familiar sights to the judges, who already knew about the project and who would ultimately have the power to decide whether or not we would be allowed to film any given trial. We hoped that our respectful behavior and appearance would reassure them (it was the first time either of us had ever worn a jacket and tie to work). We figured out who the key players were: the bailiffs, who ran the courtrooms for the judges, and the clerks, who managed the judges' schedules. When we could introduce ourselves without being disruptive, we would explain to them, as a courtesy, who we were and why we were there.

At the same time, we were learning how the process worked—for example, that "voir dire" (jury selection) could take anywhere from a couple of days to several weeks. Since we were prohibited by law from filming jury members, we knew we had to build this dead time into our schedule.

Finally, we used this research period to improve our access. We got to know some of the attorneys in the DA's office, have lunch with them, and ask if we could sit in on some of their routine interviews with witnesses.

The production office had a master database that kept track of all the cases on the docket for the next several months, along with relevant information (such as names of lawyers, possible witnesses, other potential characters, projected trial dates, strength of the case, the likelihood of going to trial rather than being settled out of court, details of the charges against the defendant, and sentencing possibilities). Gradually, cases began to emerge that both satisfied the producers' criteria for a good story and coincided with the production schedule. These were the ones we would start filming.

### Researching an Essay Film: *Where Are We?*

*Where Are We?* was conceived as a snapshot of life in the United States in the form of a road trip. We wanted the process to be jazz-like—spontaneous improvisation—but we also wanted some sort of insurance so that we wouldn't come home completely empty-handed. So even for this least conventional of our films, we did a fair amount of research. (Until this point we had worked exclusively in film. Shooting on video allowed us more freedom to film situations that might not make it into the final film, without having to worry about costs of film stock or processing.)

Originally called *Planes, Trains, and Buses*, the film was conceived as a trip across country using three modes of transportation. Thematically, we envisioned a meditation on class structure in the United States.

We started by researching routes and regional weather patterns. We made contact with the transportation companies. We got written permission from Greyhound to film on their buses and from Amtrak to shoot on the train. For the plane, we chose MGM Grand Air, a short-lived first-class-only airline that flew exclusively between New York and Los Angeles. We felt this would heighten the contrast in the economic circumstances of our subjects. We had a conversation with someone in the airline's public relations office, who seemed amenable. When it came time to start filming, though, the PR department had second thoughts and withdrew its permission. So we revised our plan: we would drive across country, supplemented with a day each on a Greyhound bus and an Amtrak train.

As we began to narrow down our shooting schedule, we tried to locate events in a handful of places across the country where we thought we would have a good chance of catching something interesting. We found a few promising leads: a miniature Graceland built by Elvis fans in Roanoke, Virginia; a gay bar frequented by marines in North Carolina; a street parade and a legendary soul food restaurant in Memphis; a nightclub performer and an AIDS hospice in New Orleans; and some senior citizen cheerleaders who were planning to perform in a Veterans Day Parade in Phoenix (the parade promised to be celebratory in the aftermath of the just-concluded Gulf War). During a six-city, eight-day trip, Sharon preinterviewed most of these people, and quite a few others who didn't make the cut, with her Hi8 camera. After reviewing her tapes and determining who worked best on film, we charted a trip from east to west that would allow us to catch the two scheduled parades, and we arranged by phone to meet and film at the other locations. We ended up using all but one of these scenes in the final film. The rest of the situations and encounters we managed to grab on the fly—which was our original intent—but it was some comfort knowing that we had a few likely solid scenes to fall back on. Even films based on capturing spontaneous moments benefit from some planning.

### Using Research to Determine the Form: *Common Threads*

When we started developing *Common Threads*, all we knew was that we wanted to make a film about AIDS, using the AIDS Quilt as a focus.

At first we considered making an observational film about the NAMES Project, the San Francisco-based community organization that created and administered the Quilt. We met with Cleve Jones and Mike Smith, the organization's cofounders and directors. We also got to know the people who were responsible for the day-to-day functioning of the organization. We needed the blessing of the leadership, but it was the everyday foot soldiers who would be in a position to make our jobs easier, difficult, or impossible once we actually started filming.

We hung out at the storefront workshop on Market Street and talked to people who were sewing Quilt panels for loved ones who had died. We were just feeling our way, trying to get a sense of what it was we were dealing with. We wanted to know if there was enough going on in the workshop to create a story, which might build to a grand unfolding display like the one we had witnessed in DC. We began reading the thousands of letters that had been sent to the workshop along with finished Quilt panels. We thought we might be able to use these letters somehow to construct a story.

Still unsure what the focus of the story would be or how it would unfold, we began identifying possible thematic subject areas and gathering relevant information. We collected statistics from the Centers for Disease Control, the World Health Organization, and community AIDS organizations. We did newspaper and magazine searches to trace how the media had covered the disease and how the national and various local governments had responded—or failed to respond.

We also had an instinct that the "sexual revolution"—from birth control in the 1960s to feminism and gay liberation in the 1970s—could provide a historical context. We found a graduate student in history at Stanford University with a special interest in the history of sexuality; she spent a semester as an intern at Telling Pictures, during which she created a chronological outline of key events in American sexual history.

Finally, we knew a central theme of the film would be death and grieving, so we started gathering information on how different cultures have dealt with these issues.

Little or none of this research may be apparent to viewers of the finished film, but the research process itself deepened our understanding of the subject and helped us focus our thinking as we developed the story.

From his archival research on *The Times of Harvey Milk*, Rob had a good contact at KRON, a local news station in San Francisco, where much of the early AIDS story had unfolded. Local news is always less expensive than national news; unfortunately, since the medium switched from film to video, many local stations haven't kept archives of their footage, often erasing and taping over their field tapes. National network news organizations are better about keeping archives, which they help pay for with license fees, and these can be steep. We knew that at a certain point in the film, as awareness of AIDS became a national news story, we would have to figure out a way to get some of this material. Since the early part of the story we were telling was San Francisco based, and because KRON had preserved its news archives from this period, we had access to a gold mine of material. What's more, our contact at KRON was in a position to offer us the footage at no cost, because he believed in the project (an example of the importance of relationships). We spent many days in the archive, viewing and cataloguing AIDS stories and making copies of clips that we thought we might be able to use.

We started a list of prominent people in the fields of health, anthropology, the psychology of death and grieving, and the history of sexuality. In some cases, we had phone conversations or meetings with them. We interviewed clinicians, researchers, and experts. Whenever possible, we asked permission to record these interviews on audio- or videotape.

We used portable home-video equipment for these preinterviews. We explained to our interview subjects that we would be using the video solely for our in-house research, not for the final film, so that they would not feel pressured to perform.

This is a practice we have continued on later films, where we typically begin with a short list of questions, which grow as we learn more about the subject. We're honest about what we know and what we don't know, expressing a sincere interest in learning more. We find that people are usually generous with their time if we can accommodate their schedules. The more we talk to knowledgeable people, the more intelligent our questions become.

Gradually, we came to the conclusion that our most compelling resource would be the collection of personal stories represented in the Quilt, as illuminated by letters that people had written and sent along with the Quilt panels they had made. We chose not to interview experts in any given field but rather to explore various aspects of the issues around AIDS as they affected people who were dealing with the epidemic most intensely: those who became ill and those who loved them.

Eventually, some of the experts we talked to would become advisors—official or unofficial—on the project. Some funders, especially foundations and humanities councils, require that you have a panel of such advisors—recognized experts in subjects related to your film. The research videotapes we came away with provided the raw material for the proposal we would write. They allowed us to assess how interviews like these could work as an element in the final film, and they helped us determine which stories and storytellers we would include. Finally, we were able to use this material to edit a six-minute sample reel, which helped convince HBO to develop the project.

## CONCLUSION

By the time we start shooting, we have loose-leaf notebooks of facts and articles and hours of videotape on every aspect of the subject we can think of. We still may not know what the film will look like, but we're learning a lot.

How do you know when to stop researching and move to the next stage? That can become a problem when there is a huge amount of information about your subject. To some degree it's a matter of experience, but there are a few clues to watch for. One is that your research is increasingly focused on the details, which means either that you've grasped the big picture and are now starting to fill it in or that you've gotten lost in minutia and need to step back and take stock. The other clue is that you begin to have a sense of how the various research strands come together into a cohesive whole. In other words, you've reached a new overall understanding of your subject. From that moment on, additional research can be more focused, aimed at filling gaps in your knowledge. Depending on your subject, research may continue throughout the making of your film, but at some point it's no longer your primary activity. You know enough to say what your film is about and begin raising the money to make it.

Once you have an idea of what elements will make up your film and how much they will cost to acquire or produce, you're prepared for the next stages in the process: writing a proposal and making a budget.

*Chapter 3*

# Make Your Case: From Story to Proposal

## DEFINE THE STORY

Most filmmakers understand that documentary films do not represent "objective reality." Every choice a director makes—from casting to camera setups to editing—is an act of interpretation. Documentary filmmakers use reality as raw material, then shape it into something in order to communicate to an audience, presumably imbuing it with some deeper understanding than, say, unedited footage of the same situation captured by a surveillance video camera. Documentaries are *constructed*.

Construction implies *structure*—indeed, the two words share the Latin root *struere* (to build, to assemble). In this chapter we will discuss the critical initial proposal writing process, which can help you discover and clarify your film's structure and identify your cinematic storytelling elements.

## FIND THE STORY ARC

Aristotle defined tragedy as rising action, conflict, and falling action. Dialectical theoreticians talk of thesis, antithesis, and synthesis. Filmmakers usually frame it more simply: every good story has a beginning, a middle, and an end. A film begins with a situation, out of which arises a conflict, which finally comes to some kind of resolution. *Once upon a time* . . . and . . . *they lived happily ever after* are tropes that seem imprinted on our genes. What comes between—the evil ogre, the external or internal dragons to be slain, the physical, social, or bureaucratic hurdles to be surmounted—are the conflicts that can make the story a fun, moving, or thrilling ride.

In conceiving a documentary, you might think of these story elements as acts:

*Act 1*: setup, in which the characters are introduced, the situation is established, and the seeds of potential conflicts are hinted at.

*Act 2*: conflict, in which the competing interests of the characters we've met in act 1 lead them to pursue conflicting goals, building to a big clash or emotional event, or to a crisis point.

*Act 3*: resolution, where we learn what, if anything, has changed for the characters or in the world. A satisfying ending lets viewers feel that they've been taken on a journey.

In Hollywood it seems most everyone worships at the altar of the three-act structure. In this model, act 1 establishes the situation and the characters (protagonist and antagonist) in the first 30 minutes or so. Then a "plot point" occurs that propels the characters into the main conflict situation of the film. In act 2 this conflict is played out, building to another plot point, usually an emotional climax. This begins act 3, in which the plot is resolved, the loose ends are tied up, and the dramatic arc of the main character or characters is completed.[1]

While it's tedious to adhere slavishly to formulas, this structure generally works, and just as well in nonfiction narrative as in fiction. It's possible to create an engaging structure without a traditional three-act dramatic structure—but any good film needs a solid beginning, middle, and end.

A rule of thumb we abide by: if there is not a strong three-act structure inherent in the material, the film probably shouldn't be longer than an hour. With films of an hour or less, it's easier to hold the viewer's attention even without a strong narrative drive. A 60-minute film could be made up, say, of several thematically related stories, interwoven or presented sequentially. Short films (40 minutes and under) work well for individual character portraits, for documenting a single event, or (as in newsmagazine segments) for presenting conflicting arguments around a single issue. However, even a short film without a narrative storyline needs a beginning, a middle, and an ending. There may not be time to develop three substantial acts, but that just changes the proportions, not the structure: the beginning might be only a minute, the body of the film might be eight minutes, and the ending 30 seconds.

By the time a film gets to the 60-minute mark, viewers are ready for something to change, to be taken someplace *new*. It's time for a third act. This is just our opinion, of course—if you feel you have an idea that can sustain

## Structural Variations

Episodic structures, such as we the one used in our road trip film, *Where Are We?*, or those that contain thematically related but distinct stories, such as Alan Snitow and Deborah Kaufman's *Blacks & Jews*,[2] are stronger when they build some overarching dramatic tension that is ultimately resolved. Even essay films, such as those by the great French filmmaker Chris Marker,[3] take viewers on distinct journeys that end far from where they began. John Haptas and Kris Samuelson's *Tokyo Waka: A City Poem*[4] has a subtle structure that's not immediately apparent but that's possible only in a visual medium like film. It uses artfully constructed montages of city scenes both large and small to link the interview segments with an intriguing cross section of Tokyo residents, while building toward its overarching themes. By taking the relationship between the huge population of crows in Tokyo and the even larger population of people as a thematic starting point, the film expands to become a lyrical meditation on the intersections of the man-made world and the world of nature in an intensely urban setting. *The Five Obstructions*[5] is structured around five remakes of a classic experimental film by Danish filmmaker Jørgen Leth. Each version is re-created with a different set of formal restriction imposed by next-generation filmmaker Lars von Trier. The heart of the film emerges between these set pieces, in the relationship between the younger and older filmmakers. Their conversations about this project they are collaborating on—the results of which we see—are rigorous, respectful, and strangely tender.

a viewer's interest beyond 60 minutes with another structure, go for it! But bear in mind that if you want an audience larger than family and friends, fellow skateboarders, or early Warhol enthusiasts, those who don't know you or share your particular passion will want a story line to follow.

As you start to lay out the story, think about possible dramatic or emotional moments you can imagine arising. Each of these can be thought of as a *story beat*—an event that moves the narrative forward. Can you shape the story around these dramatic high points, to give the film some kind of elegant structure? If you're working toward three acts, can you imagine some meaningful turns of events to serve as the climaxes of each act? As you're thinking about these questions, start considering the materials you will use to build your story.

While specifics of the story structure will be provisional if you're making an observational documentary, these questions can help you choose what to shoot and whom to follow, as well as how best to adapt to changing dynamics when unpredictable events unfold before you and your camera crew.

Essentially, the more you can imagine the film you want to make, the easier it will be to make it. It's never too early to think about structure—even if you decide to reject the three-act model, it's useful to have a clear idea of where you're beginning and where you hope to end up. Try to imagine visual and story elements that will make your film come alive, both on paper and on the screen. Keep this in mind as you proceed to the next step, imagining your film on paper. In order to make their films, most documentary filmmakers must first make the case for their films to funders, which means writing proposals.

## WRITE YOUR FILM

It's often said that documentaries are "written" in the editing room. Especially in observational documentaries, which by definition are unpredictable, the true structure of the film often doesn't emerge until the editing process. This is where you'll determine who the central characters are and how they develop, what the pivotal events in the story are, how it begins, and where it ends. But documentaries also often require—and will usually benefit from—real old-fashioned writing.

The written version of a film generally takes two main forms: the *proposal* and the *treatment*. The proposal can be thought of as a presentation or sales tool where you clearly articulate the cultural, political, historical, or scientific issue or theme the film will address. It makes the case for your subject, your film, and you as the filmmaker. If you need to raise money, you must have a persuasive proposal. The treatment is a more detailed blueprint of how the film will unfold. Consider it a stand-in for your film until you've begun shooting. Later, depending on how you tell your story, the treatment and proposal will be good resources if you require writing for the film itself, such as narration or explanatory on-screen text, or, after the film is completed, for publicity or educational outreach materials.

Proposal writing is work, but in addition to helping you craft your sales pitch, it forces you to refine and articulate your idea and thus helps sharpen the film itself.

## DEFINE THE STORYTELLING ELEMENTS

Every film conveys information. The manner in which that information is conveyed determines the style of the movie. In nonfiction film, there are two primary modes of storytelling:

*Observational* (sometimes referred to as "direct cinema" or "cinéma vérité"), in which the filmmaker is present to record real-life events as they occur, and then shape them into a narrative; and

*Historical reconstruction*, in which the filmmaker uses a variety of elements to re-create an event that has already happened.

In both forms, filmmakers have developed a number of useful storytelling tools over the years.

## STORYTELLING TOOLS

Film is an amazing medium. It's visual, and it's also kinetic—it moves through time. And it's aural (sound is surely the element most overlooked by beginning filmmakers).

Throughout the process of conceiving your film and writing proposals and treatments, keep asking yourself *What will we see on the screen?* Think visually. Start thinking about what techniques you will use to tell the story. What are the elements you can find or create to move the narrative forward? What materials will you use to construct the story?

Here are some of the most useful and common techniques and elements. For convenience, we've organized some of these elements into three broad, sometimes overlapping categories, which we'll call *objective*, *subjective*, and *directorial*.

### "Objective" Elements

*"Objective" elements* are real-world phenomena that you can find and appropriate to tell your story. These might include:

Observational footage—original footage you shoot following characters through real-life situations; and

Archival materials—*archival* is an umbrella term that includes any photos, film and video, preexisting audio recordings, and any other documentary artifacts that relate to your subject. These can be researched and licensed from photo and stock footage libraries and archives (hence the term *archival*), or they can be personal artifacts like home movies and photo albums belonging to individuals connected to the story. This category also includes newspaper headlines, printed documents, and any other found artifacts that can help you tell the story.

Any of these elements can feel obvious or surprising, depending on how they are used—but they all have the potential to make strong, direct, visual statements. Home movies, especially, seem to evoke deep emotions almost

## Archival Footage Possibilities

Archival material can serve multiple purposes, so cast a wide net when you begin your search. In *Common Threads*, we used archival news footage as punctuation between longer stretches of personal stories. It chronicled the growing mortality rate of people with AIDS and provided other factual information about public and governmental reactions to the AIDS crisis. In addition to providing this kind of historical context, the news stories served as breaks or pauses for the viewers between the intensely emotional personal stories being told by our characters.

In *Paragraph 175*, we sometimes used archival footage as emotional counterpoint to the story being told. For one scene we chose rarely seen archival footage of pre–World War II German families picnicking in parks, with baskets, blankets, baby carriages, and children running on the grass. The unself-conscious behavior of the families gave the scene a home movie-like quality, which was further enhanced by the damage that had been done to the source film. The film damage worked to our advantage in another way, because it meant that these scenes had not been recycled in earlier documentaries about the Nazi era. Under this happy, pastoral scene of children and their mothers, we selected incongruously dark and dissonant music. Narration noted that while new laws targeted gay men, lesbians were largely ignored because the Nazis believed that women's primary role in society was to reproduce, and they didn't consider being lesbian an impediment to that role. This of course put the smiling women and happy children in the park in a different light.

indiscriminately: we can get nostalgic looking at home movies of complete strangers.

### "Subjective" Elements

*"Subjective" elements* are storytelling devices with a more inherent point of view. The most obvious—and important—are first-person storytellers. These are your characters, your protagonists and antagonists, telling their stories directly to the viewer, whether on camera or in voice-over. While we discuss casting for nonfiction films in a later chapter, the primary task at this early stage is to imagine what kind of people your ideal characters would be. Later you'll go look for the real people who meet your criteria.

Interviews can be conventional "talking heads" or "action interviews," in which the subject is engaged in an activity while the filmmaker is asking questions. The interviewer can be either on-screen (à la Michael Moore) or behind the camera (which is our preference), or even in another room (Errol Morris uses his own Teleprompter-like "Interrotron" device, which gives interviewees the illusion they're looking at him while they're actually looking directly at the camera lens. This gives viewers the impression that the storytellers are addressing them directly rather than looking slightly to the left or right, addressing someone off-screen).

Talking heads are often disdained as a tired technique, but if the person speaking has something meaningful to say and expresses it candidly, this can be as dramatic as any other element. A compelling story told by an engaging person can form one of the strongest links between a film and its audience. We like being told stories, we are accustomed to having them told to us, and we know instinctively how to respond to a storyteller's directness or evasiveness. A close shot of someone in a heightened state talking directly to the filmmaker can have an immediate, direct impact: the filmmaker disappears, and the film and viewer are locked into what feels like an intense personal relationship. The great strength of the classic, must-see documentary *The Sorrow and the Pity*[6] derives largely from such interviews.

Start to come up with an ideal "cast of characters" with a variety of experiences and points of view. First, ask which people—or kinds of people—will most effectively tell your story. Then consider how these personal stories fit into the overall narrative of the film. Just as a narrative is built of *story beats*,[7] so each character's story has its own beats. Assessing how each character's story fits into the overall structure of the film will help you determine how or if you will use them. If you're able to find plausible story beats for each of your characters in each of your acts, you're off to a good start.

The subjective category also includes interviews with "experts": these are people who have valuable information to convey and who are recognized authorities in their fields. The problem with experts is that often they have no personal, emotional stake in the specific story you're telling, so their perspectives can feel somewhat distanced, their presentations dry. An ideal situation is an expert on a subject who is also somehow personally involved in the situation, even if only peripherally. Alternately, look for an expert who is passionate about his or her subject. Some experts love what they do, and their enthusiasm is clearly visible when they speak. Be aware that the most respected expert in a particular field might not have a good on-camera presence. Since you're making a film, not writing a book, go with the lively, engaging expert over one with a bigger name but monotonous voice. Shelby Foote was not the most famous Civil War expert when Ken Burns made him a household name in 1990.[8]

Experts can sometimes be intrinsic parts of the story you're telling. In *Crime & Punishment*, we had to convey a lot of legal information to make the defense and prosecution strategies comprehensible; the show was conceived as pure cinéma vérité, which precluded interviews. To solve this problem, we tried whenever possible to be in the room filming when lawyers were discussing these issues among themselves. These were central characters who, in effect, also served as "experts."

In *The Celluloid Closet*, the on-camera interviewees/characters expressed a range of subjective relationships to movies. There were gay and lesbian movie-goers such as Susie Bright and Harvey Fierstein who spoke with passion and wit about the effects on their lives, both negative and positive, of specific films and characters. There were actors like Tom Hanks and Shirley MacLaine, who described their reactions to seeing gay characters on screen as well as their own experiences playing them. Screenwriters Gore Vidal, Stewart Stern, and Jay Presson Allen recalled their intentions in creating gay characters in particular films. And finally, film historians brought out telling details in scenes casual viewers wouldn't have noticed. By balancing these varied perspectives as we tracked the evolution of on-screen gay and lesbian characters through time, *The Celluloid Closet* anchored its viewers in the universally shared film-going experience while also making them privy to some juicy Hollywood insider anecdotes.

Years later we were hired by the History Channel to produce an episode for a series called "Ten Days That Unexpectedly Changed America." Our show was about the day gold was discovered in California, as well as its repercussions. For *Gold Rush* we shot traditional formal interviews in a studio with experts—authors and historians who had studied the history we wanted to tell. Then, working with DP Buddy Squires,[9] we filmed gorgeous re-creations of wagon trains and gold panning with historical reenactment hobbyists who dressed in period costume. Rather than trying to perpetuate the artifice of the re-creations, we chose to break the illusion by making contemporary characters out of the reenactors: they served as secondary, amateur experts, adding texture to the studio interviews with historians, and allowing us to experiment with conventions of the form.

### "Directorial" Elements

The techniques we've discussed up to now are generally most effective when they are transparent—the typical viewer is not thinking about storytelling strategies, but rather is experiencing the film directly.

By "directorial" elements, we mean those that are clearly imposed by the director and so represent the filmmaker's voice and point of view. Some examples would be:

Narration (whether first-person "subjective" or third-person "objective")
On-screen text or graphics

Re-created scenes (live action or animated)
Music

In each case, the viewer is aware of the director's hand at work, communicating something *directly*. Let's look briefly at each of these techniques.

### Narration

When we use narration in our films, we use it very specifically to move the story forward in ways that our individual storytellers cannot. When conceiving the narration we think of the narrator as a character—an authoritative voice that guides the story. If not overused, the narrator can be someone the viewer will be happy to hear from.

In adapting Vito Russo's book *The Celluloid Closet*, we wanted to communicate some of his political and social theory about the root causes of homophobia. Whenever possible we tried to get our on-screen interviewees to address some of these themes, but it often made for tedious viewing. We decided the most elegant and efficient way to convey the information concisely was through narration. Similarly, in *Paragraph 175* there were historical events that needed succinct explanations—the rise to power of the Nazis, the burning of the Reichstag—which we conveyed through narration.

### On-Screen Text

In recent years, increasing numbers of nonfiction filmmakers have used text over black in lieu of narration, which can work well if the information to be conveyed is brief and easy to comprehend, and does not excessively interrupt the narrative flow. In *Xtreme: Sports to Die For*, we used brief text cards to give information to the viewers: we defined "extreme sports" and its risks, and provided factual information about the contestants. In *Crime & Punishment*, text was used to create urgency and momentum in the style of *Law & Order*, the dramatic TV series that inspired this nonfiction series. *Paragraph 175* used both narration and on-screen text: we used the text only to quote historical figures and give brief updates on our interviewees at the very end of the film, and we used narration to provide historical context.

### Reenactments

These can be painfully hokey, but with imagination, creativity, and good camerawork and lighting, reenactments—also known as re-creations—can be evocative and effective, particularly if they're brief and not overly literal. In *Paragraph 175* we had very little personal or archival visual material to work with, so we created impressionistic images to illustrate parts of our characters' stories—a park at night, a disorienting stairway, an exam room in a concentration camp.

In *HOWL*, we stretched reenactments to the point of making a hybrid film based on actual transcripts, which we edited for dramatic effect, to create an effect one reviewer called "A Reality Sandwich."[10]

*Music*

Direct-cinema purists originally eschewed any musical score, but music has become a common element in nonfiction film. This can include "source music" (that is, music that's playing in the background of a scene, which can then be used editorially to create a mood); prerecorded period music; original score, composed specifically for the film; or a combination of all three.

* * *

These are partial lists, of course, and they will vary from film to film depending on the subject and the materials available. Bear in mind that these techniques are so familiar because they have been proven effective; if they are not used imaginatively, they can feel stale. Can you come up with something new?

## Storytelling Strategy Case Study: *Common Threads*

In *Common Threads* we used some version of each of the storytelling strategies we've described. We used on-screen interviews to move the personal stories forward—to show how individuals were personally affected by the epidemic. Periodically, we cut to archival news footage, followed by images from the Quilt accompanied by narration—we used these elements to convey an overarching historical narrative through which the individual stories unfolded. We ended each of these sequences with on-screen text to convey simple, stark numbers indicating the rapidly increasing numbers of AIDS cases in the United States. Our version of re-creations was to film empty spaces related to our characters' stories, echoing the absence of people who had died. We used music for mood and transitions, and to strengthen our other formal choices (a cappella vocal themes for personal stories, percussion for news, and so on). We could have made other choices, but the important thing for us was to establish some storytelling rules and stick to them. The viewer should not be consciously aware of these formal rules, but by using them consistently we can provide a comforting narrative framework on which less predictable life stories and historical events can unfold.

## THE PROPOSAL

A proposal can be anywhere from a few paragraphs to several pages. Two or three pages are usually enough, though foundations and government granting agencies usually specify the length they want. Plan to write a "template" proposal that addresses the key points detailed below, then tailor your proposal to the requirements of individual funders. (See chapter 6, "Financing.")

If you're looking for development funding, a good typical proposal will include:

- An introductory section, explaining the purpose of the film, why it is important, and why this subject can be illuminated by a documentary.
- A description of the film itself: what we will see on the screen, how the story will be told, and who the characters are. It's helpful here to include pictures that give a sense of the visual style you have in mind. These could be photos that you've taken of locations or characters, for example, or pictures from books (you'll need to get the rights if you use these images in your film).
- Ideally, you would include a short section on why you are the right filmmaker to make this film. Why is this something you feel passionately enough about to document on film? What unique access to the characters or situation have you—or will you—secure?
- Key personnel: this is you and any crafts people with credible industry credits whose names you can convince them to let you use. (Generally, the understanding is that their commitment to actually work on the film is contingent both on your raising the necessary funds to pay them and on their availability.)
- A list of deliverables: items you promise to produce in exchange for development funding. Typically, these are:
  ○ a detailed treatment;
  ○ a full production budget;
  ○ a production schedule;
  ○ a distribution plan, and
  ○ a sample reel (this is optional).
- A rough development budget, totaling the amount you are asking for and indicating how you will use it. This section should include a development schedule, and the budget itself can be just a handful of broad categories, such as:
  ○ fees and salaries (for writers, researchers, possibly an associate producer; typically, producers don't get paid for development);
  ○ travel (if applicable);
  ○ sample reel production, if you plan to cut a reel for further fundraising (line items here should include any shooting you'll need to do, the editor, the edit system, and supplies); and

- ○ administrative expenses: these are estimated hard costs, such as phone, copying, shipping, legal expenses, and, if you are shooting with a crew, production and liability insurance.
- Additional funding sources: If you've already raised some development funding, include those amounts and their sources here and deduct them from the amount you request—funders find this reassuring. If you know you need more than your funder is willing to give toward development, you can either lower the budget or include credible sources you intend to approach for the remaining funding. You can be creative here: for example, pull the sample reel costs out and present them as a separate budget that you intend to raise from other sources. Most funders, though, will want to know that for the money they give you, however little it is, you will be able to produce something in return. It often makes funders more comfortable with less experienced or first-time filmmakers to include an experienced filmmaker as a consultant. If appropriate, this person might eventually become your executive producer.
- Appendix: This can include new articles relevant to the subject, reviews of your previous films (or those of your consulting filmmaker, DP, or editor if you have no filmmaking track record), and letters offering support or granting special access (to a person or a situation).

* * *

Keep in mind that these contents are variable; you may have a very clear idea of why the story is important and why you are the right person to tell it, but only a sketchy notion of how the film will actually unfold. This is fine—one of the reasons you are asking for development funding is to figure things like this out. So play to your strengths, and be as up front as you can: if you are planning, say, to use the development period to secure firm commitments from well-known scholars, say so. You can also include a wish list of those scholars you hope to get, even if you feel insecure about delivering them—you're not promising anything more than to ask them, and you'll never know if they'll accept or refuse until you do. (Some people may be more likely to agree to participate if you can demonstrate that you've already raised some funding.)

Writing a proposal may seem like a lot of work to do before you start actually making the film, but in fact it's the beginning of the filmmaking process. Until you have started to shoot and edit the film, the proposal will be the only tangible representation of your film in the world. Just as having the rights to a book can make a project seem more substantial, so a polished proposal can begin to give your project the semblance of life. Eventually, the film will start to take on a life of its own.

### Case Study: *Paragraph 175*

When we agreed to take on *Paragraph 175*, we felt that our strongest selling points were that (a) we had come upon an important and startling piece of history that had been inadequately documented and understood; (b) we were working with Dr. Klaus Müller, who had a relationship with the U.S. Holocaust Memorial Museum and through whom we hoped to have access to eyewitnesses for the film; (c) these witnesses were quite old, so there was some urgency to record their stories sooner rather than later; and (d) we had proven storytelling and filmmaking skills. Here is an early development proposal, based on information supplied by Klaus, for what would eventually become *Paragraph 175* (originally conceived as a television hour and with a title derived from the concentration camp tag that homosexual prisoners wore):

---

## PINK TRIANGLE
## Proposal for a One-Hour Documentary

### HISTORICAL BACKGROUND

Between 1933 and 1945, according to Nazi documents, approximately 100,000 men were arrested because of their homosexuality. Roughly half of them were sentenced to prison and approximately 10,000 to 15,000 were incarcerated in concentration camps. The death rate of homosexual prisoners in the camps is estimated to have been as high as sixty percent, meaning that in 1945 only about 4,000 would have survived.

According to liberators' and survivors' testimonies, the fact that gay men were imprisoned in concentration camps and branded with a pink triangle was common knowledge. What perhaps was not common knowledge was how gay survivors were subjected to on-going persecution in post-Nazi Germany, where they were recognized not as political prisoners but as criminals indicted under the Nazi sodomy law. Many were re-arrested as repeat offenders and imprisoned again. All were excluded from reparations by the German government, and their time spent in concentration camps was deducted from their pensions. Escape by suicide, marriage or complete isolation was common. In the 1950s and 1960s the number of convicted homosexual men in West Germany was as high as it had been during Nazi rule, and the Nazi sodomy law remained on the books until 1969.

When the International community sought atonement for the victims of Hitler's Germany at the Nuremberg Trials of 1946, neither the atrocities committed against gay men during Nazi rule nor the anti-gay legislation and measures were mentioned. Homophobia and anti-gay persecution were accepted as normal in post-war Europe and the United States. Holocaust research and museums also ignored the fate of homosexual concentration camp inmates in exhibitions and documentation.

In the 1990s, researchers began to document the histories of the men who wore pink triangles. The United States Holocaust Memorial Museum in Washington D.C. changed public perceptions by including the Nazi persecution of homosexual men in their exhibits—the first and only institution to do so. Encouraged by historians and the Museum, gay survivors started to testify, some of them in their late 80s and early 90s. In 1995 eight survivors issued a collective declaration for the first time, demanding the juridical and moral recognition of their persecution. Still today, however, the German government refuses to officially acknowledge homosexual men as victims of the Nazi regime.[11] Other European countries have similar policies of exclusion and non-recognition.

Gay survivors of the Nazi era are still fighting for their recognition. They are exceptional human beings—bitter, but sometimes full of humor; humiliated throughout their lives, but often proud and courageous; tortured by their memories, but possessing a strong will to live. Their collective story will fill a crucial gap in the historical record. And it will be a powerful testament to the endurance of the human spirit in the face of relentless persecution.

## THE FILM

According to a 1993 survey commissioned by the American Jewish Committee, only about half of the adults in Britain and a quarter of the adults in the United States knew that gays were victims of the Holocaust. And while the pink triangle has been appropriated by the modern gay rights movement, even a great many gay people are unaware of the symbol's Nazi origins. For years, gay Holocaust survivors have been forced to hide, seeking anonymity as a means of survival. Now, for the first time, several of these men have come forward to tell their stories, ending decades of unnatural silence, isolation, and shame.

*Pink Triangle* is a one-hour documentary built around the stories of three to six gay men who survived the Nazi era. Their filmed testimonies, woven together with stock footage, personal photos and memorabilia, and original, evocative footage that will be shot for this film, will tell an epic story of suffering and survival. The structure, which we will build upon in the Development period, is roughly as follows:

Act 1—the heady, libertine world of Weimar Germany in which an active gay subculture is beginning to flourish. This comes to an abrupt end when Hitler and the Nazi party come to power.

Act 2—the war years, as Jews and other ethnic minorities are persecuted and murdered. We dramatically evoke the terrifying stories of our protagonists, from their arrests, to their incarceration in the concentration camps . . . and finally to their liberation by the Allies.

Act 3—After liberation, continued persecution—and the nightmare of being re-arrested by the German authorities to serve out the remainder of their "sentences" in prison.

Coda—Putting their lives back together: how these men have reconciled—or not—with these horrendous experiences, and what their lives have become since.

## RESEARCH AND DEVELOPMENT PERIOD

September–December

During the development period, the producers will work closely with Dr. Klaus Müller, consultant for the United States Holocaust Museum, to find gay survivors, research their stories, and conduct pre-interviews. The producers and/or Dr. Müller will pre-interview these potential subjects on audio tape and Hi-8 video. Since these survivors live all over the world, extensive travel will be required.

Additionally, we will research visual materials for the film such as artifacts, photographs and stock footage. Finally, we will write a film treatment, devise a production budget, and propose a production schedule.

If an additional development partner can be obtained, we will shoot interviews with some of the older survivors, at least one of whom is in his nineties, and perhaps shoot a reunion gathering of some of the remaining survivors.

## SCHEDULE

September–October: Research and pre-interview potential participants.
November: Write treatment; Shoot the most pressing interviews.
December 15: Submit development materials, including:
Treatment
List of interviewees
Production schedule
Production budget and sample interviews
Distribution & outreach plan[12]

This was followed by a very rough R&D budget, totaling just under the $40,000 we expected our first funder to provide, as well as paragraph-long biographies of the directors and of Klaus Müller and a vague distribution plan indicating that we would work to get the film widely shown (see Outreach/Distribution Plan, below).

\* \* \*

No matter how good you think your idea is, you can't assume others will feel the same way. Particularly if you are seeking funding, you need to make a convincing argument as to why this film is necessary. Funders often seem to be looking for reasons to say no: we've already done World War II; our audience wouldn't get it; it's not important we just did a film with a lot of old people in it . . . In our case, we were facing resistance from broadcasters who were coming off the tail end of a long series of 50th-anniversary films remembering the Second World War and the Holocaust, so we felt it was especially important to distinguish our film from previous ones. Hence, the emphasis on how poorly understood this aspect of the history was by the general public.

We also feared that funders and broadcasters might have reservations about such a dark subject. We tried to allay this concern by describing our characters—who were, remember, still largely hypothetical—as "exceptional human beings—bitter, but sometimes full of humor."

And we implied that the film, far from being depressing, would uplift with inspiration: "a powerful testament to the endurance of the human spirit in the face of relentless persecution" (a phrase contributed by coproducer Janet Cole).

Once we had development funds in hand, we proceeded to do what we had promised: we researched characters and expanded the concept into a detailed treatment. Again, this may seem like a lot of extra work, but none of it was wasted: with every new iteration, the film became clearer in our minds. All the reading, thinking, and writing that went into the various proposals and treatments would inform the choices we made at every stage—from shooting through editing—as the film took shape.

\* \* \*

*Paragraph 175* was about a historical phenomenon; we used what information we could quickly gather to make our best pitch. What if you have an idea for an observational film for which it seems no historical research will be helpful? Then you really have to start inventing.

### Case Study: *Where Are We?*

The proposal for *Where Are We?* was written in response to a request for proposals from the CPB. The mandate was to conceive a documentary to commemorate the 500th anniversary of Columbus's voyage to the New World. We had a rather vague idea that we presented this way:

### Planes, Trains, and Buses

Americans love to travel; certainly it's something we take for granted. Whether it's for business or for pleasure, to fulfill a family obligation or to satisfy our wanderlust, at one time or another most of us venture out and hit the road. En route, our lives intersect—criss-crossing the nation's landscape, forming a web of American life: all ages, races, classes, covering every conceivable geographical terrain.

Whatever its immediate purpose, travel carries emotional, intellectual and symbolic value as well. Leaving the familiar and set adrift in a new, constantly changing landscape, we participate in a ritual of renewal. Our eyes are opened to what is around us. We find time to reflect. We make a fresh start.

*Planes, Trains, and Buses* is a film about people on the move. Making a grand circle of the continental United States, we travel on a Greyhound bus; on an Amtrak train; and on the exclusive MGM Grand luxury jet. Each provides the traveler with a different experience. The plane is literally sealed— a lulling interior voyage designed for networking, cocktails, or rest, disguising the fact that it is hurtling through space. The train, with its romantic history and visceral appeal to the child in all of us, encompasses both past and present, interior and exterior. The bus, utilitarian and without glamour, makes frequent stops at tiny towns no one has heard of who wasn't born in them, and provides the most tangible experience of the places travelers are passing though.

Along the way, we meet a rich variety of Americans and foreigners—each experiencing the country from a unique perspective. We might meet a European student traveling the States by bus for the first time, or an American soldier on leave from the service; a truck-stop waitress traveling to her son's graduation; a school teacher crossing the country by train because of his fear of flying; or a Japanese executive flying to New York to negotiate a film contract.

We accompany these travelers as they encounter people, settings, and situations both more real and more fantastic than their everyday lives bound by daytime work and evening television. In the air, they participate in sky-high power meetings, make the deal of the century, or fall in love. On land, they come face to face with an iconoclastic, eccentric, and distinctively American tradition, that is at once appealing and appalling—one part naive creativity and one part P.T. Barnum hokum. They might stop at Rapid City, South Dakota's Reptile Garden, where goats, pigs, chickens, rabbits and a calf present a scene from the Wild West complete with outlaws, sheriffs, and a shoot-out. Or take a moment to reflect on the earnest marriage of religion and commerce at Heritage USA in Charlotte, North Carolina. Or ponder the transplanted London Bridge, nestled in the Arizona desert. Conceived by American originals, dependent on travelers, these quirky sites continue to defy the onslaught of franchises, standardization and malls.

The on-going journey leads each person to shed daily preoccupations. One business traveler might address what she feels are the world's most pressing problems; another, returning from tending to his mother's death, ponders the direction of his own life; while a third, a retired man on his way to visit a newborn grandchild, regales fellow travelers with stories of eccentric and rather alarming relatives from his immigrant childhood.

The style of the film will combine vérité scenes and interviews in which travelers tell their life stories and comment on their travel experience directly to camera. The voice of the filmmakers will be present and interactive. Dialogue between passengers will be encouraged, and intercut with impressionistic sequences of the cities, towns, roadside attractions, and landscapes where we briefly stop, then continue on our way.

*Planes, Trains, and Buses* will be an odyssey for the filmmakers as well as the travelers we encounter. The cast of characters, their stories and interactions, their destinations and adventures en route will not be known until we set out on each journey. In the course of our travels we will explore the everyday hopes and fears, the concerns and the obsessions, the universalities and the vastly different realities faced by the extraordinary variety of people who make up America.

What will bring these disparate elements together is our documentary experience: in casting, in drawing out stories and feelings, and in capturing spontaneous events. We feel confident that we will find people and stories as rich as America itself—full of humor, depth, tragedy, loneliness, looniness and joy.[13]

\* \* \*

As you can see, this proposal is closer to fiction than to reportage. We did a minimal amount of research into American roadside attractions and then tried to imagine a film and communicate what it might feel like. This kind of imaginative labor helped us set the tone of the project throughout. It informed the interviews we conducted, the style of Jean de Segonzac's shooting, and the choices editor Ned Bastille made in shaping the journey after the fact. In the end, the tone is one of the few elements of this pitch that wound up in the final film. And although our "confidence" expressed in the last sentence was shamelessly overstated, the proposal did the trick—it got us the grant.

## OUTREACH/DISTRIBUTION PLAN

To show that you're serious—and to make your plan financially feasible—you might include a realistic outreach/distribution budget in your proposal. This can be a section at the end of your production budget (which has the disadvantage of inflating your production total) or as a separate budget. Ideally you would budget a year of festival travel and office overhead for when the film is launched.

Jeffrey Friedman, director of photography Jean de Segonzac, Rob Epstein, and producer Pam Moscow on location—*Where Are We?* 1991. (Courtesy of Telling Pictures)

How do you imagine getting your film out to the largest possible audience? The distribution plan for each film will vary, depending on the subject, the format, the intended audience, and the funder. Will there be a festival rollout followed by a limited theatrical release? Will you try for a television premiere? Can you imagine a way to distribute effectively—and profitably— via the Internet? The answers to these questions will form the basis of your outreach/distribution plan.

*Distribution* is the all-encompassing industry term that includes exhibition release strategies and advertising. *Outreach* comes from the nonprofit lexicon and refers specifically to methods of getting the word out to interested constituencies (in this case, your potential core audience).

Outreach events for a social issue documentary might include benefit screenings for organizations with an interest in the subject of the film, followed by moderated discussions (as we had with *Paragraph 175*). Or you might propose a targeted mailing of DVDs to key activists or politicians.

Many funders now expect the distribution strategy to include plans for a related website. Depending on your subject, this can be as simple as an advertisement for the film (preferably with a short clip for online viewing) or a comprehensive source of referrals for people wishing to get involved or to find out more about the issues at hand. The most ambitious web outreach component would offer a space where people can post and discuss ideas or plan activist events—but bear in mind that someone will have to build and manage such a site, and budget accordingly. Can you use free video-sharing and online networking sites to spark interest in your film? Or give your site a head start by looking at websites of organizations that specialize in issue-based outreach, such as Active Voice (http://www.activevoice.net, "putting a human face on public policy") or Working Films (http://www .workingfilms.org, "linking non-fiction film with cutting edge activism").

The distribution section of your proposal need not be long or detailed, particularly while you're still in development, but any funder will want to be assured not only that the film will get finished but that it will be seen. For a broadcaster, the potential to exploit press attention at festival screenings may be a plus. Investors (more typical for fiction films) and donors will want to know that their money will be used effectively. In addition, investors will want to know you have a plan to recoup their investment. While it's unlikely you will have any realistic knowledge of how the film will be distributed until it's finished, you can at least demonstrate that you are thinking about it and that you have a plan.

## CONCLUSION

As your film evolves, continue to update and refine your proposal not only to reflect the film's most up-to-date approach but also to list the milestones you've reached in moving your film toward completion. Bear in mind that when your film is finished, your proposal-writing days are not: you'll be busy writing detailed outreach proposals for this film and development proposals for your next.

*Chapter 4*

# The Treatment

Now that you have a sense of your story and the elements you will use to tell it, you're ready to expand your initial proposal into a full-scale treatment, in which you describe more fully how the film will unfold.

If the proposal explains why a film should be made, the treatment should make readers want to see the film by conveying what it will feel like. The treatment will flesh out the structure and characters you have established in your proposal, and lay out the story in more detail. The treatment should also convey the tone you want to achieve. It should complement and support, through evocative storytelling and visual descriptions, the assertions you made in your proposal. Writing a treatment is designing a creative blueprint for a film. Like the proposal, the treatment will be the most tangible manifestation of the film you intend to make—at least until you start shooting. It is what you will use to present the project to film instructors, potential funders and broadcasters, as well as to people you hope to convince to participate in the project—whether as on-screen subjects (your "characters"), advisors, or crew.[1] In essence, you are imagining your film on paper. While the treatment will be useful for fundraising, it may be even more helpful to you in deciding when and whom to shoot, and how to edit your material.[2]

Observational documentaries like *Where Are We?* may be able to get by with nothing on paper more detailed than our short proposal (see chapter 3), since one can never really know what will happen once the camera starts to roll. It is possible—and helpful—to imagine likely twists and turns of events, and even possible outcomes that could make a satisfying ending to an observational film. In a competition film, for instance, you could be following five contestants, one of whom ends up winning the big prize. But what if none of them wins? You may decide this isn't a big problem, since losers are at least as interesting as winners, but it might make for something of a downer ending. Or—a bigger problem—the winner could be a dark horse that you never imagined had a chance and so have no footage of. How will you handle this situation?

Historical films require much more writing up front, since the history is past and will need to be re-created, often with narration or on-screen text. But even these films usually include interviews, and while you can phrase the questions to guide interviewees toward making the points you need them to make—whether developing the story or commenting on it—the best moments will probably be those you never anticipated and couldn't possibly have written in advance.

Still, once you have some basic understanding of your subject, you can start to define the contours of the story and imagine how to tell it.

## CASE STUDY: *COMMON THREADS*

In historical documentaries—or any film that deals with events already past—the structure can be easier to discern in advance. Since you know the overall chronology from having done your research, you can choose the key events you'll need to build your film.

When we decided to make a film around the NAMES Project AIDS Memorial Quilt, we were responding to the emotional impact of the Quilt itself. How could we turn this into a story? We immediately saw possibilities within the Quilt itself: each panel was sewn by someone, or a group of people, who had lost someone to AIDS, and each panel suggested the details of a life. So the idea to make film stories out of the stories in the Quilt seemed natural. But the Quilt is an installation piece designed to be walked through—a kind of portable, experiential monument. How could we sew together individual stories into a coherent overarching narrative that would hold a viewer's interest over 60 or 90 minutes?

When we watch the film now, the structure seems inevitable. It didn't seem that way when we started. After several months of research, still uncertain how to proceed, we went on retreat with writer Cindy Ruskin, who had written a coffee-table book about the Quilt. Our goal was to brainstorm, come up with a structure, and begin writing a treatment.

Our coproducer Bill Couturié encouraged us to conceive the film as a patchwork equivalent of the Quilt, which might comprise 40 or 50 mini-stories, each told in a different style (documentary, dramatization, animation, and so on) that cumulatively would have the same overwhelming emotional impact as the Quilt, the patchwork structure of the film resonating with the patchwork structure of the Quilt. The elegance of the concept and the prospect of working in different narrative forms were both appealing—but we couldn't figure out how such a project would sustain an audience's interest. (Today, this seems like an ideal format for a web series.)

So we tried another tack: a history of sexuality and sexual liberation over the course of the twentieth century, told through old movies, sex education films, newsreels, and TV news reports, interspersed with historical facts (through either on-screen text, narration, or—our least favorite option—interviews with historians). We started working on a narrative on paper. The problem with this structure was that it seemed to lead to the conclusion that sexual freedom inevitably leads to disease and death—not a message we were interested in promoting, especially during the puritanical, sexually repressive backlash of the 1980s.

Finally, we decided to focus on telling a manageable number of representative biographical stories from the Quilt. The story of each person we chose would be told through the intimate memories of someone who loved him—ideally, the person who had sewn a Quilt panel in his memory. These personal histories would be intercut with one another and with archival material, which would provide historical context.

Once we began working with individual stories, the structure started to reveal itself. Act 1 would be life before AIDS. Act 2 would be about dealing with the disease itself. And act 3 would be life after AIDS.

Act 3 was always the most perplexing, since we were making the film in 1988 and the epidemic was only just beginning to be understood. What would life after AIDS look like? And if the first two acts were duets between bereaved loved ones and the people they were remembering, what would the third act be? We weren't sure—except that we knew the actual unfolding of the Quilt in Washington, DC, would be a big part of it. And frankly, it wasn't until we were well into the editing process that we found a satisfactory solution to the "third-act problem." But we had enough to start with: before AIDS, dealing with AIDS, life after AIDS. Three acts.

As we struggled with the structure, themes began to emerge. One of the most striking aspects of the Quilt was the diversity of people who had been affected by the epidemic. Gradually, this observation evolved into the dominant theme of the film, that despite surface differences, we share a common humanity. This sounds trite when put so bluntly, but as we wrote the treatment, and as we shot and edited, this notion stayed in our consciousness and infused the entire film.

Once we had our three acts, we began thinking about how many storytellers we could include in the film. Audiences need to spend real time with characters in a film, to feel that they know them and can identify with them. A further complication in our case was that the stories we were telling were all about people who had died. We had to allow time for the audience to develop a relationship with the storytellers who were remembering their loved ones, as well as to get some sense of the person whose story they were telling. We thought of them as biographers and subjects and grouped them in pairs, each biographer-subject pair representing one story. How many of these stories would the film be able to hold?

We calculated in terms of screen time. In a one-hour film for television, there is at most 55 minutes of actual storytelling time; in a 90-minute film, no more than 87 minutes.[3] We figured a minute or so each for the opening and closing credits, and three minutes for an opening tease (a precredit sequence to hook the viewer, required by most broadcasters).

We allocated 10 percent of the screen time to historical context. We figured our big "production number" in act 3, the Quilt unfolding, would take another 8 to 10 minutes. So the breakdown would be roughly as shown in Table 4.1.

We calculated that in an hour-long film we would have around 36 minutes to tell our five stories; a 90-minute film would allow us 63 minutes. We had to allow time in act 1 to introduce each story, then enough time in act 2 to tell their AIDS stories, and some time in act 3 for each story line to conclude. Our instincts told us we needed a minimum of 10 minutes to develop each of our

Table 4.1  *Common Threads* Timing Table

|                              | 60-minute Film | 90-minute Film |
| ---------------------------- | -------------- | -------------- |
| Total running time           | 55:00          | 87:00          |
| Subtract                     |                |                |
| Open, close, and tease       | −5:00          | −5:00          |
| Quilt unfolding              | −8:00          | −10:00         |
| Historical/archival (10%)    | −6:00          | −9:00          |
| Time remaining for stories   | 36:00          | 63:00          |

*Note*: Courtesy of Telling Pictures.

characters so that they would become more than two-dimensional cutouts from the Quilt. Finally, we felt we needed at least five stories to fairly represent the diverse demographics of the epidemic and to coherently advance our theme.

More simple math:

> For a 90-minute (feature length) film: 63 minutes of story time divided by 5 stories = 12 + minutes per story.
> For a 60-minute film (a TV hour): 36 minutes of story time divided by 5 stories = 7 + minutes per story.

Seven minutes per story seemed like too little. So now we were confident that we could make a convincing argument for a feature-length film rather than a short.[4] Each story would average 12 minutes, roughly broken down as follows:

> Act 1: 2–3 minutes
> Act 2: 7–8 minutes
> Act 3: 2 minutes

In fact, the film ended up being about 75 minutes, but the proportions still apply.

Once we had established this formula for our protagonists, we then tried to imagine our antagonist. Was it HIV itself? Was it possible to make an antagonist out of a virus? Could we find microscopic footage to represent it? Would this be effective or hokey?

As we started to delve more deeply into the individual stories, we began to see another potential antagonist emerge: the fears and cultural prejudices that stigmatized people with AIDS and their families. Eventually, we began to see that these attitudes could be represented by news reports of AIDS-inspired discrimination and violence and personified by government spokesmen in other news footage. President Reagan himself would become a minor but important figure in the story.

Here is an excerpt from the treatment for *Common Threads* as we imagined it with writer Cindy Ruskin, based on research she had done for her book and on notes from phone interviews we had conducted ourselves. Note that unlike the previous examples, it is formatted like a script. Documentary treatments have no set formats, so choose the approach that will be most helpful for you and your film. This section of *Common Threads* comes toward the end of act 2:

*HOME MOVIE—a girl taking her first steps—FREEZE-FRAME*
  *Tom Waddell*

When Jessica was born, Tom had no idea he had AIDS. But then he began developing symptoms. In anticipation of an uncertain future, Tom began keeping an audio diary for Jessica.

We hear TOM'S VOICE as we see a PHOTO MONTAGE of a loving father and daughter together:

  TOM'S VOICE
  Tonight when I was brushing my teeth I noticed small white patches on my tongue. Sweetheart, I hope it's nothing. But there's a possibility that this is an early sign of AIDS. The fear of leaving you before you ever really know me is my greatest concern . . . You'll have to understand me in order to understand your own life, and how you came to be . . .

Tom's final months were spent fighting the US Olympic Committee in court. The USOC sued Waddell and his organization for using the term "Olympics" in conjunction with the Gay Games. The US Supreme Court eventually ruled against Waddell and his organization, and the USOC sought $96,000 in attorney fees, placing a lien on the home he had planned to leave to his daughter Jessica.

  *Over more HOME MOVIES of Jessica:*
  Tom Waddell (vo)[5]
You're so delicate and charming and bright as a precious stone, you're a miracle to me, my sweet darling . . .

                                                                    CUT TO:

*NEWS REPORT—OUTSIDE A HOSPITAL—*
*MONTAGE of RADIO VOICES and HEADLINES—*

Radio Announcer
  Actor Rock Hudson, last of the square-jawed, romantic leading men, known recently for his TV roles on *McMillan & Wife* and *Dynasty*, is suffering from inoperable liver cancer possibly linked to AIDS, it was disclosed Tuesday . . .

  *NEWSPAPER MONTAGE—beginning with*
  ROCK HUDSON HAS AIDS!
We see newspaper after newspaper—AIDS is finally on every front page of every Sunday paper in the US.
  *Begin a MEDIA MONTAGE—AIDS HYSTERIA—*

> *TV PROGRAM—William F. Buckley's "Firing Line." Buckley suggests that AIDS patients be tattooed.*
> *NEWS REPORT—KOKOMO, INDIANA—Honors student Ryan White, 14, is barred from attending school because he has AIDS.*
> *NEW YORK POST HEADLINE—L.I. GRANDMA HAS AIDS!*
> FADE UP TITLE CARD:
> 1985:
> 12,000 cases reported.
> 6,000 dead.[6]

As often happens, when we were making the film we put the treatment aside and didn't look at it again until we were finished. Once we had real footage to work with, we had to go through the process of discovering the structure all over again in the editing room. We were surprised how faithfully the finished film adhered to our initial concept.

## CASE STUDY: *THE CELLULOID CLOSET*

For *The Celluloid Closet* we went through a process very similar to *Common Threads*, trying and rejecting structure after structure before arriving yet again at a solution that, in retrospect at least, seems glaringly obvious.

Our first treatment (based on our proposal) was organized thematically, according to categories of queer stereotypes—the Sissy, the Bull Dyke, the Drag Queen, the Predator, the Gay Best Friend, and so forth. The result was a fascinating catalogue, but it lacked narrative drive. So we started over, this time telling the story chronologically. Now we had an interesting progression of gay and lesbian images, but it lacked coherence. There was no evidence of an organizing intelligence; it was just a survey (*first this happened, then this happened, then this . . .*).

Finally, we hit on the notion to combine the two ideas: Sharon wrote a treatment that was built around categories of stereotypes *grouped chronologically*. We decided to deal with each stereotype in the era in which it predominated, and we used the Hollywood Production Code to build the narrative around. Act 1 is before the Code; act 2, the Code years; act 3, after the Code. This worked on paper, and as we began editing we found it worked on the screen.

Sharon crafted a 50-page narrative treatment that became the template for the film. Here is a short excerpt from act 2 (the Code years):

# The Lovable Sissy Turns Sinister

Though openly homosexual characters were now taboo on film, indirect references to homosexuality flourished in the cynical, danger-filled world of film noir.

This new film genre combined the cynicism of 1930s gangster films, diluted by Production Code restrictions, with German Expressionism, which émigré directors and writers grafted onto their American productions. Film noir epitomized the social, political and personal uncertainties of the war and post-war years. It presented a morally ambiguous world of confused male protagonists, femmes fatales, lurking evil, and moody black and white photography. It also began a continuing Hollywood tradition of using homosexuality as an identifying trait for villains.

MALTESE FALCON (1941) Directed and written by John Huston, based on Dashiell Hammett's novel the MALTESE FALCON, contains two gay characters. While the novel had explicitly described the Joel Cairo character as gay, his homosexuality is toned down in the film. Still a sissified character, Joel Cairo (Peter Lorre) is sophisticated and deadly. The character of Wilmer is implicitly homosexual. Labeled a "gunsel" by the Sam Spade character and called "sonny," "boy," "kid" by other characters, his gayness—and his obvious discomfort at challenges to his masculinity—are subtle elements of his explosive personality.

The Sissy was no longer the charming, asexual, unthreatening companion. He had become malicious. Homosexuality was now inextricably linked with evil.

GILDA (1946) Directed by Charles Vidor. Glenn Ford, ostensibly Rita Hayworth's love interest, played his character as a gay man who is both in love and in competition with an older man.

LAURA (1944) Directed by Otto Preminger. Clifton Webb portrays a bitchy gossip columnist.

INTERVIEW: Film historian Richard Dyer observes that while film noir made the Sissy evil, it also made him powerful and a major character, i.e., the Villain, for the first time.

ROPE (1948) Directed by Alfred Hitchcock. Two pretentious homosexual lovers, played by John Dall and Farley Granger, believing themselves above the rules of ordinary morality, murder a former prep school roommate on a whim. Afterward, they describe their pleasure in the act of murder in blatantly sexual terms.

INTERVIEW: Scriptwriter Arthur Laurents describes how American censors labeled such script lines as "my dear boy" (in the British manner) as "homosexual dialogue." At the same time, the censors did not grasp the essential nature of the characters themselves, who made it to the screen with all of their perversity intact.

---

## FROM DIFFERENT TO SICK

Throughout the 1920s and early 1930s, the gay character, while always an outsider, was still human—often affectionately so. By the mid-1940s and increasingly through the 1950s, sexual and other differences were viewed with suspicion by a society which increasingly valued conformity. By mid-century, the gay film character was seen as an alien creature. His coldness, his perverse imagination and his edge of elitist superiority made him inhuman, and worse, un-American.

*Visual: Newsreel footage of HUAC hearings.*

These changing portrayals of homosexuals took place in a climate of increasing political fear and repression. The year 1947 saw the first loyalty investigations of federal employees, and the first HUAC (House Un-American Activities Committee) hearings in Hollywood. The containment policy against the USSR was adopted, and the Cold War formally began.[7]

---

In writing the treatment for *The Celluloid Closet*, as with *Common Threads*, we were able not only to work out a structure but also to establish some basic storytelling rules for ourselves. Analysis would be illustrated by clips from movies, while archival news footage would provide historical context. We had yet to decide how the analysis would be delivered (interviews? narration? text cards?), but we had a solid structural foundation on which to build.

Our other films follow similar patterns.

## CASE STUDY: *PARAGRAPH 175*

*Paragraph 175* uses the rise and fall of the Nazis as act markers: the three acts are, respectively, before, during, and after the Nazi regime.

Working again with Sharon, we expanded the proposal for *Paragraph 175* into a more fully imagined film treatment. Our sources were information provided by Klaus Müller; books written by two of our potential storytellers, Gad Beck and Pierre Seel; and several history books more broadly focused on the culture of Weimar Germany and the rise of Nazism.

---

## The Pink Triangle
## (working title)

### DRAFT TREATMENT

Note to readers: initials rather than full names have been used for individuals whose participation is still tentative.

---

Act One—Weimar

A 94-year-old man sits in his New York apartment crowded with memorabilia, and begins to tell his story: the son of a liberal German Jewish family in Berlin, "D" met his lover while very young. As he talks, we cut away to archival photos and footage of post–World War One Germany, family photos, and portraits of "D" as a boy and young man. He wistfully and vividly describes the world of Weimar Berlin—dozens of gay bars, an atmosphere of cultural and sexual experimentation. As archival footage and stills reveal the extent of open homosexuality in late 1920s Berlin, "D" tells how he reveled in it and so did thousands from throughout Europe drawn by Berlin's glittery allure.

GAD BECK's telling of his story is intercut with interviews with his twin sister MIRIAM. Born into a Jewish-Christian family in 1923, Beck enjoyed a seemingly untroubled childhood. Archival photos reveal a happy bourgeois German family. That world ended for the Becks with the Nazi election victory in 1933. Labeled half-Jewish, the two Beck children experienced rising anti-Semitism at school. Gad convinced his parents that he no longer could stay at the German school due to harassment by fellow pupils, and in 1935, the 12-year-old started attending the Jewish boy's school. There Gad had his first sexual experience. He blushes and smiles, then reveals that he seduced his teacher. He remarks that he unhesitatingly told his mother. His parents had no trouble accepting his homosexuality. Gad Beck's parents proved to be the exception.

Even in such a liberal and libertine atmosphere, "D" found himself advised to seek medical help for his homosexuality. He tells how he made an appointment to see the famous Dr. Magnus Hirschfeld. Still photos accompany the story of "the Einstein of sex," as related by narration and Holocaust scholar KLAUS MÜLLER. An interview with one of Hirschfeld's assistants, a woman who still lives in Berlin, gives a sense of the doctor's strongly principled beliefs. In the closing scene from the 1919 film "Different From the Others," we see Hirschfeld himself give an impassioned plea to end the ban on male homosexuality, a legal clause known as Paragraph 175.

It would take 50 years, thousands of deaths, and many more damaged lives before Paragraph 175 was deleted from German law. Over archival footage of May 1933 Nazi attacks on buildings, we learn that one of the targets was Hirschfeld's Institute for Sexual Science. Hirschfeld's assistant recalls how they were able to destroy all his files containing names and addresses of homosexual clients before the S.S. arrived, but that his extensive library about sexuality formed a large part of the burning pyre on which the Nazis tossed the accumulated wisdom of Western Civilization.

Act Two—The Thousand Year Reich

Newsreel footage of Germany's invasion of Poland signals the beginning of World War Two. We view seemingly endless rows of battle supplies and materials, as Nazi soldiers march into Warsaw. Cut to Warsaw today, where we first meet "S" strolling down the same street shown in the newsreel footage, now lined with sidewalk cafes. He recalls the affair he'd begun with a Nazi officer in occupied Poland, and tells how he was imprisoned when a letter to his lover was intercepted. "S" would spend much of the war in various youth camps, traveling from one to another in aptly named "Death Marches."

By 1937, even a hint of homosexuality was extremely risky. The Nazis had expanded the grounds for arrest under Paragraph 175 to include anonymous tips. Men were arrested for what was deemed an "offensive glance."

Over a photo of KARL GORATH as a young man, he begins to speak, recounting that he was 26 and living in Bremerhaven, Germany, when he was denounced by his jealous lover and arrested. Gorath describes signing a confession while an SS guard pointed a gun at his head. Sent to Neuengamme concentration camp, he was forced to wear a pink triangle along with the other "175ers." He was assigned to a prison hospital there, and recalls the horrific conditions. When he disobeyed an order to decrease food rations for Polish patients, he was transferred to Auschwitz as punishment.

As Gorath describes his camp experiences, we come to realize that wearing a pink triangle meant even harsher treatment. Gay men ("175ers") were at the bottom of the pecking order, unable to form alliances with other prisoners, which was critical to survival in the camps. They found themselves reviled and abused by prisoners and guards alike. Gorath's account is amplified by Holocaust scholar KLAUS MÜLLER, who discusses the bitter irony of portrayals of Nazis even today as sadistic homosexuals, despite their own rabidly homophobic policies.

Over a slow pan of gently rolling farmland, we hear that Alsace-Lorraine was a region long claimed by both France and Germany. When the Nazis annexed it in 1940, they set to work systematically weeding out "anti-social" elements. German commanders directed the cooperative French police to establish the notorious "Pink Files" to keep track of such undesirables. One of their targets was 17-year-old PIERRE SEEL.

We meet Pierre at his home in France. Over archival and personal photos, Pierre tells how he was arrested after reporting a theft that occurred in a gay neighborhood. He was interrogated both about his homosexuality and about his suspected involvement in resistance activities before being sent to the concentration camp at Schirmeck.

Over long tracking shots of the concentration camp today, Pierre describes how inmates were forced to build their own crematoria; how he himself was violated with broken rulers and used as a human dartboard for syringes thrown by camp orderlies; and how he was commanded to witness the brutal murder of his young lover.

Over a photo of Gad Beck as a young man, he tells us that in 1941 he joined "Chug Chaluzi," a Jewish resistance group that welcomed gay men. He was 17 at the time. Archival photos and contemporary footage of former hiding places accompany his description of how they organized safe places to hide, procured food, and provided care for Jews in the Berlin underground. Gad then reveals he had personal reasons for joining the resistance.

Gad describes how in 1942 he tried to liberate his lover Manfred from a Gestapo transfer camp. He borrowed a uniform, confidently marched into camp posing as a Hitler Youth member, and demanded that Manfred be released into his custody. His dangerous charade succeeded, but as they walked away, Manfred told Gad he could not leave his entire family in the camp. Gad watched helplessly as Manfred returned, never to see him again.

At the end of 1941, having proven his mettle by simply surviving, Pierre Seel and thousands of other Alsatians were enlisted in the German army. This was the ultimate humiliation: to be forced to fight on the side of the enemy. Archival footage of German soldiers in boot camp takes on new meaning with the knowledge of some men's forced participation—and their homosexuality. Men like Pierre Seel were sent to fight against men like Gad Beck.

By 1944, Gad had become head of his resistance group, but was imprisoned when the group was betrayed, shortly before the Russians liberated Berlin. He was not arrested for homosexuality, however. He was arrested for being Jewish.

Having survived several Allied bombings, Pierre Seel was eventually taken prisoner by the Russians, who gave him his freedom.

Act Three—Liberation?

Over archival footage of Allies liberating concentration camps, we hear that of the approximately 50,000 gay men sentenced and jailed by the Nazis, only 4,000 walked out of the camps.

After the war Pierre Seel made his way back to France, where his family accepted his return only on the condition that he never reveal the true circumstances of his arrest. Over revealing photos of himself during the postwar years, he tells how he went into a downward spiral, entering a marriage of convenience and eventually becoming suicidal—until deciding to take a stand and make his story public. Today he continues an ongoing struggle for official recognition of the persecution suffered by homosexual men under the Nazis.

When his resistance group disbanded after the war, Gad Beck headed to Munich and began working with Ben-Gurion in displaced persons camps. He tells about counting survivors and preparing them for emigration to Palestine, and how he chose to emigrate to Israel himself in 1947, together with his lover.

Freed by the allies, Karl Gorath had survived three concentration camps as well as a death march. He describes returning home to a society that continued to regard him as a criminal. Even his mother was so ashamed of his homosexuality that she preferred to tell everyone he had been in the army— better a Nazi than gay. Over mug shots of Gorath, we learn that he was

> re-arrested and sentenced to prison for violation of the sodomy law—a revised
> version of Paragraph 175. He spent four years in a German prison.
>
> Over archival footage of post-war Germany, we learn that time spent in
> concentration camps did not apply toward prison sentences, and that con-
> centration camp survivors jailed for homosexuality during the Nazi period
> were actually returned to prison by German authorities to complete their
> sentences in the late 1940s.
>
> It was not until 1969 that Germany's sodomy law was finally repealed.
>
> The film closes on the only known remaining pink triangle, on display at the
> Holocaust Museum in Washington, D.C.[8]

As you can see, we've come some distance from the original proposal toward a clearer idea of what the film will actually look like. When we became aware of new possible characters, we plugged their stories into this structure. At the same time, we had come up with valuable language that we could adapt for other uses.

As you develop an idea and start talking about it, you should be able to articulate the story and themes succinctly. Once we had a clear understanding ourselves of how *Paragraph 175* would be structured, we were able to boil it down to a one-sentence pitch: "the untold story of the persecution of European gay men under the Nazis, as told by gay and lesbian witnesses and concentration camp survivors."[9]

This would be useful later on, when we had to fill out applications for film festivals or provide brief texts for festival catalogues, which might require a synopsis of no more than 25 words. And when we had more space, we could add our tagline: "a powerful testament to the endurance of the human spirit in the face of relentless persecution."[10]

Sharon later wrote a 32-page treatment for *Paragraph 175*, which we continued to call *Pink Triangle* until we had begun editing. (An excerpt from that treatment is included in appendix 3.) This treatment was much more detailed, and like the excerpted treatment for *Celluloid Closet*, it was intended to be a production and postproduction guide as much as a fundraising tool. Complex historical feature documentaries such as these—as well as *Common Threads*, with its five interwoven personal stories told against a larger historical narrative—benefit from this kind of detailed preproduction research and storytelling. With observational films, treatments of three to five pages generally suffice for fundraising purposes. At the same time, the more you can figure out a realistic structure and ideal characters in advance, the better prepared you'll be for the unexpected once you've started shooting.

## CASE STUDY: TAKING *HOWL* FROM DOCUMENTARY
## TREATMENT TO NONFICTION FEATURE SCREENPLAY

Few documentary filmmakers write scripts; they are simply not necessary or helpful to the nonfiction filmmaking process. Those who do are usually making historical films and seeking production funds from NEH, which requires scripts.[11] With *HOWL*, we went from documentary treatment to narrative screenplay, a step we had never taken before—but one we considered necessary when we realized that a film about the creation of the poem "Howl" was also a film about the young poet, Allen Ginsberg. There were few photos and hardly any footage from that period of his life before he became famous. We realized that to make the poem's creation come alive, we would have to re-create the young poet. However, we decided to rely exclusively on historical sources—interviews with Ginsberg that referenced the poem and court transcripts of the publisher's obscenity trial—as source material for our script.[12] The words that Allen Ginsberg and the other historical characters spoke would be their own. We spent months working with the documentary texts, cutting and pasting them into a narrative and interweaving these elements with excerpts from the poem.

Once we had freed ourselves from the constraints of strictly documentary visual conventions, there were two more key turning points in developing the story. One was a semipublic reading of the script, which helped us see ways to edit and rebalance our various story elements to make them flow more smoothly. The other was being invited to the Sundance Screenwriters Lab, an exceptionally generous program offered by the Sundance Institute.

At the Lab, each of the dozen projects was assigned six very experienced screenwriters as advisors. They had all read our script, and by the time we met they knew it as well as we did. We spent half a day with each advisor, who essentially tore the script apart and then coached us on to how to put it back together. One consistent message was that we were not taking full advantage of the story's dramatic possibilities. Several advisors suggested we build up Allen's tortured relationship with his mother, who was mentally ill and institutionalized for years. They also urged us to make the film more sensual to reflect the overt sexuality in the poem, which we tried to do by incorporating flashbacks. As a result of the workshop, we also added a major scene showing Ginsberg's first public reading of "Howl" at the Six Gallery in San Francisco.

However, after years of struggling to get financing for *HOWL*, we had just signed a production agreement with producers and were about to begin preproduction with our earlier script. Our producers estimated that the changes we proposed based on the Sundance Lab would raise the budget by one million dollars. We had two weeks before pre-production to come up with a solution that would work financially and artistically. We began to frantically rewrite our just-rewritten screenplay to bring the costs down. Our new romantic/sensual flashback scenes had dialogue, which we eliminated, making those scenes more impressionistic. We trimmed and shaved other spots, then went through the entire script with our producers, page by page, in a marathon telephone call. When we hung up, we had a shooting script and a green light to begin pre-production. Perseverance, panic, understanding what's essential and what can go, and knowing how to bargain enabled us to navigate through a seeming impasse. (See appendix 4 for excerpts from the *HOWL* documentary treatment and the script.)

## CONCLUSION

The written version of your film, as you imagine it, will help you think about what to film and how to structure it. It will also become the basis for all the funding proposals, sales pitches, narration, festival entry forms, awards applications, and website copy you'll ever need to write.

Throughout the research phase, continue to revise the treatment—replacing hypothetical events and characters with real ones as you find them. This may sound like busywork, but particularly if the real characters and circumstances turn out to be significantly different from your original treatment, you have a chance to restructure on paper without putting a dent in your budget. If the changes don't work on paper, you know you have a problem. Even if they do work, there will still be many creative and structural challenges ahead, but you will have avoided some pitfalls.

By the time you start shooting, you may no longer need to revise your original treatment, although you may want to refer to it from time to time. And whether or not you revise what you've written, as you begin to collect real footage you will continue to refine the story and hone your themes.

Once you know what your film will look like, you're ready to think about the nuts and bolts of budget and scheduling.

## Chapter 5

# Development Materials: The Budget and Sample Reel

Now that you have a subject and approach, it's time to figure out how to translate your idea into a movie. In concrete terms, you need to devise a production schedule and a budget—two essential items not only for your own use but also as part of any development materials.

## PRODUCTION SCHEDULE

The number of days you'll need to shoot to gather enough material to build a story depends, of course, on what you're shooting.

If you're following a process, ask yourself how long it takes to play out. D. A. Pennebaker's _Company: Original Cast Album_[1] observes the creative process of recording a Broadway cast album; the bulk of the action takes place over one long night. In a situation like this—with a limited time frame and one-time-only performance moments—you'd want to shoot as much as you possibly could, ideally with multiple cameras, to ensure you have enough material to work with.

_Pumping Iron_, _Paris Is Burning_, _Wordplay_, and _Spellbound_[2] all follow groups of competitors over many months as they prepare for their respective face-offs. _Harlan County U.S.A._[3] followed striking coal miners through a struggle that lasted several years. Barbara Kopple and her crew shot hundreds of hours of film on _Harlan County_ and _American Dream_,[4] and it took a team of experienced editors many months to wade through it all and make sense of it and shape it. Their efforts paid off with two Academy Awards.

You have to allocate shooting days based on the exigencies of the stories you're following. An experienced producer or production manager can be helpful here. You might need to check in with your characters every day or week, for example, and plan on filming them at least three times each over the course of a year. The more spread out the shoots with each character, the likelier their stories will develop over time. Unfortunately, there is no rule of thumb here.

How much footage will you actually shoot? The number of hours shot compared to the number of hours used in the actual film is called the "shooting ratio," and it can vary widely from one filmmaker to the next. Saving money on film stock is no longer an issue now that almost everyone is shooting digital. This gives you incredible freedom in production, but it can also create big headaches in the editing room, when you have to sift through hours and hours of tedious footage looking for useful gems. Typical ratios can vary from 20:1 (that is, 20 hours shot for each hour of edited film) to 60:1 or greater. Some directors have shot upwards of 500 hours of film for one feature-length documentary. If you average 4 hours of tape per shoot day, a 60:1 ratio would mean 15 shooting days; if some days were shorter shoots, you might expand the number of days to 20. Our rule of thumb is that it takes *at least* 18 to 21 shooting days to shoot a feature documentary.

It's a balancing act between what you need to build a story and what you can afford—both in production and in editing, when the amount of footage shot will determine how many weeks or months the editor will need to make sense of it all.

We've had the luxury of long editing schedules on our documentary features, from eight months to over a year. But our experience has not been unique; most feature documentaries have lengthy edit schedules. The advantage to taking this much time is that you get to live with the material that much longer. Digital editing has made many of the mechanical and technical processes of editing faster and easier, leading many producers and broadcasters to shorten postproduction schedules, even though the new technology has done nothing to accelerate the creative process. It takes time to try things, live with them, and then put them aside and come back to them, in order to make a story unfold smoothly and flawlessly. We always try to make our nonfiction features work dramatically, as a narrative film would work, with emotional peaks and valleys, elegantly presented. It usually takes us about 10 months of editing to get a film to this point. This would be an extremely luxurious schedule by television standards, and over the years we have worked with schedules from as short as one week for a 12-minute newsmagazine segment to 12 weeks for a television hour (actually about

43 minutes of screen time when you account for the opening and closing credits and commercials). Typical editing schedules for one-hour television documentaries are 12 weeks at the most.

You will also need to determine the size of your crew. Do you want to maximize mobility and unobtrusiveness, with just a couple of people and a small camera? Or do you need multiple cameras to cover a complicated event?

## CASE STUDY: FILMING *COMMON THREADS*

Our first shoot on *Common Threads* was of Tracy Torrey, a former naval commander who had lost his lover to AIDS. As part of our research we had had a phone conversation with Tracy, who told us he himself had AIDS and was coming to San Francisco very soon to visit the NAMES Project workshop where the Quilt was being assembled. He planned to sew a Quilt panel for his deceased lover, as well as one for himself. Even at this early stage of the project, before we knew what form it would take, we recognized this story as too potent—and urgent—to forgo.

Since we had not yet raised any money, we called in favors to film for a day with a minimal crew: one camera person, one sound person, and an assistant.

Filming the NAMES Project AIDS Memorial Quilt on a sound stage, 1988. (Courtesy of Telling Pictures)

We tried to pack as much as we could into that day, including getting some general footage of the NAMES Project workshop, to give us potential material for a sample reel.

Our next shoot was a different story altogether. The Quilt was scheduled to be unfolded on the Washington Mall, in front of the U.S. Capitol, in October. We were already talking with HBO about doing a film based on the Quilt, but we didn't have a deal yet. We convinced them to give us development funding that would allow us to shoot this unique event, which we felt certain we would want to use in the film.

This time, we had a crew of five cinematographers, including a Steadicam operator (for smooth, fluid moves over the Quilt and through the crowds), three sound recordists, and a crane. The entire unfolding would take no more than an hour or so at sunrise, and we had one chance to capture it. In the cold dark before dawn, we placed our five crews around the vast Mall, each with a specific filming assignment. We had a rough choreography in mind, based on what we knew about the plans for the unfolding. We tested our walkie-talkies, so we'd be able to communicate any last-minute changes—and hoped for the best.

The footage was beautiful, and we were able to edit a 20-minute sequence out of it that helped convince HBO to fund the entire production. In the final film, the sequence of the Quilt unfolding lasted about 14 minutes.

By this point, we had decided on five storytellers and budgeted two days with each of them: one day to spend time with them and make them comfortable and one day to shoot the interviews and additional visual material such as vérité scenes and family photos. We also budgeted a day for each story in which to shoot more impressionistic visuals. Rather than stage reenactments, we had decided to film environments that had special meaning for each of the characters whose stories were being told, such as the San Francisco Bay Bridge, where Tom Waddell and Sara Lewinstein were driving when they first discussed the notion of having a child together, and the hospital room where Sallie Perryman's husband Rob died. Two of our storytellers lived in New York, one in San Diego, and one in San Francisco, where we were based (the fifth was Tracy Torrey, who lived in Washington, DC, but we had already filmed him in San Francisco). So our budget for the shoots included days for travel, hotel, and per diem for the producer-directors and film crew. On this film we also had the luxury of an associate producer, who managed the storytellers and crew and helped us keep on schedule.

* * *

Once you have all the parameters sorted out—number of shooting days, size of crew, editing schedule—you can start sketching in a budget.

## BUDGET

Budgeting movies properly—allocating adequate funds to get the job done, while staying within the inevitable financing limitations—is a skill in itself. If you're planning a do-it-yourself (DIY) approach to filmmaking and don't expect to spend more than a few thousand dollars, you'll primarily need some planning, common sense, and self-discipline. While you want to cultivate these qualities regardless of your budget, they're critical for DIY filmmakers. Once you start talking about raising sums of money from financers, you would be wise to consult with a producer or production manager who knows the film business.

There are several ways to organize your budget. Feature films divide costs into "above-the-line" and "below-the-line" expenses, for instance. Above-the-line costs include the key creative personnel, such as director, producer, and writer, who usually receive flat fees; while below-the-line includes costs relating to production and postproduction crew, equipment, and services. Needless to say, the director of photography and editor, who are both considered below the line, make major creative contributions to a film, as do other crew members, but traditionally these jobs are compensated at a daily or weekly rate.

Documentaries can also be divided into preproduction costs, production costs, and postproduction costs. Some funders have their own budget templates to which you'll need to make your budget conform, a time-consuming and dreary task. Just as proposals and treatments are ongoing processes, so is budget making, and you can expect to revise or at least reformat your budget periodically throughout the making of your film.

Table 5.1 is a sample budget for a one-hour documentary, with line-by-line annotations, using an organizational approach that we've developed over the years. There are professional budget software packages you can buy, but those are designed primarily for fiction films, and we've found it easier to create our own template for our documentary projects than to adapt a preexisting one. This budget was produced with a simple spreadsheet program.

## BUDGET NOTES

We're assuming a basic knowledge of spreadsheets: *cells* arranged in vertical *columns* and horizontal *rows*.[5] The ability to work with spreadsheets is one of those unglamorous skills that you'll find really helpful.

An important caveat: *do not assume any of the rates quoted in the sample budget are accurate!* Many will vary wildly, depending on such factors as the scope of your production, the experience of your crew, and where you are

Table 5.1 "Sample Budget"

| | A | B | C | D | E | F | G |
|---|---|---|---|---|---|---|---|
| 1 | | PRODUCTION | | | | | |
| 2 | 8 | **Months total project length** | | | | | |
| 3 | 34 | **Weeks total project length** | | | | | |
| 4 | 6 | Weeks preproduction | | | | | |
| 5 | 4 | Weeks of production | | | | | |
| 6 | 20 | Shooting days (local + distant) | | | | | |
| 7 | 3 | Distant shooting days | | | | | |
| 8 | 2 | Travel days | | | | | |
| 9 | 24 | Weeks postproduction + finish | | | | | |
| 10 | | | | | | | |
| 11 | Acct # | Item | Rate | Per | # Units | Cost | Subtotal |
| 12 | | **Production Staff** | | | | | |
| 13 | 1 | Director** | | Fee | 50,000 | 50,000 | |
| 14 | 2 | Executive producer | | Fee | 10,000 | 10,000 | |
| 15 | 3 | Line producer* | 1,200 | Week | 34 | 40,800 | |
| 16 | 4 | Writer/researcher | 2,000 | Week | 5 | 10,000 | |
| 17 | 5 | Director of photography | 800 | Day | 22 | 17,600 | |
| 18 | 6 | Sound recordist | 500 | Day | 22 | 11,000 | |
| 19 | 7 | Production assistant | 150 | Day | 30 | 4,500 | |
| 20 | 8 | Office manager/prod. secretary* | 800 | Week | 34 | 27,200 | |
| 21 | 9 | Production accountant | 320 | Week | 34 | 10,880 | |
| 22 | 10 | Archival researcher | 300 | Day | 10 | 3,000 | |
| 23 | | | | | | | 184,980 |

| | | **Equipment** | | | | |
|---|---|---|---|---|---|---|
| 24 | | **Equipment** | | | | |
| 25 | 11 | Camera package rental | 400 | Day | 20 | 8,000 |
| 26 | 12 | Sound package rental | 250 | Day | 20 | 5,000 |
| 27 | 13 | Lighting supplies/purchases | Allow | | | 1,000 |
| 28 | 14 | Expendables | Allow | | | 2,000 |
| 29 | 15 | Camera purchases (HD camcorders) | 500 | Each | 3 | 1,500 |
| 30 | 16 | Accessories and rigging (HD camcorders) | Allow | | | 1,500 |
| 31 | 17 | 1-TB field drives | 200 | Each | 6 | 1,200 |
| 32 | 18 | HD camcorder flash drives | 50 | Each | 3 | 150 |
| 33 | | | | | | 20,350 |
| 34 | | **Talent/Location** | | | | |
| 35 | 19 | Honoraria (incl. interviewees) | Allow | | | 3,000 |
| 36 | 20 | Location expenses | Allow | | | 5,000 |
| 37 | | | | | | 8,000 |
| 38 | | **Travel/Accommodation** | | | | |
| 39 | | Item | # People | # Days | Unit Cost | Total |
| 40 | 21 | Airfare | 3 | 5 | 360 | 5,400 |
| 41 | 22 | Per diem | 3 | 5 | 60 | 900 |
| 42 | 23 | Lodging | 3 | 5 | 250 | 3,750 |
| 43 | 24 | Auto rental | 125 | 1 | 22 | 2,750 |
| 44 | 25 | Ground transportation | Allow | | | 1,000 |
| 45 | 26 | Gas/tolls/mileage | Allow | | | 1,500 |
| 46 | 27 | Parking | Allow | | | 500 |
| 47 | 28 | Tips/porters/petty cash | Allow | | | 500 |
| 48 | | | | | | 16,300 |

(continued)

Table 5.1  (Continued)

| A | B | C | D | E | F | G |
|---|---|---|---|---|---|---|
| 49 | **Catering** | | | | | |
| 50 | Crew meals | Allow | | | 3,000 | |
| 51 | Craft service | Allow | | | 2,000 | |
| 52 | | | | | | 5,000 |
| 53 | **Stock Footage/Archival Stills** | | | | | |
| 54 | Footage license fees | 1,500 | Minute | 5 | 7,500 | |
| 55 | Librarian/lab prep fees | Allow | | | 2,500 | |
| 56 | Film/video transfers | Allow | | | 2,000 | |
| 57 | Photo license fees | Allow | | | 5,000 | |
| 58 | Still photo reprints | ALLOW | | | 2,500 | |
| 59 | | | | | | 19,500 |
| 60 | **Postproduction Picture Editing** | | | | | |
| 61 | Editor | 2,500 | Week | 26 | 65,000 | |
| 62 | Assistant editor* (half-time) | 500 | Week | 13 | 6,500 | |
| 63 | Transcribing | 90 | Hour | 85 | 7,650 | |
| 64 | Editing facility | 1,000 | Week | 21 | 21,000 | |
| 65 | Technical consultant | 40 | Hour | 25 | 1,000 | |
| 66 | Editing supplies | Allow | | | 4,000 | |
| 67 | Transfers | Allow | | | 3,500 | |
| 68 | | | | | | 108,650 |
| 69 | **Postproduction Sound** | | | | | |
| 70 | Sound editing | 250 | Hour | 40 | 10,000 | |
| 71 | Sound effects/library usage | Allow | | | 1,000 | |

| | | | | | | | |
|---|---|---|---|---|---|---|---|
| 72 | 45 | Editing supplies | Allow | | | 500 | |
| 73 | 46 | Deck rental | 300 | Day | 10 | 3,000 | |
| 74 | 47 | Import digital audio files | 60 | Hour | 15 | 900 | |
| 75 | 48 | Final mix | 400 | Hour | 24 | 9,600 | |
| 76 | 49 | Layback | 175 | Hour | 3 | 525 | |
| 77 | 50 | DAT stock | 10 | Tape | 35 | 350 | |
| 78 | 51 | Narration/voice-over recording | Allow | | | 1,000 | |
| 79 | | | | | | | 26,875 |
| 80 | | **Titles and Graphics** | | | | | |
| 81 | 52 | Graphic design | 5,000 | Fee | | 5,000 | |
| 82 | 53 | Title design | 5,000 | Fee | | 5,000 | |
| 83 | 54 | Graphic animation | 400 | Hour | 15 | 6,000 | |
| 84 | | | | | | | 16,000 |
| 85 | | **Music** | | | | | |
| 86 | 55 | Original music composer | 12,000 | Fee | | 12,000 | |
| 87 | 56 | Musicians/studio/engineer | Allow | | | 4,000 | |
| 88 | 57 | Music clearance | Allow | | | 10,000 | |
| 89 | 58 | Purchases/scratch track | Allow | | | 1,000 | |
| 90 | | | | | | | 27,000 |
| 91 | | **Video Finish** | | | | | |
| 92 | 59 | Online edit | 600 | Hour | 30 | 18,000 | |
| 93 | 60 | Color correct | 250 | Hour | 6 | 1,500 | |
| 94 | 61 | Digital effects session | Allow | | | 4,000 | |
| 95 | 62 | Master transfers | 145 | Hour | 4 | 580 | |
| 96 | 63 | Online stock | 260 | Tape | 4 | 1,040 | |

(continued)

Table 5.1  (Continued)

| | A | B | C | D | E | F | G |
|---|---|---|---|---|---|---|---|
| 97 | | | | | | | 25,120 |
| 98 | | **Administrative** | | | | | |
| 99 | 64 | Production office rent | 500 | Month | 16 | 8,000 | |
| 100 | 65 | Phone/fax/e-mail/web | 750 | Month | 16 | 12,000 | |
| 101 | 66 | Office supplies/petty cash | 350 | Month | 16 | 5,600 | |
| 102 | 67 | Shipping/postage/messenger | 500 | Month | 16 | 8,000 | |
| 103 | 68 | Legal fees | Allow | | | 5,000 | |
| 104 | 69 | Insurance (liability) | 3,500 | Fee | | 3,500 | |
| 105 | 70 | Insurance (E&O) | Allow | | | 10,000 | |
| 106 | 71 | Insurance (production) | Allow | | | 5,000 | |
| 107 | 72 | *Payroll taxes, benefits, and workers' comp | 19% | | 74,500 | 14,155 | |
| 108 | 73 | **Guild fees | 12.5% | | 50,000 | 6,250 | |
| 109 | 75 | Bank charges | Allow | | | 1,500 | |
| 110 | | Budget subtotal | | | | | 536,780 |
| 111 | 76 | Production contingency | 2% | 536,780 | | 10,736 | |
| 112 | 77 | Production services fee | 5.0% | 536,780 | | 26,839 | |
| 113 | | | | | | | 37,575 |
| 114 | | | | | | | |
| 115 | | **Total production** | | | | | 574,355 |

*subject to payroll taxes (see account 72)
**subject to Guild fees (see account 73)

located. You'll need to do your own research to make a budget that will accurately predict your costs.

We've arbitrarily set some parameters for our hypothetical production of a one-hour documentary. We estimate the whole project will take eight months (34 weeks) from start to finish, including 20 days of production over a period of 4 weeks, 3 shooting days in a location that will require travel, and 24 weeks of postproduction (20 weeks of editing and 4 weeks for final video and sound finish). The total project length will be useful for costs that continue over the duration of the project, such as overhead.

Note that the days and weeks of project duration are segregated in their own cells, so that they can be used as "global" values—that is, values that are referred to throughout the budget (cells A2–A9). This is very useful when you want to compare the costs of different numbers of shooting days, for instance; you need only change the actual number once (the global value), and all references to that cell throughout the worksheet will adjust accordingly. So you can see the difference in cost between 20 and 21 shooting days simply by changing this global value from 20 to 21 (cell A6). All the line items that are calculated on the basis of production days will automatically be adjusted, as will the bottom line. This should become clearer as we proceed.

Column A: Account numbers (see heading at A11: acct #): If you use bookkeeping software, you should set up a *chart of accounts* to track your budget items. You can set up your chart of accounts before you write your budget, or you can generate it as you write and transfer these account numbers to the bookkeeping program afterward. For simplicity's sake, we've just used consecutive numbers that will help us refer to budget lines in the notes below (cells A13–A112, account numbers 1–77). The following notes are numbered to correspond to the account numbers in the sample budget.

## Production Staff

1. Director: Figure out what you need to live on for the duration of the project, and balance that with how much financing you think you can raise. Then divide that number by the number of weeks in the project to figure your weekly rate. In this case, we're budgeting $50,000 for the whole project. The double asterisk (**) indicates that this position will entail guild fees if the director is a member of the Directors Guild of America (DGA). (see account #73).

2. Executive producers who have raised or contributed funding might negotiate, as part of their compensation, "a piece of the back end"—that is, a percentage of the film's future earnings—so they may agree to take a lower fee or no fee up front.

3.  Line producer: Once again, depending upon her professional experience and what responsibilities she will take on, this fee is negotiable. It could even be placed above the line, as a set fee. In this case, we're estimating a weekly rate that we feel would attract a producer with previous experience. The asterisk indicates payroll taxes, which are calculated on their own line (row 107, account #72).

4.  The researcher and writer could be the same person—you, for instance—or you could have a team of researchers feeding raw material to a writer. If you're good with words, writing your own treatments and scripts helps you define and then refine your vision for the film. If you don't have time, or if you don't trust your writing abilities or need help organizing your thoughts, you might want to hire a writer. When we work with writers, we often begin by putting our initial ideas down on paper, both to focus our thinking and to give the writer some place to start that reflects what we're after.

5–6.  Director of photography and sound recordist: These are crew that will travel with you. In this budget their time is calculated at 20 shooting days plus 2 travel days. Some crew will make deals for half their daily rate for days on which they travel and don't do any shooting, but since in theory they could be working elsewhere, many will want to be compensated at their regular rate, which seems only fair if you can afford it.

7.  Production assistant (PA): We've budgeted a PA for 20 shoot days and added 10 extra days to help prep, pick up and drop off equipment, and so on.

8.  Office manager/production secretary: If you have an office manager who will be coordinating logistics such as travel and lodging for the production, it's legitimate to budget him as a production secretary, at least through preproduction and production. In this case, we're keeping him on for two weeks of postproduction as well. The asterisk indicates that this position is payrolled (see notes for accounts #72–73, below).

9.  Production accountant: This is the person who will be helping you track your budget, pay your bills, prepare payroll taxes, and keep you honest. Here we've calculated her hourly rate at $40, or $320 for an eight-hour day. We've estimated that she would average one day a week on this project.

10.  Archival researcher: Any miscellaneous production personnel may be added to the production staff category. For this film we've included an archival researcher to help us track down rare photos and stock footage.

## Equipment

11–13.  Camera and sound packages and supplies: These prices are easily found by contacting local rental houses. Although you will try to make deals for the best prices and will likely rent the equipment belonging to the DP and the sound recordist you hire, it's fine to use the standard "book rate" in your budget (you'll find plenty of things to spend the savings on).

14. Expendables: This is a catchall term, for all those miscellaneous expenses inevitably incurred in production: batteries, tape, marking pens, whatever. There's always something you won't have budgeted for specifically.

15. Camera purchases: For this project, we're planning to use three HD prosumer camcorders for secondary footage (video diaries, perhaps). Rather than rent these cameras, we'll just buy them and have them on hand for future productions (on which we will then be able to charge a rental fee).

16. Accessories and rigging: All the peripheral items that fill out the camera package add up: microphones, carrying cases, tripods. Often these items are included in the rental price of the camera and sound package, but if you need an additional lighting kit or multiple radio mics, expect to pay extra for them.

17–18. Video stock or digital memory: Twenty years ago, this line item would have been film stock (and there would have been additional line items for processing and printing). Then the medium switched to video, then from standard definition to high definition,[6] and at this writing it is moving to digital. The relevant question here is how much material you will be able to shoot in a day. Two or three hours is pretty good, particularly if you're filming two scenes in different locations requiring travel and separate setups. Assuming HD tapes at 30 minutes per tape, that's six tapes per day. If you're downloading directly to hard drive, factor in the cost of memory and backup. In this budget we've assumed that the primary camera would be shooting HD and that there would be secondary cameras shooting HD prosumer camcorders.

## Talent/Location

19. Honoraria: Your "talent" could include a narrator or other voice-over actors to whom you might have to pay a SAG (Screen Actors Guild) day rate. Depending on their celebrity status and where you are filming, you might need to budget for taxis or limousine service. (On *The Celluloid Closet*, almost all the talent managed to get to the set themselves. Our added expenses on that project were hair and makeup.)

20. Location expenses: This is another catchall category, which might include actual location fees (for instance, you might agree to pay the costs of a security guard if required by the management) as well as miscellaneous expenses incurred at a location or in getting to and from a location.

## Travel/Accommodation

21–23. These are self-explanatory—figure out whom you need to get where and how much it will cost to get them there. Per diems are allocated for crew living expenses when away from their home base. The amount varies, but assuming you're paying for lodging, you need to allocate adequate per diems for three restaurant meals. New York City will be a more expensive location than Tuba City, Arizona, and each must be budgeted for accordingly. Note that some funders either do not allow per diems or have specific rules about them. In that case, you'd need to increase your catering budget. The amount spent on food for crew will be the same; it's just renamed and categorized differently. We've calculated a total of five per diem days (three shooting days at a distant location plus two travel days).

24. We're allowing for a car (or van) rental for each of the shooting days, whether local or distant, as well as the two travel days.

25–28. Ground transportation includes taxis to and from the airport. These are all ballpark estimates.

## Catering

29–30. You might not actually provide lunch, but you will need to provide some basic snacks and water (known as "craft service" in the industry), and there are usually a few meals for which the producer ends up with the bill.

## Stock Footage/Archival Stills

31–35. Estimate the total amount of screen time you want to devote to archival footage and stills, and budget according to average license rates, which you can determine by contacting two or three archival sources. Note that some archives require a minimum license fee—for example, for 30 seconds of footage, regardless of your chosen clip's length.

## Postproduction Picture Editing

36–37. Editor and assistant editor: Give yourself adequate time to finish the film, and then if possible add a week or two. This is not the category to shortchange. Editing is painstaking and creatively challenging—it's where the film really comes to life. As we've noted, digital technology has made the process easier in many ways, but it hasn't changed the speed at which the creative process unfolds. Allow time to really absorb the material, try things, put sequences together, make changes, have screenings—and then to throw everything up in the air and restructure.

38. Transcripts are crucial, especially if you do interviews. Some transcribers charge by the hour of screen time, others by how long it takes them to do the work. Get quotes and make your best estimate.

39. Editing facility: Either you'll pay an editor for the use of her system, or you'll use this line item to help offset the cost of your own system.

40. Technical consultant: This is the person you call in when the computers crash. (Don't forget to back up your work!)

41. Supplies: This covers everything from tapes, blank DVDs, and additional hard drives to notebooks and pens.
42. Transfers: This is in case you need to pay an archival house or a sound library to make copies of material you want to use.

## Postproduction Sound

43–51. This category assumes you will be using either a sound editor with his own software and equipment or an audio postproduction facility. In either case, you can ask for guidance on which line items to include and how much to budget.

## Titles and Graphics

52–54. If you're not a graphic artist, you might want to pay someone to help you create a stylish opening for the film and design a title treatment and end credits. You can find someone to work with and get rates from her when you do your budget, or you can decide what you think is a reasonable amount and then find someone who is willing to do the work for that price.

## Music

55–58. Will you use an original score? Or period music that you license? Or a combination of the two? Composers come at all prices, depending on their experience and how attractive your project is. Experienced film composers can make invaluable contributions to your film. "Purchases/scratch track" covers the cost of downloading or buying CDs you will use for temp music. (Temp music is simply the music you use while editing to explore the tone or mood you'd like to achieve. There's no need to pay license fees for temp music unless you become so attached to it that you decide to keep it as your final score.)

## Video Finish

59–60. This is your online, which is when the low-resolution versions of files you've been using are replaced by high-resolution ones. In addition, the color tones in people's faces and their backgrounds are "corrected" to the best possible color values, and digital or video glitches and other visual problems are fixed using After Effects, Photoshop, or another software program. You may elect to do some or all of this yourself, or your editor might be able to do it. Depending on the scope of the project and where it will be shown, you might want to go to a professional online house where you will be guaranteed a broadcast-ready master. In this case, again, your best bet is to consult with an online facility and ask for estimates.

61.  "Digital effects" is an item that could come in handy if you have some problem shots that need special processing for technical reasons. This is especially important if you will be using archival material. Most archival footage, even if originally shot on film, is available only in standard-definition video with an aspect ratio of 4:3—the familiar rectangle shape of old movies and pre-flat-screen TVs. You will likely be shooting high definition, with an aspect ratio of 16:9, that is, widescreen. At the very least, the archival footage will need to be processed to improve the image quality, but you'll also have to decide whether you want borders on both sides of your archival footage to make the entire image visible. The other option is to enlarge the image while cropping the top and bottom, so that it fills the screen. Unless you are finishing the film yourself with your own editing software, either of these options can become expensive, so consulting an online house in advance will help you avoid budget shortfalls.

## Administrative

64–75.  This is how you keep your operation going—your overhead. Funders, especially broadcasters, can be very picky about what they'll pay for in this category. They might balk at covering your ongoing expenses, especially if you have multiple projects going simultaneously. We try to be reasonable but realistic: we don't pad our office rent, but we try to include a production services fee (line 77), sometimes called "cost of doing business." This can be a percentage of the budget subtotal, as in this case, and the amount of the percentage is almost always a topic of discussion in budget negotiations. An argument can be made that overhead items like office rent and phone should be included in the production services fee, in which case the percentage should be raised sufficiently to cover those costs.

65–67.  Office line items are self-explanatory, based on estimated monthly average expenses.

68.  Legal fees cover production matters on which you will need to consult a lawyer, such as rights agreements, releases, and contracts with funders or broadcasters. The estimate should be based on a conversation with your entertainment attorney.

69–71.  Insurance is often overlooked by first-time filmmakers. You'll need liability insurance (to cover injuries, legal disputes, and so forth), production insurance (to protect you in the event your exposed film, shot tape, or hard drive is physically damaged, for example, and you need to reshoot), and errors and omissions (E&O) insurance, which protects you from licensing and release disputes and is required by broadcasters. Some broadcasters provide their own production insurance, and some provide E&O. If you have a broadcaster funding your project, these are things to ask about.

72–73.    "Fringes," as they're called in the industry, refer to payroll taxes, union and guild benefits, and workers' compensation, calculated as a percentage of the salaries paid to those employees who are not independent contractors. Talk to your accountant about this. A rule of thumb is that if someone is working for you at your place of business, under your direction, at hours set by you, and on equipment you provide, then that person is an employee and must be payrolled (that is, you must pay employer payroll taxes and deduct employee taxes from their paychecks). People who work for you but make creative decisions with some degree of independence, have flexibility in determining their schedule, and use their own equipment can legitimately be considered independent contractors. As you can imagine, this quickly gets fuzzy. Is a director of photography, using her own camera, meeting you on location at a time determined by you, and working under your direction an employee or an independent contractor? Again, this is a question for your accountant and for hers. Often freelancers prefer to be paid as independent contractors, and if your accountant agrees, then it's to your benefit as a producer to do so, as you'll save money on payroll taxes. Just be sure to include a paragraph in their deal memo indicating that they are responsible for any taxes incurred as a result of their work for you (see Sample Deal Memo in appendix 2).

   Some craft workers, such as editors, might belong to a union to which you will have to pay pension and welfare benefits. It's helpful if you have these people on board when you're making your budget, so that you can estimate these costs accurately. You may decide it makes sense to break this line down into two or three lines, to keep things simpler and your budget more accurate.

   Guild fees ("pension and welfare") should be included if the director or writer is a member of the Directors or Writers Guild.

74.    Bank charges: You will likely have miscellaneous expenses when you set up a checking account and order checks.

## Budget Subtotal

This is the total of all the costs budgeted above (accounts 1–74) and is used to compute the next two items:

76.    Production contingency: Producers usually include a contingency to cover unexpected overages. Broadcasters have varying policies on this. Our position is that with a reasonably accurate budget, the producer has too little cushion for when things go wrong: a shoot doesn't work out and you decide you need an additional shooting day; a piece of equipment breaks down—anything at all that can go wrong and cost you extra money. The contingency protects you

from having to go into your own pocket in such cases, or going back to your funder and asking for more money. And if by some miracle everything goes exactly as planned, then the production contingency should be considered a bonus to the producer for coming in on budget. Of course, broadcasters may have different opinions about this, so it can be a subject of negotiation and compromise.

77. Production services fee: This is another tricky item, which some broadcasters will try to whittle down or eliminate. We feel strongly that it is justified, and we make the argument that we have ongoing overhead just as the broadcasters do. Without maintaining a production office infrastructure, for example, we would have to incur expenses such as buying a copy machine and installing phones for each new project. If you have a thriving production house with multiple projects, you can share these costs among their respective budgets, but the costs are real and should be accounted for.

\* \* \*

So that's a rough overview of how to create a budget. Just fill in the numbers and add them up. If the total is too high, start looking for places to cut back. If you are a first-time filmmaker making your own budget, you would be well advised to have an experienced producer at least look it over before you go into production, to make sure your forecasts are realistic. Once you are in production, you will want to keep your budget at hand, to compare it with actual costs and adjust your plans accordingly.

## CREATE A SAMPLE REEL[7]

For many filmmakers, the first money raised for their films goes toward shooting and editing a sample reel.[8] Sometimes a film subject will raise questions in potential funders' minds about how you will approach it visually. Is your main character really strong enough to carry a film? How can you make a film about radio, for example, which is an audio experience? Do you actually have the access you claim to certain key people? How will you make a film about a public policy issue (say, water use) more than just an illustrated lecture? A compelling sample reel that suggests how you'll accomplish what your proposal promises will make your fundraising efforts more successful.

A sample reel is like an advertisement for your film—think of it as a coming-attractions trailer for a film that hasn't been made yet. It could be as short as a couple of minutes, like the trailers shown in movie theaters before the feature, or as long as 15 minutes, although 9 to 12 minutes are probably the most common lengths.[9] And just as you may need to tailor your proposal to fit the needs of different funders, you may need to make multiple sample reels for funders with different priorities, or as more footage becomes available.

The sample reel can serve several functions. Besides helping you sell the film to potential funders, it can help you convince people to participate in the project, whether as subjects or as support crew; and it can help you start to define the creative language that will most effectively convey your story. As you start to edit your sample reel, you are really starting to make your movie.

### Work with What You Have, Play to Your Strengths

You have to start somewhere. What materials do you already have? Are there preinterviews from which you can pull a few compelling moments to give a sense of the characters and the stories you will be telling? (Sample reels are yet one more reason to record decent picture *and audio* in your preinterviews.) Is there archival footage you can get copies of to add a sense of historical context? Are there photos you can scan to help convey the visual language of the film? Find some music that expresses the mood you want to evoke. Then start weaving these elements into a sequence or two that best exemplify the film you intend to make. This is a great opportunity to get your feet wet—and to see some of the problems and strengths in the material.

### Case Study: The Sample Reel as a Creative Tool for *The Celluloid Closet*

We started with transfers of film clips that Vito Russo had collected for the traveling lecture/clip-show presentation he had developed over the years. We went back to the Museum of Modern Art archive to view the films from which they were excerpted, and we added a few clips that we found on our own. We cut these together with music and title cards, organizing the clips by stereotype: The Sissy, the Predator, and so on. The message was that gay and lesbian characters have been in the movies since the birth of the medium (already a surprise to most people), and their manner of presentation provides a telling commentary on our attitudes toward gender. This was more or less spelled out in various incarnations of the sample reel, which we reworked several times—sometimes through narration, sometimes with title cards. We always made sure to mention that the film would be "based on the landmark book by Vito Russo" and ended with the promise "Coming soon from Telling Pictures!"

One version of the reel included a reenactment of a young Vito character watching his first same-sex kiss on screen in a movie theater. We were looking for a way to avoid a traditional narrator, so we thought of using Vito's

DVD Cover—*The Celluloid Closet*. Poster design by Juan Gatti. (Artwork from *The Celluloid Closet* appears courtesy of Sony Pictures Classics Inc.)

voice—or an actor reading his words—in the film as an audio element. We sketched this sequence on videotape using amateur actors and a theater that allowed us to shoot there one afternoon. When we sent this cut of the sample reel to executive Sheila Nevins at HBO seeking her support, she told us we were "working too hard." She urged us to use the traditional storytelling tools we had been using for years and trust that the material would be strong enough to drive the film. She was right.

When Lily Tomlin joined the project, we used her to narrate the sample reel. Our most successful version of the sample reel advertised our strongest selling points: entertaining movie clips, a book with a core following, a celebrity narrator, the promise of movie star interviews, and what we thought was an intriguing theme.

As much as possible, try to include examples of all the different storytelling tools you will be using in your film—stock footage, intimate interviews,

## Lead with Your Strongest Footage

Documentary filmmaker Jon Else was on a PBS panel that awarded *The Times of Harvey Milk* a grant at a critical time. Else had never heard of Rob Epstein or his producer, Richard Schmiechen, before, but he and other panelists were so impressed by Rob's sample reel that they gave all the available money to *Harvey Milk*. What was so compelling on that reel that it led to a unanimous agreement of the panel? Instead of a summary or survey of the larger film, which wouldn't have been possible at that stage anyway, Rob had sent an edited scene of the huge, peaceful candlelight march held in San Francisco on the night of Harvey Milk and Mayor George Moscone's assassination. It's crucial to know what material to emphasize.

evocative visual re-creations, period pop songs—whatever works to tell the story. If it's simply impossible to include an important element, then find a way to indicate what's missing, as we did with the title card at the end of our *Celluloid Closet* sample reel: "Still to come: interviews with the actors, writers and directors who made the movies."

* * *

Our sample reel for *Common Threads* was a 15-minute sequence we edited from our first shoot of the Quilt being unfolded in Washington, DC. Except for the music, which we borrowed from a preexisting film score, that sequence stayed pretty much intact and forms the heart of the third act of the finished film. When we were raising money for *Paragraph 175*, we used an excerpt of the one interview we had completed—a particularly moving three-minute talking-head anecdote that we knew had a disproportionate impact on audience's emotions for such a short clip. Often, though, the sample reel is an entirely different animal than a scene or sequence from the film—again, think *movie trailer*.

There is no formula for sample reels, other than to play to your strong suit. Try to convey the look and feel of the film you're proposing to make. And—very important—*you want to leave the viewer wanting more*. Don't try to create the whole film in miniature, with a beginning, middle, and end. You want to leave room to imagine possibilities that go beyond the material you already have—otherwise, why make the movie? When you think it is finished—or when you get stuck editing—show your sample reel to people whose judgment you trust before sending it off to potential funders.

## Sample Reel: Dead End or Fork in the Road?

Our sample reel for *HOWL* was what convinced us to strike out in a different direction. When we started *HOWL*, we fully expected it to be a documentary. With some development money in hand and several months of research behind us, we decided a sample reel was the next step. The sample consisted of existing archival footage of Allen Ginsberg—all featuring the poet as middle-aged or older—as well as portions of an audio recording of the older Ginsberg reading the poem and footage and stills from the 1950s accompanied by a jazz sound track. Reactions from colleagues and Rob's film students convinced us that this approach was a dead end. Ginsberg had written "Howl" as a young man; it was his first major poem and the work that made him a poet. Our choices were stark: give up a project to which we had already devoted some years, or figure out another way to do it. We decided we needed to re-create the world of the young Allen Ginsberg. That meant making an entirely different kind of film, in which the dialogue would be authentic but the speakers would be actors. The path we took to our hybrid nonfiction feature film began with that sample reel.

CONCLUSION

The *development* period usually refers to the process of raising money. It's also when you determine the parameters of your film, as well as the practical conditions that will make it possible to produce. This process also allows you to develop the concept and your style of storytelling.

A sample reel combined with a strong proposal or treatment, a realistic budget, and a viable production schedule together form the basis of a credible production. You can use these materials to help get potential funders excited about your project. The care with which these materials are prepared and presented will demonstrate that you're serious about making this film, and that you're up to the job.

*Part Two*

# Preproduction

_Chapter 6_

# Financing

Fundraising is onerous and unavoidable. No matter how successful you become as a filmmaker, you will inevitably find yourself in the position of having to sell your idea—and yourself as a filmmaker. Salesmanship is a surprisingly large part of making movies. Even if you don't have to raise production funds, eventually you will have to sell your films to distributors, exhibitors, and audiences. And regardless, you'll need to convince people to participate in your project, whether as subjects in the film or as members of the crew—and that involves selling. It all boils down to convincing other people that your project is important, that audiences will want to see the film, that you are the right person to make it, and that it's worth the time, effort, and money you propose to invest in it.

All the persuasive arguments you can muster should be well laid out in your development materials: the proposal and treatment, the budget and production schedule, and, when possible, the sample reel. It may feel more comfortable to think of it as showmanship rather than salesmanship. Either way, your enthusiasm for the project needs to be infectious—and genuine.

## DEVELOPMENT FUNDING VERSUS PRODUCTION FUNDING

If you are just getting started with your project, you might want to seek development funding. As the term implies, this is money to help you do the research and development required to go into production. The advantage of asking for development funding is that because the amounts are generally quite small, there's less risk to the funder. On the other hand, there is a greater risk that the project will never get completed.

Generally, a development agreement with a broadcast entity or commissioning organization, for example, includes a set of deliverables and an agreement by both parties (filmmaker and funder) to move into production together if the funder finds the deliverables satisfactory. (Otherwise rights to the project revert to one of the parties, either the party that initiated the project or the one that financed development.) The development agreement might also set out some general parameters of the potential production partnership, such as the terms of the projected license.[1]

Development grants from foundations, state humanity councils, and the NEH or NSF may facilitate but do not guarantee production funding from these sources.


## FOUNDATIONS

The advantage of foundation money is that it usually has few strings attached beyond some reasonable reporting paperwork, and since the money is in the form of a grant, it does not need to be paid back. In addition, support from one funder can encourage others to consider your project more favorably.

The disadvantage is that grant proposals often require a fair amount of work for a relatively small amount of money. Government funding sources such as NEH or private funding sources such as the Corporation for Public Broadcasting (CPB) or the Independent Television Service (ITVS) that receive and distribute federal funds may require reviews of rough cuts but otherwise attach minimal strings to their awards, and even that filmmakers pay back grant money with profits from their films, but since documentaries rarely make a profit, it's generally a moot point. As a rule, the bigger the grant, the bigger the grant-writing job. NEH gives very generous grants, for example, but the grant preparation process is arduous and time consuming. NEH does make successful sample proposals available, something few other funders do.

Foundations are generally wary of film projects, especially those in development. The fear seems to be that, because filmmaking is such an expensive proposition, projects may not come to fruition. That's not an unreasonable concern: a history of unfinished films over the years has led some foundations to stop funding media at all. The remaining funders are far more likely to consider a project favorably in the later stages of editing. Many foundations limit their grants to "finishing funds." ITVS also stipulates that it wants to be the "last money in." Getting involved at this late stage reduces the risk of supporting a project that will never come to fruition.

An Internet search can guide you to foundations whose interests align with those of your project (see, for example, the Foundation Center's comprehensive website: http://www.foundationcenter.org). Go to the websites of foundations you're interested in and read their guidelines carefully. Try to find ways to emphasize those aspects of your concept that support the foundation's mission statement. Be sure also to review their lists of grant recipients, which usually describe the funded projects and note the amounts granted. Sometimes these lists will reveal more about a foundation's current interests than its mission statement does, and reviewing amounts awarded as percentages of projects' total budgets will help you determine how much to request.

You may have to tailor your proposal and sample reel, shifting the emphasis for various potential funders. Let's say you're making a film about an inner-city literacy center. You find a foundation that gives film grants to projects concerned with issues of women and poverty. You might consider featuring the story of a woman with a dead end, minimum wage job learning to read as one of your story elements. As long as you intend to include such a story in your film, there's nothing dishonest about moving it front and center for the purposes of this proposal. Just as in another proposal—for a foundation concerned with immigrant issues, say—you would want to feature your immigrant story. It may require a bit of cursory research to be sure you can find such a person, but then it's really a matter of taking the proposal or treatment you've already written and refocusing it.

It's up to you to decide at what point you've shifted the emphasis so far that you would be requesting the money under false pretenses. Be a responsible member of the nonfiction film community: make the film you say you're going to make, and let your funder know if circumstances beyond your control force you to make significant changes in your story. In other words, don't poison the well for the filmmakers coming after you.

Whenever possible, try to make contact with one of the foundation's program officers, who act as liaisons between grantor and grantees. They can advise you of the suitability of your project for grant submission. This will save you and them from wasting time, and a program officer who likes your project can offer helpful advice about how to position your project to elicit the most favorable response. NEH and NSF assign program officers to shepherd film projects through their procedures. If you plan to go this route, ask recent NEH or NSF grant recipients how helpful their program officers were and how best to navigate this very important relationship.

## BROADCAST PARTNERS

One of the most common sources of funding for documentaries is television. U.S. public television money is harder and harder to come by, and it's a complicated web to sort out. There is local station funding, which offers relatively small amounts, as well as national broadcast funding, which generally originates with the CPB and is filtered through an ongoing series (such as *American Masters*, *The American Experience*, *Nova*, or *Frontline*[2]) on the Public Broadcasting Service (PBS) or through ITVS, which was established to encourage "creative risks . . . [and] voices and visions of underrepresented communities."[3]

As with most funding, there are strings attached. Making a program for one of the established series—with their signature styles and structures—will offer filmmakers the least creative autonomy but the best chance of having their work broadcast in prime time. Making a film with ITVS funding offers greater autonomy but no guarantee of national broadcast. However, ITVS has an interest in getting its programs shown, since its reputation and clout in the media world increase in proportion to the number of broadcast slots found for films it has funded. Many films it supports do air on the ITVS spin-off series *Independent Lens* or on *POV* ("point of view"), a public television series that has featured independent documentaries since 1988. *POV* itself provides acquisition/finishing funds for the films it accepts, but with restrictions for those that have already received money from ITVS or other public broadcast-related sources.

For-profit broadcasters (such as cable networks) are generally less bureaucratic so easier to deal with, and sometimes offer less restrictive standards (as in use of vulgar language, for instance)—but they will almost certainly want to have a strong hand in shaping the final product. It's a trade-off.

When is the best time to involve a broadcaster in your project? That depends on your project and the broadcaster. Waiting until you've raised at least a portion of the budget and begun making the film—whether you've just shot and assembled some footage or you're on your way to a rough or fine cut—gives you the advantage of having a more persuasive pitch, since you can show a work in progress. It also puts you in a stronger position when negotiating creative decisions, especially if you have financed a significant portion of the budget. Like foundations, broadcasters are often more comfortable providing finishing funds than development money, for the same reasons—they're investing in a known quantity. They can see from the rough or fine cut what the film is going to be, and the fact that the film is already so close to completion resolves concerns that it won't get made. All that broadcasters need to be convinced of is that the film has a respectable likely viewing audience. They may also respond to the importance of the subject and the film's potential to make an impact and garner positive publicity for the broadcaster.

Generally, your options are to sell broadcast license rights to the finished film, sell the film before it is finished (a "presale"), or partner with a broadcaster during production (a "coproduction"). Each of these scenarios presents distinct advantages and disadvantages.

## SALES

The simplest arrangement—and the most advantageous if you can afford it—is to sell the film after it's finished. You get to make the film you want to make, and if the film is accepted by festivals, you will have a launch venue where audiences can respond. The better audiences respond, the better your chances of making a profitable sale. This scenario is also the most risky if you don't take into consideration the length, style, and content preferences of your potential broadcaster. The sale price should include, along with your fee, the cost of a cutdown[4] if necessary, and any processes required to make your film meet that broadcaster's technical specifications—which vary from one broadcaster to another. If music rights are prohibitively expensive, you may, for example, have negotiated a lower rate for festival-only distribution. A broadcaster might agree to pay for expanded exhibition rights as part of its licensing deal—but this will likely lower the licensing fee the broadcaster will offer you. (See Music Rights in chapter 8.)

If you decide that you need the financial backing of a broadcaster in order to get your film made, you can structure the relationship either as a presale or as a coproduction. These are vague terms, each implying a different business and creative relationship.

## PRESALES

Generally, a *presale* implies that you are making the film independently and that the broadcaster is buying a license, before the film is made, allowing it a limited right to broadcast it. The actual amount of a presale is typically less than either that of the sale of a finished film or that of a coproduction.

The obvious advantage to the presale is that if you find a broadcaster who likes your project and is willing to fund it, it can take a lot of pressure off you. You have financing and you know the film will eventually have a broadcast home.

On the other hand, by going to a broadcaster before you've started production, you'll have less to tempt them with, so your sales job becomes all the more challenging. The funders will have to base their decision on faith in your idea, your proposal (and sample reel), your access, and your track record. And once broadcasters do start putting money into your film, they are likely to start taking a proprietary interest in it—it's their money, after all. So creative control can become an issue.

## COPRODUCTIONS

Coproductions are like presales in that the broadcaster provides funding before the film has been made, but in return the broadcaster becomes a part owner of the finished film. The usual limits on their *broadcast window* (number of showings over a period of time) may not apply for a coproduction. The broadcaster's financial commitment will probably be significantly greater— and the broadcast executive assigned to your project may insist on more involvement in the shaping of the finished product.

Involving the network during production can be an advantage. Making your executive part of the creative process invests him in your project and can help avoid last-minute demands for changes. It can also be frustrating if your visions for the film diverge, though it's probably best to know this early on.

Although some filmmakers might see this as unwarranted interference, films can benefit from critical input from perceptive broadcast executives, especially if the executive is smart and her network is the ideal home for your film. When we submitted a one-hour version of *Paragraph 175* to HBO executive Sheila Nevins, she responded that the film warranted a feature length and offered to pay for it. (See also the case study on *The Celluloid Closet* in chapter 5.)

## INTERNATIONAL OPPORTUNITIES

If your film has international potential—and that's a big *if*—you can look for coproduction partners or try to make presales outside your home territory. Broadcasters license programming for exhibition in specific territories; thus an American presale does not preclude sales to other territories such as Germany, France, or Japan.

A few words of caution, though.

First, specifically American subjects rarely appeal to international buyers. Films with many talking heads in particular are difficult to sell abroad.

Second, if you sell off valuable territories too early, you may not be able to find a sales agent later on when you need to sell the film to the rest of the world. Sales agents work on commission, and a film with valuable markets already sold will be less attractive to them.

Finally, without a real understanding of the international broadcast market, you can unintentionally spoil valuable sales by selling to less lucrative territories. A sale to one of the Benelux countries (Belgium, the Netherlands, Luxembourg), for instance, can spoil your chances in neighboring markets like Germany and France. You're better off working with—or at least consulting with—a knowledgeable sales agent, if possible.

## PITCH MARKETS

Pitch markets can be a good place to find potential partners, or at least start a buzz about your project. The Toronto Documentary Forum at Hot Docs (the documentary festival held each spring in Toronto) and the Forum at the International Documentary Film Festival Amsterdam (IDFA) in November are two well-regarded venues that attract most of the international commissioning editors[5] that you would want to meet.

Naturally, these are highly competitive affairs, packed with aggressive filmmakers eager to get noticed. Attendees are assigned mailboxes, which are generally overflowing with postcards and promotional materials, often quite slickly produced. Having some nice-looking graphic materials— whether it's a polished presentation packet, glossy postcards with catchy artwork, or even a poster mock-up—can help get your project noticed. The better your presentation looks, the more attractive your project becomes.

At Hot Docs and IDFA, the sessions are something of a spectacle. Each filmmaking team is assigned a time slot of a few minutes in which to make a presentation to a room full of commissioning editors from around the world. This presentation may (and should) include a short sample reel, giving a sense of the filmmaker's approach to visual storytelling as well as the strength of her story and characters. Bleachers of seats are filled with an audience of other filmmakers waiting their turn to pitch or just observing competing pitch techniques.

In recent years, Great Britain's Channel 4 BRITDOC Foundation and the Sundance Institute Documentary Film Program have joined forces to stage "Good Pitch" sessions on both sides of the Atlantic (http://britdoc.org/real _good/pitch). At these events filmmakers make their pitches and show clips to nonprofits that might be able to offer the pitching filmmakers funds, connections to other resources, outreach partnership, and other assistance.

## Refining the Pitch

*HOWL* was accepted to No Borders, the domestic pitch forum run by the Independent Feature Project (IFP) in New York. We had a beautiful proposal and an attractive package, including some well-known actors. In fact, ours was the most sought-after project the year we attended. We had one-on-one meetings with over 60 potential financers in a five-day period. While we raised no financing there, it was a great opportunity to make contacts and to refine our pitch. By gauging which parts "landed" with our listeners as well as those parts where they seemed to drift off, we were able to hone our presentation. By the end of the five days, it was pitch-perfect.

What we learned about our pitch at No Borders did help us later with other funders on *HOWL*, and there's always a chance that a funder who saw our pitch and passed will be more willing to support another film of ours in the future.

Because pitching is performance, it helps to rehearse in front of people. We think it's essential. Try out your pitch on friends and colleagues, and listen to their feedback.

We prepare our pitch sessions as if they were little productions, carefully scripted to hit all our sales points, and structured for maximum effectiveness. We practice with colleagues and friends until we feel comfortable making the presentation without reading from notes. Pitching is a performance art. Your enthusiasm and passion are as important as the subject matter you are promoting.

Our own experiences at pitch forums have been mixed. We pitched *Paragraph 175* at IDFA. We showed a sample reel that was simple in the extreme: three minutes of a very moving story told by a man who lost the love of his young life to the Nazis. The response was overwhelmingly enthusiastic. People had tears in their eyes. Several of them told us that ours was the most successful presentation of the session. We were elated. And we never received a penny of development funding from anyone in that room—though many of them would eventually license the film once it was finished.

We had a happier outcome when we applied and were invited to bring *The Celluloid Closet* to CineMart, another development market (a sidebar of the Rotterdam International Film Festival). A catalogue was distributed containing proposals for the 30 or so films that were chosen, and one-on-one meetings were scheduled with interested broadcasters. We were able to make an important connection there to a commissioning editor from ZDF television in Germany, who, along with Channel 4 in the UK, would be our first coproduction partners on *The Celluloid Closet.*

Even if the pitch market doesn't yield immediate results, it can be valuable in making your project known to broadcasters who may be interested in seeking it out for licensing once it is finished. At the very least, pitch markets are excellent opportunities for networking, which is a vital part of the filmmaking business. We have no way of measuring what effect, if any, our IDFA pitch had on future sales, but it did create interest in the film, which is never a bad thing.

## INDIVIDUAL DONORS

If you have a project that you think individuals or communities might be interested in seeing made, by all means, ask them for financial support. You may decide to use this method as a part of your fundraising strategy. Films dealing with social issues affecting specific groups are good candidates for targeted fundraising.

## TARGETED FUNDRAISING CAMPAIGNS

Consider allying yourself with an appropriate organization that might be willing to make its mailing list available to you. In exchange, you might have to offer something—a limited number of DVDs or streaming rights to distribute to the organization's members, for instance, or benefit premiere screenings that the organization can use as fundraising events. Or you may get lucky and find an organization that just wants to help you get the word out.

When we were developing *The Celluloid Closet*, we waited until we had two coproduction partners on board (Channel 4 in the UK and ZDF in Germany) before we went to the gay community asking for support. We wanted to be confident that we would actually be able to finish the film before we started asking individuals for personal money. We met with a very smart direct-mail consultant who had an extensive gay and lesbian mailing list. He was so confident in the prospects of a direct-mail campaign that he was willing to finance his costs out of the first money he intended to raise for us. This was too good an offer to refuse. We produced a very slick package, including a letter from Lily Tomlin, and a souvenir poster of Vito Russo memorabilia (we were targeting an audience that was familiar with Vito's work as the author of *The Celluloid Closet* and as a community activist). The mailing was indeed tremendously successful, putting us well on the road to production.

In recent years, e-mail and the Internet have made the cost of mounting a targeted fundraising campaign much less prohibitive. An e-mail targeting members of a specific audience can direct their attention to your production website, where they can view a sample reel, read about you and the project, and of course make a contribution.

Crowdsourcing has increasingly become an effective means of fundraising. Crowdfunding websites have made it possible to raise cash quickly by setting deadlines and offering a tiered array of thank-you gifts based on the amount individuals donate. This kind of time-limited, intensive fundraising by way of online social networks can generate excitement and publicity along with much-needed funds. As with any possible funding source, do your research: analyze recent successful campaigns, poll everyone you know who has done one, and then design your own campaign so that it will be both successful and manageable.

## FUNDRAISING EVENTS

Big, splashy fundraising events with famous performers or public figures donating their time are a huge gamble, and often much more expensive to mount and time-consuming to organize than anyone anticipates. Further, they're appropriate only for certain kinds of documentaries: those with either a clearly identified well-heeled constituency or those with large, enthusiastic audiences who might not be wealthy but are able to make donations. If your film fits into one of these categories and there are people working around you who can take on much of the organizing burden, you might want to consider such an event, which can not only raise money but also provide publicity and generate goodwill with your potential audience. But first, carefully evaluate how realistic your fundraising prospects are.

While Rob and Jeffrey were making *Common Threads* Sharon worked on a documentary biography of Supreme Court Chief Justice Earl Warren, titled *Super Chief: The Life and Legacy of Earl Warren*.[6] The producers were Bill Jersey, a veteran documentary filmmaker, and Judith Leonard, a first-time filmmaker who was also a lawyer and a prodigious fundraiser. During post-production, Judy conceived the idea of holding an Earl Warren Dinner, which eventually grew into an entire weekend. The event was held at the Fairmont Hotel atop Nob Hill in San Francisco, and notable politicians and senior partners from major law firms from across the country attended, along with two sitting Supreme Court justices: William Brennan and Thurgood Marshall. The event raised a substantial amount of money and generated goodwill for the film because, along with all of the production team's hard work, the constituency was the elite of the legal profession and the weekend offered a unique, prestigious—and tax-deductible—networking event for that group. (A second film came from the event as well. The morning after the dinner, NPR's Nina Totenberg moderated a debate about Earl Warren. Panelists included Anthony Lewis, then the *New York Times* legal reporter, and Robert Bork, who had been denied a seat on the Supreme Court. This was filmed and edited into a companion piece.)

Some years later, when all three of us were working on *The Celluloid Closet*, we held a fundraising evening at the Castro Theater in San Francisco, a landmark movie palace in the center of the city's gay community. Lily Tomlin was the headliner for a sold-out evening that included performances by Marga Gomez, Harvey Fierstein, and Robin Williams. Like the Earl Warren event, this evening raised critically needed funds and gave back something unique to the community most interested in the film's subject. What's more, the evening was about as much fun as a filmmaker could hope to have—and to offer an audience—while fundraising.

## COCKTAIL PARTIES

Filmmakers sometimes organize small gatherings, often at the home of a supporter of the project who has influence in the community, to make a presentation and ask for donations. If you have such an ally, strategize with her about the guest list and the refreshments, and as with any pitch session, plan your presentation with care. Prepare a short sample reel and printed materials—whatever you can offer that shows both the urgency of your project and your talent at presenting it. Then write the script for your presentation. In the typical scenario, your host introduces you, explaining why she feels the project is so important and why you are the right person to get it made. Then you give a short presentation, no more than 5 or 10 minutes, including an effective sample reel. And your host closes with a request ("the ask") that people write checks—as she has—to support this worthy project.

Again, this method can produce varying results. You might leave the party with checks for a few hundred dollars in your pocket and promises (of varying reliability) for bigger ones to come. You might luck out and meet some wealthy individual who is so excited he wants to fund the whole project— unlikely, but you never know. Or you might strike out completely. These parties can be a lot of work to pull together, so weigh the efforts and costs against the possible benefits and decide if it's worth it.

We tried fundraising cocktail parties twice with *Paragraph 175*, once in San Francisco and once in New York. Both times, all we went home with were leftover hors d'oeuvres. Maybe the subject, while important, was too grim for that kind of social setting, or perhaps because it was historical, attendees felt it lacked the urgency of a film addressing contemporary issues. Or maybe we just didn't sparkle enough on those particular evenings.

On a happier note, Rob raised one-third of the $300,000 budget for his film *The Times of Harvey Milk* from community fundraisers and cocktail parties. This was a film with a community base who understood the importance of getting it made. (The remainder of the budget came from foundation grants and public television.)

## INDIVIDUAL SUPPORTERS

If you know—or have some way of getting to—one or two wealthy individuals who you think might have an interest in helping you get your project made, write them a letter. Be professional and passionate, and offer them the chance to get involved in your exciting, important project. Offer to meet with them individually at their convenience to discuss the project or the details of their contribution.

Individuals will want to know the terms of their involvement. This is for you to determine. Grants from individuals will usually be in one of two forms: as a contribution, preferably tax-deductible, or as an investment.

## INDIVIDUAL CONTRIBUTIONS

Some people may be willing to make a contribution with no strings attached, perhaps in exchange for only an on-screen credit. These people are rare, though. At the very least, you want to offer contributors a tax write-off. To do this, you will need to establish a nonprofit corporation (time consuming but not that difficult in consultation with your attorney and accountant). Alternatively, you can find an existing nonprofit media organization to serve as *fiscal sponsor* for your project, usually for a small administrative fee (7% is typical). It's even possible for the charitable organization with which you've allied yourself (see Targeted Fundraising Campaigns, above) to set up a fund to accept contributions, earmarked for your project, that they pass directly on to you. Take care, however, that your contracts protect your creative control of the project when you get involved financially with a more powerful organization.

Organizations expressly intended to service filmmakers often offer not only nonprofit sponsorship but also valuable fundraising advice. Some even handle certain bookkeeping tasks, such as issuing checks and 1099 tax forms to independent contractors. It might make sense to work with one of these organizations on your first few films before you consider setting up your own nonprofit.

## INVESTORS

Investors will want to see a business plan demonstrating your intention to maximize the monetary value of your finished film, the amount it will cost compared to the amounts similar films have earned, what markets you intend to exploit, and so on.

Investments can be simple loans, or you can get fancy and formally offer shares of ownership in the project. In the loan scenario, you might promise to pay back the loan amount plus 20 percent from first monies received. If there is more than one lender, the loans will be repaid *pari passu*—that is, to each lender in proportion to the amount of his respective loan. (If investor A loans you $20,000 and investor B loans $80,000, the first monies received from distribution would be distributed 20% to A, 80% to B.)

Investment shares can be structured similarly, with the added incentive of profit sharing: the investors might share in 50 percent of any of the producer's future net profits from exploitation of the film. Smart investors will understand—and you should make it clear—that film is a particularly risky business and that there might never be any profits. In the worst-case scenario investors get to write off their investment as a business loss. You should stipulate that all financial arrangements and promises of screen credit (such as executive producer) are subject to any restrictions a future broadcaster may impose; an investor may object to this unless you grant her the power to participate in distribution decisions. Again, you'll need to work with (or be) a lawyer to do this properly.

## CONCLUSION

Maybe you can make your film with your own equipment and without paying a crew. Maybe you already have all the money you need to hire a crew and rent equipment and make the film exactly as you had hoped to. Or perhaps you've raised just enough money to feel confident that you can finish your film, one way or another. In our experience, there comes a moment when we know we have adequate resources to make a film—even if it's not the film we originally expected to make. For each of our films, we had fallback scenarios—a shorter film, say, or one with fewer archival clips (hence lower licensing fees)—so we felt confident we would end up with a finished product to present to the world. That's the moment when we've gone into production. At some point, you have to stop preparing and start making the movie.

_____ *Chapter 7* _____

# Casting the Nonfiction Film

You may have heard directors of fiction films say that 90 percent of their work is done during casting. There's some truth to that hyperbole, and it applies to nonfiction as well. You can think of your documentary subjects as actors who will, in effect, be improvising their scenes. There have been films with great premises that floundered because of poor casting. On the other hand, you could discover a real star—someone with whom audiences will connect and remember for years to come. Choosing the right subjects to follow can make or break a documentary.

Discussions of "casting" documentary films may seem a bit weird at first. These are real people, after all, and often in fraught circumstances—indeed, that might be what initially makes them compelling subjects for a documentary. And as we mentioned in chapter 1, we would never to refer to people as "characters" while we're filming them. It just sounds too objectifying. Once they have been filmed, however, their stories inevitably become objectified to some extent, as their interview bites and screen moments are evaluated and used to build a dramatic narrative.

Whatever you call them, the process of choosing those people who will best convey your story is very much like casting actors for parts in a fiction film. Whether you're making a vérité documentary about an institution or reconstructing a historical event, you will have to make choices about whom to film. Sometimes a good strategy is to develop a profile of the kind of person you'd like to film, then find likely candidates who meet your criteria. If you take that approach, bear in mind that real people are almost always more complicated than you will have imagined, and part of your task is to adapt your expectations to their lived experiences. Depending on the situation, your pool of potential players could be tiny or vast—and either extreme can be a source of anxiety.

In an observational film, you have to use gut instinct to guess which characters are most likely to lead your film in interesting directions. How long are you prepared to follow this story? What do you think the chances are that the people you're following will undergo some significant change—in their situation, their psychology, or both—within that time frame?

## CASTING CRITERIA

There are other basic questions we ask when we're casting people: Does their personal story fit in to the larger story the film is trying to tell? Are they good storytellers? Do they have screen presence?

## HOW DO THEY FIT IN?

Whatever kind of documentary you're making, your characters should have personal stories that make them compelling and contribute to a larger story, which represents the narrative arc of the film (see chapter 3.)

If it's a vérité documentary about an institution, then you will be looking for people within the institution who are compelling in themselves and whose experiences express something about the institution as a whole. *Welfare* by Frederick Wiseman is a good example: a film in which observed interactions, often seemingly endless and meaningless, build a vivid picture of a deadening bureaucracy.

In a historical film, you may be looking for living witnesses or writers or historians who have studied the events at hand; in either case, each of your storytellers will contribute pieces of the larger story. In films about long-ago events, with no surviving witnesses, you will have to rely more on experts. In *A Midwife's Tale*,[1] producer-writer Laurie Kahn-Leavitt and director Richard P. Rogers focused on a single historian and made her research process part of the story, while also using reenactments to develop a parallel story of the eighteenth-century frontier midwife whose records this historian had uncovered and pieced together.

## CAN THEY TELL A GOOD STORY?

Not everyone can tell a good story. In fact, plenty of people can take a perfectly good story and mangle it with unnecessary details and digressions.

Sometimes the digressions turn out to be more interesting than the story. Often they are simply distractions.

If you ask a potential interview subject to tell you about his wedding and he begins by trying to remember the exact date, month, and year, then follows with a list of the guests, their relationship to the bride and groom, where they came from, and how they got there, but he never gets around to describing the ceremony or how he was feeling—either you've phrased the question wrong, or he's not the right person to talk to.

Sometimes people go to the other extreme, giving monosyllabic responses to questions. This might indicate cultural or social barriers you'll need to overcome—such as being in a society where women speak freely only when men aren't around—before this person opens up to you, or it could be that she is simply taciturn. Sometimes you, the filmmaker, may represent a class or a nation that has oppressed a potential character's culture or society, in which case you'll need to spend time with this person and his community to establish trust. In most situations and for most documentaries, however, an initial meeting, a casual chat over coffee, or even a phone conversation can tell you a lot about how good a storyteller someone is.

## CASTING HISTORIANS AND OTHER EXPERTS

How do you find out which experts will likely be good on camera—in other words, how do you audition them—without being blatant about it and without going to the expense of meeting them all in person? How do you avoid being in the awkward situation of finally getting access to a world-renowned expert only to discover that he speaks in a rapid, low monotone with no facial expression whatsoever? Here the Internet can come to the rescue. See if the people on your list of possibilities are on YouTube, C-Span Book TV, or FORA.TV, a website specializing in public policy speeches and panel discussions. If they're associated with a university or think tank, their institution's website might list public appearances. They might have their own personal websites.

If your experts pass the online speaker test, don't rely on that alone. Depending on how accessible an expert is, try to have an extended phone conversation with her, and ask for permission to record the conversation for your research. This way you'll be able to have a free-ranging conversation with her without having to remember everything she said or worry about your next question. And of course recording the conversation (with her permission) allows you to share it with your filmmaking partners.

Sometimes you will have to film someone who is not particularly engaging: this is the only person who has had the experience you want to convey. In that case, when the time comes, your challenge will be to direct the interview to get what you need so that you will be able to edit it into a coherent, compelling narrative.

## SCREEN PRESENCE

This is a very vague, subjective quality, but like Justice Potter Stewart and obscenity, you know it when you see it. A character with strong screen presence is someone who has energy when she talks to you—someone whose eyes have life in them. Even if you're dealing with an individual suffering from severe depression, his suffering should be visible in his eyes. Someone who is completely shut down will make a very difficult subject for a film.

The best way to assess a storyteller's effectiveness is to do the equivalent of a screen test. In documentaries, they're called *preinterviews*.

## PREINTERVIEWS

You meet someone you think would make a good character for your film. Initial impressions are important—if this person is engaging and lively and has a good story, you would certainly want to consider them. And initial impressions can often predict how someone will come across on camera, since viewers' encounters with subjects in a film can be extremely brief.

At this point you should consider trying to get something on video. Ask if you can record your conversation, purely for research purposes. To put your subject at ease, emphasize that you will not use any of this material in the final film. Keep the atmosphere as relaxed as possible and use a minimal recording setup. Use a small video camera—something that feels more like a home video camera than a professional one. We often also use a small tripod so that we won't have to fiddle with the controls or worry about holding the image steady once the camera is turned on. Make sure the available lighting is good enough to get a proper image—no need to use professional lights at this stage. Finally, use a high-quality external microphone—either one that is mounted on the camera or, in noisy situations, a wired clip-on mic (not hidden under the subject's shirt, as it presumably would in a real shoot, but clipped onto the outside of her clothing). Keep it casual.

Then just start talking. You might start with small talk about where she's from and where she works, gradually leading to the subject you really want to discuss. If it's a particularly delicate subject, tread very lightly and try to stop before things get too emotional. You want to see how readily your prospective subjects can access their feelings, but you don't want them to have their big catharsis before the real filming starts—although we have recorded quite a few emotional research interviews that in no way inhibited equally emotional interviews when we filmed them. But to be safe, if things start getting emotional, we try to gently steer the conversation to more neutral ground.

In some cases, it's an advantage to have someone other than the director, such as a producer or associate producer, do the preinterviews. This is particularly helpful when the possible characters are not accustomed to being interviewed on film. If you'd like them to repeat a wonderful story, it may not have the same freshness if they repeat it to the same person, whereas when they have a fresh audience they might "perform" well in front of the camera when it really counts.

Another advantage to having someone other than the director do the preinterview is that the director will respond to what's really on screen instead of recalling her own experience of the encounter. Sharon thought that one preinterview she did for *Where Are We?* was phenomenal and waited eagerly for our reaction. What we saw was a crazy woman talking about ghosts and sitting in a bathtub without water. While it's true that we were looking for eccentric and unique characters, all we could say was "What were you thinking?"

On the other hand, establishing a relationship with your film's subjects may be essential to ensure that they'll be relaxed and looking at a familiar face when you return with strangers and intimidating cameras, lights, and microphones. It's up to you to gauge which approach to preinterviews will generate the best scenes when you start making your movie.

Experts usually have no problem repeating themselves, which can be a real boon to filmmakers as long as they don't sound rote. Even with experts, warm-up chitchat in a preinterview can deepen the connection and free them to speak frankly with you. Experts are people too, after all.

Finally, always bear in mind that your subjects are auditioning you during this process as much as you are auditioning them. Their level of comfort and safety in talking to you will influence their decision to participate in your film, as well as their willingness to be open and vulnerable during production.

## CASE STUDIES

### Casting an Interview-Driven Documentary: *Common Threads*

*Common Threads* was a film about very recent history—a medical and political story that was still unfolding. Our criteria in casting the film were

very specific to the project. Without being heavy-handed about it, we wanted
our cast of characters to be an accurate representation of the demographics
of the disease, which at that point in the late 1980s primarily affected gay
men, and increasingly intravenous (IV) drug users, people with hemophilia,
and heterosexual women.

Similarly, we were looking for a variety of relationships. Since each story
would be built around the life of someone who had died, we wanted our storytellers to represent the breadth of relationships affected by a disease like
AIDS: lovers, spouses, parents, children. So in a sense, we really were casting
*roles*—we knew we needed parents, for instance, but we didn't know if they
would be parents of a gay man or of someone with hemophilia or of an IV
drug user.

Finally, we looked for people whose stories had strong elements for each of
the three acts we envisaged in the treatment. Act 1 would be life before AIDS.
Act 2 would be about dealing with AIDS, emotionally, physically, and politically. Act 3 would be the creation of the AIDS Quilt, as well as life after
AIDS, whatever that would turn out to be. To some degree we were relying
on our interview subjects to help us understand what their third acts would be.

Working with writer Cindy Ruskin, we combed through some 2,000 letters
that accompanied the Quilt panels people had created and sent to the NAMES
Project from around the country. We sorted these letters into piles—*yes*, *no*,
and *maybe*. This may seem coldhearted, given the intense pain pouring forth
from each of the letters, but we had to make choices. We were able to winnow
the candidates down to about 200.

We divided this list between us and started the next phase, phone interviews.
We called and explained who we were and what we were doing, always men-
tioning that we were working with the NAMES Project, an organization the
letter writers knew and trusted. If they were receptive we asked them a few
questions about themselves and the person they had lost. We took detailed
notes about their stories and what we could glean of their personalities.

We used these notes to flesh out our treatment, plugging new anecdotes
into our existing structure, replacing hypothetical storytellers and stories
with real ones. Through this process we further refined our story, and we
shortened the list of potential storytellers to about 30. Then we set out to
meet and videotape preinterviews with as many of these as we could.

Finally, we went to a friend's house outside the city for a weeklong creative
retreat. We screened our research tapes and reviewed our notes. We used
color-coded index cards to represent different storytellers and broke down
their stories into self-contained anecdotes or "story beats." We laid them

out on a table in three separate sections, one for each act. We integrated the story beats of various characters and juggled their order, trying to create a progression that had some narrative and emotional logic to it. We knew, for example, that people would start learning about AIDS in act 1, that people would start getting symptoms in the first part of act 2, and that all the deaths would happen somewhere toward the end of that act.

We made lists of possibilities for each of our "roles": the parents, the lover, the wife, and so on. And we started to make painful choices. We had two wonderful sets of parents, for instance, and we loved them both. One couple had lost a son who was gay, and the other had lost a son with hemophilia. We already had our quota of gay men, and we were short on hemophiliacs. The decision came down to demographics.

### Casting a Vérité Documentary: *Crime & Punishment*

For observational documentaries, our process is very similar. Preparing for the nonfiction network series *Crime & Punishment*, we spent months meeting with attorneys—mostly prosecutors but also defense attorneys who had cases we were interested in—to assess who would give us the best access and who had the most interesting cases. These were the primary criteria we used:

How good a case does the prosecutor have? (Ideally it was good, but not so good that there would be no plausible defense.)

How comfortable were the crime victims, attorneys, and defendants likely to be with a film crew following them around?

How would they come across on camera? Were the victims sympathetic? Were the attorneys dynamic?

If we knew which judge would preside, how likely would she be to let us film in the courtroom?

What possibilities would there be to shoot scenes outside the courthouse and DA's office? (These could include visits to the crime scene, visits to the victims' homes, or meetings between lawyers and their investigators in restaurants.)

How likely was the case to go to trial during the period we would be set up for production?

Finally, how "telegenic" was the potential cast? In other words, were there enough players that viewers would want to spend time with for the length of the program?

In the end, the choice of stories was based on casting, story elements, and scheduling.

## PITFALLS AND OBSTACLES

In the previous examples, we cast a wide net, improving our odds of find-ing the right people. You might find your options severely limited by circum-stances. We've faced this situation a couple of times, and for very different reasons.

### Reluctant Storytellers: *Paragraph 175*

For *Paragraph 175*, as with *Common Threads*, we had three acts in mind. Act 1 would be Weimar Germany (life before the Nazis came to power, when lesbian and gay subcultures began to blossom in Berlin). Act 2 would be the Nazi years and repression. And because the history we were telling was half a century further in the past than that of *Common Threads*, we had a better grasp of our last act: act 3 would be about the postwar period and the linger-ing stigmas related to homosexuality.

But half a century is a long time, and that presented other problems. We were looking for a subgroup of gay people who had been affected in some way by the Nazi regime in World War II. Our director of research Klaus Müller had been seeking out gay victims of Nazi persecution for a decade, and he was aware of only a handful. Most men of that age who had been openly gay during the Nazi era had perished during the war or in the interim since, or they were very old or in poor health. Those who survived were usu-ally wary of broadcasting their sexual orientation publicly. Gay people of that generation generally tended to be reticent about their sexual orientation. Add to that repeated imprisonment, years of forced labor and often torture, as well as decades of societal rejection after the war, and it was no wonder these people were reluctant to tell their stories in front of a camera. Then there were questions of memory, only somewhat reliable even in the best of circumstances. How would 50 years of aging affect the accuracy of the sto-ries we would hear? Would memories be repressed? Embellished?

For a long time we were worried that we would not be able to find enough storytellers to fill out a feature-length film—or even a television hour. We augmented Klaus's research with our own, making contact with other histor-ians in Germany and Amsterdam, who gave us new leads. These contacts were always indirect. Usually the older people had young helpers or activist friends who helped care for them, serving as their liaison to—and protection from—the outside world. So we began the laborious process of convincing each of these young protectors—and waiting for them, in turn, to try to con-vince their older charges—that we were trustworthy and that the project was worthwhile.

Eventually we had assembled a small group of known survivors and witnesses. One died before we had a chance to interview him. Another demurred
for health reasons, and a third panicked on the day of the interview when his
neighbors learned that a documentary crew was in the building and he feared
they might start asking questions. A fourth was willing to let us interview
him, then changed his mind on the day of the shoot and would talk only
about why he didn't want to be interviewed. Eventually, we had three relatively reliable commitments for significant interviews, and on that minimal
basis we moved into production.

We were ultimately able to find seven storytellers to interview. We even
ended up using the man who didn't want to be interviewed—he would serve
as a vivid illustration of why this story had taken so long to come to light. Of
the remaining interviews, only one or two fit our original notion of the ideal
storyteller—that is, a quintessential victim of Nazi persecution. So we ended
up expanding the scope of the story: instead of being only about homosexual
victims of Nazi persecution, we made a film about the experiences of homosexual men and women during the Nazi regime. One had been a young vol-
unteer in the Berlin underground during the war; another was a Jewish
lesbian who escaped Germany before being arrested. As circumstances forced
us to expand our ideas of who the storytellers would be, our concept of what
the film was about broadened to include their stories. As often happens, this
seeming impediment ended up improving the film—in this case, adding layers
of complexity.

One of the most surprising interviews for us was Albrecht Becker, a
93-year-old flirtatious dandy who had served prison time under the Nazis
for being homosexual. After his release, he found himself one of the few
young men remaining in his village. Feeling lonely, he left to join the
German army, which was still fighting against the Allies. His only explanation was "I wanted to be with men!" At first we had serious reservations
about including Albrecht, simply because his story was so unexpected. Did
we really want to tell the story of a gay German soldier? On further reflec-
tion, we saw that Albrecht's story might provide some insight into how ordinary Germans were able to reconcile—or remain oblivious to—conflicting
values. His story added a level of moral ambiguity that we never could have
imagined when we first got involved in the project.

The person who came closest to what we originally had been looking for—
the quintessential victim—was Heinz F. He agreed to tell his story, which he
hadn't told anyone before, but stipulated that his family name not be revealed
and his face be unrecognizable. We agreed to film him in silhouette—we
needed the story! Although we wouldn't see the emotion in his face, we hoped

to hear it in his voice, and his choice to stay in the shadows, we rationalized, would make a vivid statement about the stigma that still clings to this story. Thankfully, when coproducers Michael Ehrenzweig and Janet Cole showed Heinz the playback monitor to reassure him that his face was obscured, his response was, "But it's so dark!" We later joked that his vanity had won out, and we were grateful, as his beautifully expressive eyes provide some of the most poignant moments in the film. His story was so strong, and the pain in telling it for the first time in 50 years so palpable, that it supplies much of the film's emotional power.

### Celebrity Storytellers: *The Celluloid Closet*

*The Celluloid Closet* presented an entirely different set of challenges. The story was built around the history of Hollywood movies. The subject demanded interviews with industry insiders, including movie stars.

The key to approaching public figures—movie stars, writers, or figures in the news—is to know just how and when to try to make contact with them. Before making your approach, you should have a clear idea of what you are asking of them.

We've made cold contacts with well-known people over the years; with a little bit of perseverance and wiliness, this sometimes works. When we decided we wanted Bobby McFerrin to create a score for *Common Threads*, for example, we found out who represented him and wrote a personal letter explaining who we were and what the project was about. Within days, we got a call from his manager to say he was interested.

When it came time to approach big Hollywood movie stars, though, we felt we needed an ally in the world we were dealing with. Producer Howard Rosenman, a well-known figure in the entertainment industry, had worked with us previously on *Common Threads*, having introduced us to our narrator, Dustin Hoffman. This time we asked Howard to use his connections to convince movie stars to be interviewed on camera.

From our wish list of actors, Howard started with the biggest name with whom he had a close personal relationship. Once he had gotten one big star on board, it became easier to convince everyone else.

We knew that at the celebrity level we would not have the luxury of preinterviews. (Divas do not audition for documentary interviews![2]) Even without knowing what, if anything, of interest they had to say about the films, we decided that if they agreed to participate, the value of their participation outweighed the risks of an unhelpful interview. Had we had made the film today, we could have searched online for interview clips to assess what kind of conversationalist each star might be before initiating contact or preparing interview questions.

In general, you can expect the first response to be no. Don't be discouraged. Very often the request will never have reached the intended recipient but will instead have been intercepted by a protective staff person. Agents have little incentive to pass these kinds of requests to their clients, as documentary projects are notoriously unlikely to generate income for the client or the agency; and publicists are deluged with requests like this, especially for their more famous clients. If your only access is through an agent or a publicist, try to find someone in their office with whom you can establish a relationship and get them excited about your project. Be persistent but not obnoxious. You want them to take your calls and to think of your interactions as pleasant breaks in their routine, not annoyances. Most important, you want to give them a reason to want to help you.

But you're always better off avoiding the gatekeepers altogether, if possible, and finding a personal connection to the person you want to approach. If you don't have a friend in Hollywood, someone you know might. If you can't find a personal connection, then look for other affinities between the person you'd like to reach and yourself.

We knew, for example, that Susan Sarandon had been active politically in New York in the early days of the AIDS crisis and that our friend Vito Russo had been one of the founders of the AIDS activist group ACT-UP. We wrote a letter to Susan, explaining our past work (which included by this time an Oscar-winning AIDS documentary featuring Vito as one of the storytellers) and the film we were trying to get her to participate in, *The Celluloid Closet*, based on Vito's book. This was enough of a connection to get a call back from an assistant, who was sympathetic to the project and who was instrumental in making the interview happen.

## CASTING ACTORS FOR A NONFICTION MOVIE: *HOWL*

Serendipity led to our casting James Franco as Allen Ginsberg in *HOWL*. Director Gus Van Sant was in San Francisco, where we are based, filming *Milk*, which incorporated archival footage and a number of story elements from Rob's documentary *The Times of Harvey Milk*. We had had just finished a draft of the screenplay for *HOWL* and asked Gus, as a friend, to read it. He responded favorably and agreed to come aboard as executive producer. When we asked him for suggestions in casting the young Allen Ginsberg, he immediately suggested James, who was playing Harvey Milk's first lover in *Milk*. This was a choice we wouldn't have initially made on

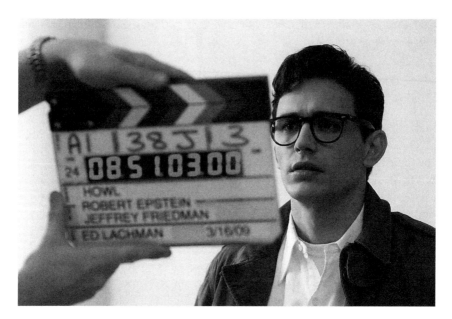

James Franco as Allen Ginsberg on the set of *Howl*, 2010. Photo by JoJo Whilden. (Property of Radiant Cool, LLC.)

our own. We looked at James's earlier work and were especially impressed by his intensity and his uncanny ability to fully embody his characters. We asked Gus to pass him the script. In our first meeting with James, we learned of his own connection to poetry in general and to the world of the Beats in particular. He seemed excited by the challenge of playing Ginsberg. James said, "I'm in, however long it takes."

Gus also introduced us to a great casting director, Bernard Telsey, who helped us cast all the remaining roles. In the courtroom obscenity trial scenes we had the opportunity to work with some truly gifted actors, including David Strathairn, Jon Hamm, Jeff Daniels, Mary Louise Parker, Alessandro Nivola, Treat Williams, and Bob Balaban. Like Franco, each of these established and respected artists joined the project for reasons other than money. They were familiar with our previous work or had an interest in unconventional filmmaking or loved poetry or had a personal connection to the poem "Howl" in particular.

## CASTING TOOLS

Assuming you cast a wide net for your documentary and your story has not already determined your principal characters, one of the big challenges will be simply to keep track of everyone you're considering. As with any kind of research, it's crucial to take good notes and keep them organized.

Video preinterviews are very useful for reviewing potential storytellers and confirming or recalibrating your original assessment—someone who seemed great at the beginning of your process might seem less stellar after you've met 30 other candidates. Photos—even snapshots taken with a mobile phone—will help you put a face to a story when they all start to blur together.

We sometimes create a form to evaluate potential film subjects. This can also be the basis of a searchable database, another useful tool when dealing with large numbers of stories. Typically, we'll devise a template that includes some basic information, as in Table 7.1.

**Table 7.1**  *Common Threads* Film Subject Scoring Table

| Name | | | | | |
|---|---|---|---|---|---|
| Description | | | | | |
| Interviewed by | | | | | |
| Contact info | | | | | |
| Story elements | | | | | |
| Act 1 | | | | | |
| Act 2 | | | | | |
| Act 3 | | | | | |
| **Ratings (5 = highest)** | 1 | 2 | 3 | 4 | 5 |
| Overall story rating | | | | | |
| Camera presence | | | | | |
| Willingness to participate | | | | | |
| Potential scenes | | | | | |
| Potential themes | | | | | |
| Potential conflicts | | | | | |
| **Overall Rating** | | | | | |

*Note*: Courtesy of Telling Pictures.

Needless to say, this is a document you would never want any of your potential subjects to see. It's a good idea to leave these pages in a notebook in the production office so that there's never a chance they'll be casually glanced at.


## CONCLUSION

Once you have chosen your "cast of characters," you enter into a special relationship with them. You need to be coolly analytical as you make your choices, but in your interactions with potential subjects you should be developing a relationship of mutual trust. Be clear about the boundaries of your relationship—ideally it's friendly, but it's not a friendship. You, the filmmaker, are in charge. Your subjects need to trust that you will treat them and their stories respectfully, and you need to trust that your subjects will cooperate during production. As true as you try to be to your subjects and their lives, you are the filter through which their reality will be presented to the world. Your perspective can never be the same as theirs.[3] In the happiest scenarios, though, the two perspectives can be harmonious.

# Chapter 8

# Legal Headaches: Releases, Rights, and Licenses

Most documentary projects involve some third-party rights or licenses that must be cleared. At a minimum, you need to get permission—preferably in writing—from everyone you film. The gold standard for releases and licenses, which might seem like overkill at first, is to request all rights, in all media, in perpetuity, throughout the world. Your goal is to avoid having to renegotiate rights *after* your film has become an acclaimed festival prize winner with a promising future—this is when rights holders will, understandably, demand the highest fees.

Even before you begin filming, you may want to purchase the rights to a preexisting story—a magazine article or book, for example. Or you may need to license the use of certain pieces of music or archival film or video clips. You'll probably need to do some detective work to figure out who owns these rights. It's never too early to figure out what rights you will need—and to start thinking about what they will cost.

Releases and licenses are binding legal documents, so it's always wise to consult with a lawyer when preparing them. The reason to have legitimate licenses and releases is, very simply, to avoid getting sued. In the United States anyone can sue anyone for anything—provided they have the resources—regardless of the strength of the claim. An individual or an organization that wanted to prevent your film from being made could even decide to litigate, knowing that they would be unlikely to prevail in the courts, just to make your life difficult. Of course you could (and probably would) countersue, and lawyers on both sides would happily put in plenty of billable hours, but presumably this is not how you want to spend your money or your time. Even if you aren't worried about being sued, broadcasters and distributors are.

One way to protect yourself against the possibility of damages from lawsuits is an insurance policy known as "errors and omissions." Broadcasters—as the "deep pockets" most likely to be named in lawsuits—will usually require that producers acquire such a policy.

This chapter will briefly explain errors and omissions (E&O) insurance policies, as well as some of the more common types of licenses and releases required in a typical documentary production.

## PERSONAL RELEASES

This is the simplest and most common type of legal agreement you will need to enter into with any clearly identifiable person who speaks, or even just appears, in your film. Networks often have existing releases they want producers to use, and these tend to be overwritten and intimidating. Whenever possible we try to reach a compromise that will let us simplify the language so that we are protected, the person we're asking to sign won't be intimidated, and a broadcaster (and E&O insurer) will accept it. These simplified releases are critical in fast-moving vérité situations, for instance, when you're asking someone who has just appeared briefly in a scene to quickly sign a release.

This became evident when we were filming *Where Are We?* The project was predicated on the spontaneity of casual encounters with strangers as we traveled across the country. Handing people two pages of legalese and asking them to sign would have been self-defeating. After several drafts were exchanged among our lawyers, the broadcaster's legal department, and us, we eventually came up with a shorter release in plain English that was acceptable to everyone.[1]

While you will often, by necessity, collect signatures on releases after the fact in observational situations, there's no excuse not to get a release signed before shooting an interview. On the other hand, don't go overboard by sending the release to interview subjects in advance unless they demand it. That allows them to mull over "grant the right to exploit" and other troubling-sounding but legally necessary phrases. We've found it's best to hand an interviewee the release (and a pen) as he's settling in his chair so that it becomes just one more preinterview step—along with getting his nose powdered and having a microphone snaked under his shirt.

Occasionally, when it has been impossible to get a signature on a written release in a fast-moving observational film shoot, we've gotten a verbal release, *on camera*, in which the subject identifies herself and gives explicit permission to use her interview (or her image or the footage of her—however we're able to get her to say it) in a documentary.

Children's releases must be signed by their parents or guardians. If you plan to film in a school, it's virtually impossible to do so without making the principal and teachers your allies. They are sometimes willing to send the releases home with the children (along with an explanation of your film) to be signed in advance, if you provide all the paperwork. And parents are more likely to sign if your project has been vetted by the teachers or principal.

Finally, in crowd scenes, such as concerts, public meetings, and parties, when it would have been logistically unreasonable to get signatures from everyone present, we have posted signs prominently visible to everyone who enters, informing them that filming is taking place and that by entering this space they give their permission for their image to be used in the film. We make sure to get a shot of the sign during the filming—this will be our only evidence of a release if we need one. We also make an announcement to the crowd when possible to the same effect, and we film that as well. In some cases (as when we filmed in a gay bar near a marine base for *Where Are We?*), we have sectioned off a part of the room that we agreed not to film, marked it clearly, and instructed the audience to position themselves accordingly. The rule of thumb is that if the camera lingers on a recognizable face in a crowd, and certainly if that person speaks, you need to get a release of some kind in order to use his image in the film.

## STORY RIGHTS

If you're making a film about public figures—for example, politicians or entertainers—you are not required to ask their permission or get rights. Of course filmmakers must respect laws protecting public figures against defamation, libel, and slander, and these vary from country to country, but assuming you are producing a fair and well-researched representation of your subject, you can reasonably hope this won't become an issue. All the same, if you're making a film about someone famous and she is amenable to the project, it is helpful to have something in writing. This will not only help you avoid lawsuits but also legitimize your access when pitching the project.

Private individuals have more privacy protection. Even if they agree to be filmed, you will need to get a personal-appearance release from them. Make it a habit to do this before you begin filming to avoid hassles and heartaches later on. Note that it's routine to include language in such releases that grants you the right to recount events or stories from their lives ("life story rights" or simply "life rights") as well as any subsequent interviews and additional filming you may do with them.

In the United States, privacy rights and the related "rights of publicity" generally end with a person's death. These rights, however, are governed by state law and therefore can vary from state to state. For example, some states have enacted laws to enable the estates of deceased famous persons to continue to control and license their image.


## BOOK AND MAGAZINE RIGHTS

If the story has been recounted in a book or magazine, then you may want to secure those rights as well. While this may not be strictly necessary, there are advantages to getting these rights. They can help you ensure some degree of exclusivity. Also, depending on how the book treated its subject and how the subject feels about it, it can help your chances of gaining access to people and situations referenced in it. The author might be a valuable resource for your film, as a consultant or as an interview subject. On the other hand, being associated with a book or an article that presents a person or organization in an unflattering light—or one that the subject perceives to be unflattering—would likely work against you.

You may have to include a consulting fee in your budget if you plan to rely heavily on the author; this could be seen as an exception to the rule about not paying interview subjects.[2] In the case of an expert whose livelihood depends on his expertise in the subject you're asking about, it's reasonable that she receive at least token compensation. Even with nonexpert subjects, while it's important to avoid the perception that their statements have been bought, modest stipends to compensate them for reimbursement of reasonable costs or lost income associated with their participation in the film might be acceptable—it's a judgment call.

To research rights to a book or magazine article, start by writing to the publisher, who will likely refer you to the author's agent. Bear in mind that you are not just shopping for these rights—you are selling yourself and the project. There may be competing offers, and the author may be interested in who has the most money, who is most likely to do the best job, or both. Ideally, the author will see your project as adding value to the book, perhaps even increasing sales. An author might just as easily perceive a film project as competing with the book, in which case your job will be to make a convincing counterargument.

## MUSIC RIGHTS

Music rights are much more complicated and surprisingly expensive. If you want to use a recording of a piece of music or a song, you will need to negotiate and pay for two separate rights.

*Sync rights* refer to the musical composition itself—the right to *synchronize* the composition with visual material. These are granted by the music publisher. With sync rights, you are paying for the composition, lyrics, and arrangement (if there are multiple arrangements, make sure you get rights for the one you want). You will be able to research and try to clear sync rights through either ASCAP or BMI, both of which have useful websites.

You will also need a *master* or *recording license*—the right to use a specific recording of the music. These are usually granted by the record label or the artist. The recording license will often be more expensive than the sync license, particularly if the recording artists are well known. Occasionally, depending on the piece in question, you can find another acceptable recording done by less famous performers. This is especially easy with classical music. Alternatively, you might arrange to have it recorded by other musicians at a fraction of the recording license fee. For one film, Sharon was able to secure a sync license for the 1940s pop song "Ac-Cent-Tchu-Ate the Positive," but a recording of the Andrews Sisters from the period was too expensive. The film's composer brought three women singers together to perform a cover version he orchestrated for a fraction of the original recording's cost. One note of caution: the law prohibits the use of "record-alike" versions, which so closely resemble the original that an audience may be confused and believe that it is the original artist.

If you are using a recording of a piece of music, even if the composition itself is in the public domain (that is, free to use because the copyright has expired),[3] you still must pay for the master license to use the recording.

Fees will vary depending on how the film will be distributed. Theatrical, home video, broadcast TV, cable TV, festival screenings, and webcasts should all have different rates. If you know that your distribution will be limited to one or two of these, you can negotiate lower license fees. If you're not sure—as is often the case—you can at least try to agree in advance with the rights holders on rates for each form of distribution, starting perhaps with festival screenings only (the least expensive). The understanding is that you will purchase appropriate rights as needed, depending on the release pattern of your film, and that the agreed-upon rates will be binding for a period of months or years (the length of this period is also negotiable) from the date of the film's initial exhibition. Getting this agreement in writing before the film is released can protect you from opportunistic rights holders if your film is a runaway success.

Here again, you will have to convince the rights holder that your project is worthwhile and won't reflect badly on the artist. If you do a good enough job, you might even be able to lower the rates or eliminate them altogether.

The one exception to securing music rights is public television. Section 114 of the Copyright Law exempts producers from paying master use licenses for public television broadcast only. In addition, the Harry Fox Agency, which represents many publishers, has a voluntary rate agreement with PBS for sync rights. Again, these apply only to the public television broadcast of your film.

While we knew *Where Are We?* was destined for public television, we wanted it to be seen in festivals and other venues as well. The budget restrained us from including pricey Elvis Presley recordings on the sound-track, even though a key scene featured a miniature Graceland built by ardent Elvis fans.

In some unusual situations, the disposition of music rights might restrict a film's distribution solely to public television. John Antonelli's *Sam Cooke: Crossing Over*, which appeared on the PBS series *American Masters* in 2009, is a case in point. Unable to secure the music rights to Sam Cooke recordings despite repeated efforts (the rights holder claimed he wanted to make his own documentary someday but never did), and having spent years making the film, Antonelli settled for an exclusive public television release.

If you're not making a film about musicians, there are ways to avoid this kind of headache. You can subcontract the task to a music clearance special-ist, or you can hire a composer to write and record original music. But good composers do not come cheap. One way to negotiate the price down is to allow your composer to retain ownership of her work and to use the music she composes for your film for other purposes. You may, moreover, be able to negotiate approval rights if, for example, another film wanted to license the music.

## FOOTAGE AND PHOTO RIGHTS

Rights for film clips and stills are a little more straightforward. Usually the rights are controlled by one party—a studio, a stock footage house or archive, or an individual. If, however, there is music in the film clip, you may need to secure the rights to any songs or musical score that the clip con-tains, apart from the rights to use the film clip itself. Typically, a license agreement will require that the licensee (that's you) take responsibility for clearing these "underlying rights." If you're lucky, the owner of the license to the clip may control these music rights as well. As you can see, this starts to become complicated very quickly.

If the subject of your film has home movies and still photos you plan to include, have him sign a materials release in addition to a personal release. This also applies for original paintings or other artwork by your subject featured prominently in your film.

For some historic photos that are in the public domain and therefore presumably free to use, be prepared to pay an access fee if a particular archive is the only source of those photos. Along with signing a materials release, the archive will at least provide you with high-resolution copies of the photos.

## FAIR USE

One has the limited right to use a limited portion of copyrighted work for one's own purposes. The Copyright Act identifies four areas to determine if a claim of fair use is valid:

- The purpose and character of the use, including whether it is of a commercial nature (as opposed to educational, critical, or artistic), and whether the use somehow transforms the original material and repurposes it in some way rather than simply copying it.
- The nature of the copyrighted work (artistic as opposed to commercial, for instance).
- The amount that was taken from the original copyrighted work relative to its entirety. (Using one minute of a two-minute song may be excessive.)
- The economic impact of the use on the original work. (Does the fair use claim diminish the licensing value of the original work in the marketplace?)

Many filmmakers share the common misperception that there is a firm rule for fair use—that if you use less than 5 seconds, say, it's definitely fair use. That is not the case; there is no bright line defining fair use. It's an evolving question of intellectual property involving gray areas of the law and judgment calls. It's best to consult with an attorney to help navigate this confusing terrain.[4]

## ERRORS AND OMISSIONS INSURANCE

E&O insurance, in theory, protects the filmmaker and the broadcaster or distributor from claims of copyright infringement and other intellectual property liability claims resulting from material in the film. Any U.S. broadcaster will require you to secure such a policy to protect them (and you) from potential litigation. Some broadcasters have a blanket policy under which independent productions can be covered.

Companies offering these policies are as cautious as any other insurance company in their underwriting policies. In cases where the underwriter feels you are especially vulnerable, he may refuse to cover the film, in whole or in part. Even then, he can sometimes be reasoned with.

## CASE STUDY: LICENSING CLIPS FOR *THE CELLULOID CLOSET*

*The Celluloid Closet* presented a daunting licensing challenge, as a good portion of the film is composed of clips from Hollywood movies. If we had to pay "book rate" for these clips, it could easily have escalated into the millions. We were advised early on to minimize the clips and use more interviews, but this was not how we wanted to make the film. We needed a different strategy.

The first problem was determining which clips we wanted to use before we tried to license them, and the only way to do that was to start editing. So that's what we did, using scraps of feature films we grabbed from TV or rented videos. We tried to edit them into a coherent story, so that we would know whether it was worth going after the rights to use them. Even then, the rights could be prohibitively expensive or our requests could be denied completely. The latter seemed like a real possibility, given the unflattering portrait of the movie industry in Vito Russo's book, on which our film was based. We were prepared to argue that Vito's criticisms of the industry were motivated in part by his passionate love of the movies, and further, that we intended not to demonize anyone but simply to use the clips to show how certain stereotypes evolved in the culture over time. We had no idea if either of these arguments would be convincing.

As a fallback, we contemplated using unauthorized copies of the clips and claiming fair use. We hoped to avoid this route for two reasons.

First, we didn't want to risk lawsuits with Hollywood studios, no matter how strong our argument. We didn't want to be a test case. The studios would have far more resources than we would, we had no desire to spend years in court, and we didn't want to scare off distributors or broadcasters with a pending lawsuit.

The other reason we wanted to avoid using unauthorized copies was that the image quality would necessarily be degraded. Film clips would have to be copied from video (already degraded from the original), and the final film would either have to remain in video or be transferred from video to film (which would degrade the image still further). This seemed a shameful way to treat any movie. As we were making a movie *about* movies, we felt a responsibility to be respectful of the work we were critiquing.

We put these worries aside for the time being and continued editing. We kept a database of the clips we were using and the rights holders of the films they came from.[5]

As we refined the rough cut, we narrowed the list of potential clips down to a number that seemed manageable—probably a couple hundred. We learned that over the years a few media companies had gobbled up most of the older film libraries, so there were really only a dozen or so rights holders we would need to deal with. We decided it was time to ask our executive producer Howard Rosenman to go to work. Howard's Hollywood credentials gave us added credibility—this film about the movie industry had a bona fide industry insider behind it.[6]

We drafted a letter with Howard to send to the licensing departments of the various studios, explaining who we were, our respectable track record, and our honorable intentions: we were out not to trash the industry but rather to take a historical perspective on the movies to educate and raise consciousness. This got us exactly nowhere. The studios were generally happy to license their clips to us—at the book rate of thousands of dollars a minute, well beyond our means.

We regrouped. A key to our success on this project proved to be our association with a respected charitable organization, Hollywood Supports, established to provide AIDS support and education within the movie industry. We met with the executive director, who responded positively to our project. We agreed to offer the organization several benefit premiere screenings and a share in any profits. In exchange, Hollywood Supports agreed to let us use its backing of the project to help get the film made.

Then we went back to the studios. Our strategy this time was similar to the one we used to approach movie stars. We started with a studio we had a relationship with from a previous film, on which we had been given a reduced rate. We told our contacts at that studio about this new project and about our association with Hollywood Supports, and we asked them to grant us the rights to a few of their films and to waive the licensing fees completely. They responded that they might be able to waive the fees if we covered their library and duplication costs, to which we readily agreed.

Once we had a signed contract with the first studio, Howard was able to go back to each of the other studios and persuade them to get on board (with the implication, of course, that it would reflect poorly on those that didn't). When this approach failed, Howard escalated to the next level, often going directly to the studio heads. Relationships matter. Within a few months, we had agreements with all the studios for every clip we wanted, with a few exceptions and conditions. In some cases we had to get prominent actors' consent, for example, which eventually led to our receiving a treasured letter from Charlton Heston—a consolation prize of sorts—in which he denied permission to use a clip from *The Agony and the Ecstasy*, insisting that the Renaissance artist Michelangelo was *not* homosexual.

Our attorneys drafted "favored-nations" agreements with each of the studios—meaning that no licensor would receive a deal less favorable than any other. The one catch turned out to be those duplication and library costs. Each studio required that we use their designated lab. We tried to negotiate separate favorable deals with all of them, with varying success. These lab costs ended up being one of the biggest line items in our final budget. Still, if we had paid for the clip rights, the film would never have gotten made as it was, in its glorious 35 mm widescreen format.


## CONCLUSION

The last thing you want is to finish your film and then find out that you can't legally distribute it because of rights infringements. Or worse: you finish and sell the film, then get sued by a media giant. The best solution is to keep track of proprietary material as you're making the film, and start investigating the issues and strategizing sooner rather than later.

While editing, discipline yourself to steer clear of footage and stills until you are confident you'll be able to get the rights for them. You don't want to have to re-edit just when you expect to be arranging your world premiere. Consult with your attorney and potential E&O insurers. In the end, for better or for worse, it's often broadcasters' legal departments and insurance companies that will determine what can and cannot be used in your film.

*Part Three*

# Production

_____ *Chapter 9* _____

# Assemble a Team

People are usually drawn to nonfiction filmmaking for its artistic or polemical possibilities, but filmmaking is at least as much craft as it is art or rhetoric. A film that grows from a strong artistic vision, filtered with skill and dedication, has a greater chance of succeeding with audiences and making a lasting impact.

Filmmaking is a collaborative process. While it's now easier than ever to function as a one-person film crew using portable video equipment and editing software (see our discussion of do-it-yourself [DIY] filmmaking later in this chapter), the business of filmmaking requires a number of skills that most filmmakers don't have. Even if you are a super brainiac with vast knowledge of multiple disciplines, the process of simply making a film is consuming enough that you will probably want some help.

There are other, less obvious benefits to having a solid team behind you. Film is a medium of communication, and the larger your audience, the more effective your film. As you get deeper into your subject, making difficult creative decisions, it's helpful to have extra eyes and ears around to help you gauge your choices. And when things are not going the way you had hoped (which will often be the case), it's comforting and wise to have a trusted colleague who can see and hear things that you might miss. "Two heads are better than one" has certainly worked for us.

The director will make the final decisions, and the crew will always look to the director to be decisive and have a clear vision. But that doesn't prevent the director from asking those around her for advice and opinions. The roles described in this chapter apply to a feature documentary with an adequate

## Partnerships and Creative Differences

Because filmmaking is such a challenge, many people seek out partners when starting films. Often they choose friends who are also filmmakers. Maybe they'll both be producers, or one will be a producer/cinematographer while the other is a director/editor. However you apportion roles, if you'd like to remain friends with your filmmaking partner, your best chance of doing so is to agree in writing, in advance, who owns the film, what each person's responsibilities are, and perhaps most important, how you will resolve differences when they arise. The number of documentaries made by people who end up never speaking with each other again is noteworthy.

After you have a written agreement, you'll still need to figure out how to work with your partner. While our filmmaking views are usually in sync, we do have disagreements. But because we respect each other's judgments and we trust that at the end of the process we'll have made the film better, we work through disagreements and usually find a third—and better—approach that manages to address our individual concerns.

budget. That will not always be the case, but the tasks enumerated need to be done regardless of your film's scope and budget. Condense and combine these roles as appropriate for your project.

## THE CHAIN OF COMMAND

Filmmaking is hierarchical. The organization of a film crew can be visualized as a pyramid, with the director at the top and beneath him the various departments and subdepartments supporting the director's vision. Each aspect of the filmmaking process—producing, shooting, and editing—is a department. Each of these departments, in turn, has a department head (the producer, the cinematographer, the editor, respectively) who answers directly to the director and supervises those who work under her. The producer is responsible for hiring and supervising the associate producer and production assistants. The camera person is responsible for the camera assistant, lighting technicians, and often the sound recordist. The editor is responsible for the assistant editor, postproduction supervisor, and sound editor. The director should be concerned primarily with his department heads.

Naturally, you want to hire the best people you can at every level. In assembling your team, you should look for qualities such as competence, experience, and compatibility. By "compatibility" we mean people whom you get along with, whom you'd want to spend time with even under trying circumstances, and who share your vision.

## PRODUCERS

Under the best of circumstances, filmmaking is a seat-of-your-pants proposition. The more you can anticipate problems before they arise, the more time you'll have to deal with the problems you couldn't anticipate. Especially if you are an inexperienced filmmaker, having someone by your side with a clear understanding of all the steps involved in making a movie will be invaluable. Furthermore, a producer or executive producer with significant broadcast credits can lend your project credibility with potential funders and broadcasters. Some broadcasters may require you to work with a producer with a proven track record before they'll agree to buy or fund your film. They want to be assured that the film will get finished and delivered properly, and that it will meet their standards. Broadcasters are generally risk-averse and tend to be more comfortable working with producers they are familiar with.

What does a producer do? There is no commonly accepted job description— the role is vague and wide ranging, particularly for documentaries. The simplest answer is that a producer *produces*: he makes things happen and creates the circumstances necessary for the film to be made. What this means in any given production at any given moment can vary wildly. Producers can help raise money. They can use their connections to attract talented people to work on the film. They can take much of the day-to-day logistical burden off your shoulders.

To complicate matters, there are different types of producers—there may be executive producers, line producers, coproducers, associate producers, and just plain producers on any given film—and the credits themselves are flexible and slippery. Their jobs may be similar or overlapping, and the precise screen credit may be negotiated—sometimes arbitrarily but preferably depending upon their experience and your budget. You should agree to all credits in writing before you start working together.[1]

A "producer" credit is more valued than "coproducer," which in turn is considered more valuable than "associate producer." The assumption is that the lesser-credited jobs entail less autonomy and responsibility. If a production includes more than one type of producer, the positions also imply different chains of accountability: the associate producer typically reports to one of the producers or the coproducer. A producer who is strictly involved in financing generally gets an executive producer credit. Line producers live with a project day in and day out, taking care of production and post-production details, often helping with fundraising, and doing whatever else needs to be done for you to get what you need on film.[2] Their responsibilities often include tracking the budget, hiring the crew, handling legal contracts and correspondence, organizing shoots, and supervising postproduction.

Let's say you are looking for—or are asked to be—a hands-on producer. What is the range of activities expected for this role? To simplify matters, we will lump all the producing tasks—whether performed by the producer, the coproducer, the line producer, or the associate producer—under the general heading of *producer*. For lower-budget documentaries, the tasks might well be performed by one person, who in some cases could also be the director.[3] Producer responsibilities fall roughly into two broad categories: handling logistics and budget, and taking care of the crew and the film's subjects.

The producer is in charge of making sure the entire production runs smoothly. Typical responsibilities include making deals for crew and equipment, arranging production logistics, formulating the budget and then tracking actual costs, seeing that crew and equipment are where they are needed, keeping the crew fed and happy, licensing footage and music, and keeping the whole production on schedule. The producer can also help locate and schedule the subjects you want to film (your "characters"). Ideally, the producer looks for ways to minimize your disruption of their lives and helps make their experience of being filmed as painless as possible. He can also help with research and writing. In short, the producer does all the day-to-day chores that go into making a movie.

A typical sequence of producing tasks on a shoot might go something like this: call an equipment rental house to negotiate a better rate on an item of production equipment, then arrange lunch for the crew, then help to find a babysitter for the person who's about to be interviewed, then reassure the owner of the location where you're filming that his property is not being trashed, and so on. This may sound completely random, but the ability to deal with a variety of problems in quick succession or simultaneously is part of the job description. A good producer anticipates and tries to mitigate problems before they arise. His goal is to create the optimal environment for the director to direct.

Will you be following one of your characters to a lunch meeting at a restaurant? If so, you'll need to get a location release from the management, make sure the noise level and lighting is acceptable, and be prepared to soothe other diners' anxieties about being filmed. You'll probably want to stake out a table in advance that works for both picture and sound. On an observational shoot, situations like this arise often and unexpectedly. You can't be everywhere at once, and a good producer can make the difference between a chilly refusal and a warm welcome.

A producer should be organized and efficient and quick with numbers, and be able to connect and relate well to different kinds of people. Like any good manager, a producer shouldn't micromanage but should instead understand the strengths and weaknesses of the team members and delegate responsibility intelligently.

Any or all of the producing responsibilities can also be handled by a competent coproducer or associate producer (AP). These credits are negotiable, and there are no real standard formulas. Bigger productions might have an executive producer who makes deals with broadcasters and distributors; a line producer who manages the daily logistics of production; a production manager who manages the budget; one or more associate producers who do all the little jobs that the producer doesn't have time for; a production coordinator who manages the logistics on the producer's behalf; a production secretary who runs the production office; and a crew of production assistants doing grunt work for everyone. Smaller productions might make do with one associate producer who ends up doing everything a producer would do—at an AP's pay but perhaps for a producer's credit, a common career stepping-stone.

To complicate matters even further, producer credits are often given away as rewards or thanks for various services or for helping to finance a film. On *Common Threads* there are three executive producers credited: one of them, Howard Rosenman, was responsible for getting Dustin Hoffman to narrate, and the other two were colleagues of his at the time, neither of whom had any direct role in the film. We were grateful to have Hoffman as our narrator, so we agreed to grant those credits in exchange. On *The Celluloid Closet* Howard also received an executive producer credit (along with two of his new colleagues), but this time he worked a lot harder for it, securing clip rights from the studios, getting several of the major movie stars to agree to participate, and helping to secure some of the financing. Michael Ehrenzweig and Wendy Braitman helped get *The Celluloid Closet* accepted into the Rotterdam development market (CineMart), where we made an important connection to a European funder; in exchange, they got associate producer credits. Rob and Jeffrey took the producer credit, as recognition of the years we spent developing and bringing the project to fruition. And Michael Lumpkin, who handled all the day-to-day details of production, got a co-producer credit. On *Paragraph 175*, Michael Ehrenzweig performed virtually the same function that Michael Lumpkin had performed on *The Celluloid Closet*; Lumpkin's credit was coproducer, while Ehrenzweig is credited as producer. Why? Because that's what we negotiated with each of them, based on what they were bringing to the table (such as funding, time commitment, previous experience) and where we each were in our respective careers.

While producing is not, strictly speaking, a creative role, a smart producer with good creative instincts can often help the director make difficult choices—and then follow through to make sure they get executed properly. A good producer can also serve as a trusted advisor, urging you to develop the story in interesting ways that might not have occurred to you. This is one reason it's important to find a producer that you feel in sync with. And because making a film can be emotionally trying, it's important that your producer be someone you like and trust.

Different producers have different styles: there are screamers or browbeaters, there are cajolers, there are seducers, and there are combinations of these and more. Decide what kind of atmosphere you want on the set, and take that into account when assembling your team. We prefer to avoid the screamers, for instance—but we also expect our producer to be able to get tough when he needs to. If you tend to hysteria, you probably want a producer who can calm the situation down. If you're more mellow and withdrawn, you want someone outgoing and assertive. (Hysteria is never useful in any crew member.) Much of the producer's job is talking to people, and talking them into doing something they might not be inclined to do. Personality counts for a lot.

When you're choosing a producer, it's essential to meet in person. Bear in mind, however, that while you can sense a great deal about someone's personality in a face-to-face interview, it's not the same as being in a high-pressure situation together. We've never interviewed anyone for any job who described himself as "a screamer," for instance. It's also vitally important to get references and talk to his former colleagues.

## THE CREATIVE TEAM

As access to digital equipment and software has expanded, many more films are being made—and standards of quality are arguably being eroded. On the one hand, broadcasters are more willing to buy programs—at lower and lower prices—that a few years ago would have been deemed technically too amateurish and rough to broadcast. On the other hand, the competition has become exponentially greater. In this competitive marketplace, more polished and professional-looking projects will have an advantage, provided the costs are roughly comparable. And there's the rub: how to maintain high professional standards with DIY budgets or, on the other hand, successfully make the case for a higher budget, which an ambitious, complex subject will require. Unless you happen to be a skilled camera or sound person, it always comes down to money. Are you willing to raise the extra money you'll need to hire people to make your film look and sound great? Can you do it yourself? Or are you willing to settle for less?

Very simply, the more talented, creative people you have working with you, the more likely you will be to produce something of high quality. It's up to you to decide whether you have the ability to shoot your own footage while also directing—or, if not, whether you can afford to hire a camera person or find a talented beginner who will work for free or a reduced rate. Certain subjects and situations will be better covered by a low-profile, DIY approach. It's up to you to balance the best production approach for your subject with your honest evaluation of your own production skills, and then balance both of those with your film's budget.

### Camera

On location, the creative person working most closely with the director is the camera person. The director relies on him to create the images from which the film will be constructed. The camera operator plays such a significant role that her screen credit is often elevated to "cinematographer," "videographer," or the loftier-sounding "director of photography" (DP).

The advantage to not doing your own camera work is that it allows you to be more aware of what's going on around you. You can direct the camera to details—an expressive reaction or a new person entering the scene—that you might miss if you were following the action narrowly through the lens or absorbed with framing the best image.

Cinematography is demanding and difficult work, requiring physical stamina and technical skill as well as a heightened, sustained awareness—the capacity for intense concentration and the ability to pay constant attention to what's happening around you at every moment.

First and foremost, a vérité camera person should be unobtrusive and unintimidating—a comfortable and benign presence. Beyond this, though, is where the artistry comes in, because handheld observational or vérité shooting truly is an art. A good camera person has a cinematic eye, able to create dynamic and pleasing compositions within a changing and unpredictable situation. She listens carefully to know at all times where the important action is happening. At her best she has what seems like extrasensory awareness of where the next important action *is about to take place*, as well as the ability to position herself in just the right spot to capture the important action

## Working with a Feature DP on *HOWL*

James Franco described *HOWL* as a feature film with the soul of a documentary. Our experience with DP Ed Lachman on *HOWL* convinced us he was a feature DP with the soul of a documentary filmmaker and a poet. Ed had briefly worked with us on *Common Threads*, and having followed his work on countless features since then, we looked forward to working with him on a dramatic narrative.

We met with Ed and agreed on different stylistic approaches for each of the four types of live-action segments in our script. The scenes of the obscenity trial would be brightly lit and shot traditionally, like a 1950s courtroom drama. The extended interview with the young Allen Ginsberg would be intimate, with framing that was idiosyncratically off-center, inspired by photos taken by Ginsberg and his contemporaries. For the black-and-white reenactment of Ginsberg's first reading of "Howl" at the Six Gallery in San Francisco, we began with rhythmic floating moves that echoed the cadence of the poem. Later, as the reading picked up steam, we went after a more edgy handheld energy. Finally, for the black-and-white flashback memory scenes between Ginsberg and his friends and lovers (Kerouac, Cassady, Orlovsky), we wanted a spontaneous, erotic feel. For inspiration Ed suggested we watch Robert Frank's 1959 experimental short *Pull My Daisy*,[4] which featured Ginsberg, Kerouac, and other Beat poets. We shot these scenes in super-16 mm black-and-white and improvised with the actors for a jazz-like immediacy.

from the best possible angle. This ability to be in the right place at the right time is a mysterious skill, based in experience, observation, and instinct. The best camera work is unobtrusive, with movement that feels organic to the unfolding scene.

In addition to finding and following the action, the camera person must be mindful of technical details, such as maintaining focus and adjusting the aperture for lighting variations. Further, she must keep the frame free of sound equipment and other telltale signs that there is a film crew in the room—all the while keeping an eye on the director, who might see action elsewhere that he wants to catch on camera, which he might indicate with a nod or a glance.

A sensitivity to human behavior informs the best documentary camera work. You can see it in observational scenes, when the camera stays on someone who may not be the center of the conversation but whose face is registering intense emotion. You can see it in the timing of a subtle zoom during an emotional moment in a scene or an interview.

In addition, a good cinematographer will be aware of how scenes are edited and be sure to get enough coverage (different angles to cut to) and cutaways (reactions or physical details of the people or settings that the editor might plausibly cut to for dramatic impact, to help make a smooth transition, or to cover an awkward edit).[5]

Interviews—the perennial "talking heads"—are generally more formal, and while they are less unpredictable in terms of camera movement, they often require at least some minimal extra lighting. The DP is always in charge of creating the lighting design, in consultation with the director. When shooting an interview, he works with the director to find the best position for camera and subject. Because of the static nature of sit-down interviews, the composition and background become important factors to consider when setting up the shot. Here, too, one of the most important skills a DP can bring is close attention. Listening carefully for shifts in the train of thought, the experienced camera person can judge when to change focal lengths (for example, medium shot to close-up) to make the editor's job easier.

### Individual Supporters

Whether using a handheld camera to shoot observational scenes or filming interviews on a tripod, a good camera person creates a calm, efficient atmosphere on the set, putting subjects at ease and not intruding into the situation unnecessarily. But different situations require different skills. Your film's content and style will determine what kind of DP you will look for.

As a rule, interviews are easier to shoot than observational scenes, so if your film will have some of both, you might want to consider candidates with good vérité skills and assume they can handle the interviews. On the other hand, not all vérité shooters are great lighting designers. In this case, you might want to work with different cinematographers for different shooting situations, or you might want to budget for a talented lighting technician (gaffer) who can help the DP light the interviews. Most DPs will have gaffers they like to work with, and once you've settled on the DP, you should rely on him to recruit supporting crew, including his camera assistant (AC) if he needs one and your budget can support one.[6]

The best way to find good documentary shooters is to watch films they have shot. Many DPs have sample reels that they will gladly send you, but these will show you only that they can make beautiful shots. You want to find someone who knows how to tell a story visually, and to know this you have to watch a *whole* film—at the very least, whole extended scenes—that he's shot. It's also a good idea to talk to directors the DP has worked with, and especially with editors who have worked on films that he's shot. The directors can tell you what they feel the DP's strengths and weaknesses are, and the editor is in a privileged position to tell you how easy or difficult it was to edit scenes from his footage.

We try to work with the same DP throughout a film to ensure stylistic continuity and to get the obvious benefits of an ongoing working relationship. If your film requires extensive travel, this may not be affordable or necessary, particularly with the rising numbers of capable cinematographers around the world. Establishing and communicating a consistent visual approach is important if you're using multiple DPs in multiple locations, and it's easiest if you're primarily shooting interviews. A number of historical documentaries built around interviews and archival footage that Sharon wrote and produced managed to keep their budgets relatively low by filming with local two-person crews in whatever city the interviewees lived. The only travel expenses were Sharon's, with her hotel room sometimes doubling as the interview location if a more interesting one wasn't available. It's possible to find local crews in unfamiliar locations worldwide through recommendations on documentary filmmaker listservs such as Doculink (http://www.doculink.org) or by contacting local production companies whose business it is to vet and refer crews.

### Sound

Pretty pictures will take you only so far. Much of the content of a film comes through the ears. Sound recording is the craft most overlooked in low-budget filmmaking. If you're watching a conversation and you can't hear what the people are saying, there's usually not much point in watching. Like editing, sound recording is most apparent when it's done poorly. When it's done well, it should be transparent. But recording perfect sound, especially in observational situations, is a highly refined skill.

Unless you're an experienced sound recordist, the advantage to hiring a real sound recordist, if you can afford one, is simply superior-quality sound. Especially in complicated situations, such as large-group discussions, a good sound recordist—armed with a few wireless microphones, a boom mic (a microphone at the end of a long pole, held aloft like a fishing rod by the sound recordist), and a portable mixer—can accomplish amazing things. There is an art to sound recording that you begin to appreciate only when you've watched a pro in action.

While the built-in camera mic on a digital recorder can provide backup sound in a pinch, you would still be wise to replace the microphone that comes with the camera with one of higher quality. The limitation of this setup is that a microphone mounted on the camera will make a good recording only of whatever is right in front of it, thus severely limiting the camera person's options to cover a scene. As soon as the camera pans away from a speaker for a reaction from the person he's speaking to, the sound of the speaker will become unacceptably muffled.

The solution is to use multiple microphones—typically either hidden and fastened with a clip underneath someone's clothing or held overhead on a boom pole. Sometimes a boom alone will suffice, but if you expect that a primary character will do a lot of talking, a clip-on mic will ensure that you don't miss anything. Another option we've used is a combination of camera mic plus a directional ("shotgun") mic. In this arrangement, the camera mic records whatever the camera is pointed at and the shotgun can be aimed as needed to capture off-camera dialogue or other sounds. An experienced sound recordist can assess a production situation and recommend the best combination of microphones for the occasion.

In vérité shoots, we try to place wireless mics on one or two of the key players and have the sound recordist boom the rest. In interviews, we usually use a mic on an overhead boom, which in turn is mounted on a stand that can be easily adjusted for minor shifts in position. Sometimes sound recordists like to use clip-on mics as backups, but generally the sound from these lacks the resonance—the "presence"—of a boom mic. Before the interview, the director will decide whether or not her questions will be included in the film; to keep this as an option, the director will need to be miked as well.

Operating the boom and mixing the tracks on location requires skill, agility, and technical facility. It's worth trying to find someone who knows what he's doing. Like shooting, sound recording requires different skills depending on the situation. An interview is far easier to record than an observational scene. Interviews require technical skill and a sensitive ear. Observational scenes also require these qualities, as well as the alertness and nimbleness to be where the action is when it happens.

Like the camera operator, the sound recordist is juggling multiple tasks: watching and listening to everything that's going on in the scene, noticing outside noise that will create a problem in editing, monitoring the various tracks on which the different microphones are recording, watching the camera person and the lens, staying constantly aware of how wide the shot is (and thus how close he can move the boom without getting into the frame).

## Production Case Study: *Crime & Punishment*

On *Crime & Punishment*, we had the luxury of working with full camera and sound crews. As soon as we knew which courtroom we'd be filming in, we would carve out at least an hour—preferably four or five—for the sound recordist and his assistants to plant microphones strategically around the courtroom: on the judge's desk, the witness stand, at the jury box for opening and closing arguments. Whenever possible, we placed wireless mics on the attorneys. Often the defense attorneys were more resistant to being wired than the prosecutors. (They were suspicious of us from the outset, since the focus of the show was on the prosecution.) In these situations, the producers and APs would spring into action, strategizing, cajoling, and trying to convince the defense lawyer, for example, that if the prosecution wore a mic and the defense didn't, the defense argument would seem weaker by comparison. Many still refused. Then the sound recordist would place extra microphones in the courtroom so that no matter where the attorneys wandered while questioning witnesses or speaking to the jury, the audio would at least be usable. The recordist would then monitor and mix some dozen audio channels for use in editing.

Even in more intimate situations we depended on our sound recordist's expertise. When a producer on location saw a potential scene developing—two lawyers entering a room to discuss a case, for instance—and decided to film it, the sound recordist would make on-the-spot decisions about the best way to record the sound: boom mic, wireless mics, a microphone hidden on a desk, a (legal) phone tap, or a combination of some or all of these. Often we had to just start shooting and then adjust the mics as we filmed.

He should be ready and able to jump into action at a moment's notice, chasing action as necessary, while carrying heavy and awkward equipment.

Even placing wireless microphones on people takes special talents. The mic should be hidden but protected from clothing rustle, and placed so that fabric does not muffle the sound. Placing the mic is actually a rather intimate moment, requiring at least a modicum of sensitivity.

The sound recordist must work closely with the camera person—especially in an unpredictable vérité situation, when an expert camera-sound team engage in a kind of improvised dance around one other to get the best shots and perfect audio. It's complicated, intensely concentrated work to ensure that both picture and sound will be uncompromised—getting just the right camera angles (with no boom mics dipping into the frame, no boom shadows on the walls) while guaranteeing that no matter who is speaking, the sound will be clear and clean. For the director, it's a relief not to have to worry about whether or not the conversation you are filming will be audible.

Because the camera-sound team must work so intimately together, we generally hire the camera person first, then ask for recommendations of sound recordists she likes to work with.

### Editor

When you're filming an event or an interview, anything can happen. Once the filming is finished, however, the recorded reality takes on a new form: a series of fragmentary moments of reality that were captured on film. Sifting and organizing these moments to discover, re-create, and interpret the essential reality of what occurred is the art of editing.

Obviously, there is more to editing than cutting shots together—otherwise anyone with a powerful computer and good computer skills could edit. In all types of film—but especially in documentaries, where the story is often constructed in the editing room—the editor needs to be a skilled storyteller as well. A good documentary editor also has the ability to digest great quantities of information (visual, aural, and intellectual), and to determine which of all the footage is best suited to create a compelling, dramatic narrative.

Because editing is so central to the storytelling process, some documentary directors prefer to edit their own films. The director was on the scene following the action and knows how the story unfolds—who better to make sense of the material in the editing room? The flaw in this reasoning is that his very intimacy with the material can blind even an experienced director to weaknesses and strengths that will be obvious to a good editor. The director may recall a moment in filming as especially moving or funny—qualities that may or may not come across in the footage. It's always valuable to have fresh eyes assess your work. Even if you do edit your own film—or especially if you do—invite people to watch and critique it as it comes together, and listen carefully to what they say. It's rare to see a film edited by the director that wouldn't benefit from being shorter.

A good editor may be less inclined than the director to fall in love with shots that drag or unnecessarily divert the narrative flow. The process of losing these precious moments—whether they are favorite bits in the raw footage or scenes that have been painstakingly constructed—is sometimes called "killing your babies." An editor may be able to see more clearly than the director how dropping material will help to move the story forward, so you want an editor who will stand up—within reason—for what she believes is the best interest of the film. A fresh perspective and creative ideas about

## Killing Your Babies, aka the Cutting Room Floor

For *The Celluloid Closet* we interviewed Gus Van Sant about his 1991 film, *My Own Private Idaho*, starring River Phoenix and Keanu Reeves. Gus told us a moving story about River Phoenix's approach to his role as a gay hustler, and about the filming of one scene in particular (the campfire scene). We edited a sequence around Gus's story using shots from the original scene. It was a beautiful sequence, but ultimately we had to drop it entirely. It was a problem of rhythm. The *Idaho* sequence belonged near the end of the story we were telling, but at this point in the film we were building shorter sequences leading to a climactic ending. The campfire scene needed time to breathe—it lost its impact when shortened. It was just too late in our narrative to have a slow, reflective scene. We did, however, include the interview with Gus as a DVD extra but without the shots from the movie.

how to tell the story are exactly what you need from an editor. While the director always has the last word, it's helpful to have an effective advocate for a different point of view.

If you do work with an editor, it's important to communicate clearly what you have in mind for the footage—what you feel its strengths and weaknesses are and how you imagine it working in the overall film. You may want to sit with the editor while she is making selects (sifting out the usable bits and organizing them) so that she can better understand your tastes and intentions.

When considering possible editors, look at their work. As with cinematography, whole films (even short films) are more instructive than sample reels. A great sample reel tells you only that this editor is capable of cutting a great sample reel. What you're looking for is someone with the ability to tell a story dynamically with image and sound. A good editor shows sensitivity to characters and the nuances of their situations, as well as a visual flair and a sense of rhythm and music. An editor should also have facility with the software, of course, but this is the easiest part of the craft to learn.

Like shooting skills, editing skills vary according to the type of film. An editor may be very good at editing interviews intercut with still photos and archival material. Don't assume from this that she will be equally proficient at wrestling a story and characters out of many hours of raw observational footage. The reverse applies as well. Some editors work better in long form than short, and vice-versa. Try to get examples of films of comparable style and length to yours, so that you can get a sense of how the editing contributes to the overall flow and rhythm of the film as you're watching it. Get recommendations from other

Production still—*Where Are We?* Photo by Toni Whiteman. (Courtesy of Telling Pictures)

filmmakers. Just as editors offer valuable assessments of DPs, so DPs can provide insights into how an editor has handled their footage.

The fact that editor Dawn Logsdon had some knowledge of French and German was an asset on *Paragraph 175*, in which almost all of our characters spoke one language or the other. But ultimately it was her lyrical style and sense of pacing that helped to make that film as strong as it was. Jean de Segonzac, our DP on *Where Are We?*, introduced us to Ned Bastille, who became that film's editor. Jean intuited that Ned's ironic sense of humor would help find the right tone and make sense of a film that literally went all over the place.

The editor is probably the person with whom you will spend the most extended, intense periods of time. You might be able to shoot a documentary in a few weeks, but it will take months to turn it into a real film, with coherent story lines and well-developed characters. Think about sitting in a dark room for hours and days and weeks and even months with the person you're hiring, and make sure that this is someone with whom you want to spend that kind of time.

The assistant editor's job is to organize the material so that the editor can easily find what she needs. Assistants may also pick up slack during the editing process, adjusting levels on sound tracks, tweaking graphic effects, or adding on-screen titles to the editor's specifications. A good assistant might even be able to cut sequences—this is how assistants learn to become editors.[7]

Some editors prefer to digitize and log the footage themselves, as a way to become familiar with the material. Others will want an assistant to do this before they begin. Sometimes the assistant comes onto the project and starts organizing the footage before the editor is hired—but it's always preferable to have your editor in place before hiring the assistant. Editors often have assistants they like to work with, and in any case the editor needs to be involved in decisions about how the footage is organized and logged.

Assistant editors are often not budgeted full-time for the entire editing process. Make a realistic determination—based on your editor's needs, editing process, and level of technical self-sufficiency—as to how much assistant-editing time your project will need. Particularly if you have a firm deadline, err on the side of budgeting for more assistant time rather than less.

### Additional Crew

Production assistants can run errands on the set, fetch equipment, organize releases, order lunch. Sound editors can do much more precise and adventurous sound design than most picture editors, who will likely be too busy anyway refining the picture edit—getting the film to work—to devote her full attention to sound. A postproduction supervisor can help keep track of complicated projects that use material from multiple sources in varying formats. Generally, when a job becomes too overwhelming for one person, there's another convenient job description of someone who can help pick up the slack.

### MAKING DEALS

Your hiring options are limited by your budget. You want to find the best possible person who is willing to work for the amount of money you are able to pay. We have found many talented people who are willing to negotiate their fees, especially for a film on an important subject. Many people make loads of money working on projects they don't care about, and jump at the chance to work on something they feel is worthwhile. You may even be lucky enough to find talented people who are willing to work for free on a limited basis. Don't abuse this generosity. People have a right to be paid for their work. We always do our best to pay *something*, even if it's only a token amount. Avoid creating situations in which people working for you feel resentful.

Besides, if you are paying someone her rate, you're in a better position to demand more from her—which you inevitably will have to do from time to time.

Some producers offer deferred payments or rates that are partially deferred. Most experienced craftspeople consider this a joke, and with good reason, given the unpredictable economics of documentary filmmaking. (We are among the few producers we know of who have made deferral deals and have actually paid them—in full!)

Once you've agreed on terms, it's important to put your agreement in writing. This agreement can be as simple as a short deal memo (see appendix 2). It's important to be clear about everyone's expectations up front, to avoid misunderstandings later on. At the same time, you need to allow yourself flexibility to deal with uncertain production contingencies.

## THE BUSINESS TEAM

Filmmaking is a business, with budgets, contracts, and deal making that require professionals with special skills. Expect to spend a fair amount of time reading legal documents and looking at spreadsheets. At some point, it's usually a good idea to establish yourself as a corporate entity, which provides some protection against liability claims. You may be required to do so by a broadcaster before they will enter into a business arrangement with you.

Where you are located, the nature of your project, and your likely sources of income will all help determine what sort of corporate entity will best suit your needs. If you are planning to raise funds from foundations and individual donors, you will need a fiscal sponsor who can accept nonprofit donations on your behalf. Or you may decide to set up your own nonprofit corporation, with a 501(c)(3) designation from the IRS, so that you can accept tax-deductible donations directly. Broadcasters, however, may have policies restricting them from contracting with nonprofit organizations, in which case you will need a for-profit corporate entity. You might find that you need one of each. Sometimes, in order to meet funder restrictions or for tax purposes you might use both. The nonprofit could enter into an agreement with your for-profit corporation, which would serve as a "loan-out company" providing your personal services as producers and directors. Or the nonprofit might subcontract an entire production to the loan-out company (a "production services" agreement). It's always important to establish a paper trail to document these agreements as "arms-length transactions," so that everything is aboveboard. Most anything is possible, as long as you know the rules and follow them. Which leads us to another crucial team member you should recruit.

### Get a Lawyer!

If you make a film, at some point you will need a lawyer who is familiar with entertainment law. A lawyer can advise you on what kind of production entity best suits your needs and can help you set it up. You will also rely on him to review and suggest changes to contracts and releases and to advise you on licensing and rights issues. Unless you have legal training yourself and are familiar with entertainment industry practices, these are tasks you do not want to take on yourself. The earlier in your career you can establish a relationship with an entertainment lawyer, the better.

Here again, it pays to have someone with whom you feel sympatico, who believes in you and what you want to do. Especially when you're starting out, you want someone who will be available to answer your questions and offer advice and who won't keep the meter ticking at top dollar every time you have a question. No easy task: finding someone smart and aggressive

## Legal Emergencies

We were scheduled to film an interview for *The Celluloid Closet* with Tony Curtis, who was in the midst of a sudden family tragedy. The day before the interview it was canceled and rescheduled several times. We had already booked a soundstage and a crew, but didn't know if an interview was going to happen. When Curtis showed up on set we handed him our standard release—and he refused to sign it. It was the usual "all rights in perpetuity" legalese combined with the lack of remuneration that upset him. To him, it sounded like some form of slavery. We explained that we couldn't afford to pay anyone, and even if we could it would be unethical in the context of a documentary, and that besides, no one else was being paid. We also knew that the network wouldn't let us use his interview without a signed release. Then he offered to sign a one-sentence statement agreeing to appear in our documentary. Because we had such a good relationship with our lawyer and were able to get word to him that we had an emergency, he was able, within an hour, to negotiate vastly simplified language that still met the demands of the network's lawyers and would satisfy the insurance company. And we were able to film a highly entertaining interview with Tony Curtis that is one of the highlights of the film.

who will return your calls or e-mail promptly *and* whose knowledge of the entertainment business gives you confidence *and* who won't charge you an arm and a leg, particularly before you're even funded. A less-experienced lawyer in a firm with more-experienced partners will likely be more responsive and more willing to invest time in an emerging filmmaker's career than will an established Hollywood power lawyer.

It's important that you use your lawyer's time wisely. Don't call every time a question arises, unless it's urgent (and learn to know the difference). It's more efficient to keep a list of issues on which you want advice from your lawyer, then send a brief e-mail listing the subjects you want to talk about and schedule a phone call. Sometimes the issues can be resolved most efficiently by e-mail. Every lawyer works differently, so find a mode of communication that works for both of you.

What you want above all is assurance that in a moment of crisis, your lawyer will be there for you.

### Accounting: The Bookkeeper

Perhaps the least glamorous credit on a film, the bookkeeper is also one of your most important collaborators. Keeping track of your money is essential to getting the film done, the crew paid, and the budget balanced. A bookkeeper on your team—especially one who is familiar with the film business—will be a valuable ally. Any good bookkeeper will know the difference between an asset and a liability, but film has its own idiosyncrasies. Are these supplies to be expensed or equipment to be depreciated? Is this a production expense or a development expense? A bookkeeper who is familiar with the production process will know, without having to ask, that "color correction" should be coded as part of postproduction.

These skills become critical when you're in production, working with a budget. Ideally, you'll have a producer or production manager keeping track of the budget, making day-to-day decisions about when it's OK to exceed a line item, knowing there's extra money in another line item that will likely be unspent. A small discount in airfare and hotel rooms could mean an extra hour of filming if you're paying your crew overtime. It takes a special kind of mind—and a lot of paperwork—to keep track of things like this. A crucial tool is the cost report, which should be updated regularly, showing the budget line item, the actual amount spent, and the amount remaining (or overspent). A good bookkeeper can serve as your production accountant, generating weekly or monthly reports itemized by budget category, so that you always know exactly what your financial situation is.

Important qualities to look for in a bookkeeper or production accountant are competence, honesty, and flexibility. Unless you have a large, fully funded production, you will probably want to hire someone part-time. You may decide that one or two days a month is adequate while you're in development but that you need someone once a week or more while you're in production. There are times, though, when you'll need financial information and can't wait till the next scheduled bookkeeping day. You want someone who can give you answers when you're in a crunch.

### Accounting: The Accountant

If you form a company, you will need to file corporate tax returns. Working with a certified public accountant (CPA) who is familiar with the film business can save you a lot of headaches and money. You should meet with your CPA before you even set up your company, so that you understand the financial implications of your choices. A CPA will help determine, for example, whether your company should be on a "cash" or "accrual" basis. If you're in the middle of a project at the end of your fiscal year and have just received a chunk of money from a funder, your CPA may be able to help you avoid forfeiting it in taxes before it's spent.

## DO-IT-YOURSELF FILMMAKING

What if you, by yourself, are the entire team? Art and experimental filmmakers have almost always gone the DIY route by necessity and temperament. What's new is the growing body of DIY nonfiction filmmakers who seek a larger, more general audience for their work.

Since the advent of nonlinear editing in the early 1990s, the technical quality of both production and postproduction equipment has advanced—and the costs have decreased—to the point that it's now possible for one person to create a broadcast quality film completely by herself from concept to broadcast master. Possible, but not necessarily easy.

When does a DIY approach make sense? That question was brought home to us after we began producing an observational documentary on a community hospital in Oakland, California. We hired filmmaker Michael Palmieri to edit a fundraising clip for us. After viewing the footage we'd shot so far, he said, "You're going in with an SUV when you should be going in with a Vespa." It was good advice but we didn't have a chance to follow it. An opportunity arose to make progress on *HOWL*, which was in development at the time, and we took it. Peter Nicks, who was working with us on the hospital project, took it over and completed his film, *The Waiting Room*,[8] while we moved ahead with *HOWL*.

Based on subsequent conversations with Michael Palmieri, who makes nonfiction films by himself or with his partner Donal Mosher, we've compiled some useful guidelines and strategies for DIY nonfiction filmmakers.

First, don't quit your day job. You'll need it to buy a camera and an editing system, with the inevitable upgrades, and cover your living expenses while you make your film. Ideally, your day job is not only film related but also involves shooting or editing, because successful DIY filmmaking depends on technical expertise and skill.

Prior editing experience is critical to making a film on your own. You'll be able to think like an editor when you shoot, which will help ensure that you get the coverage you need. Prior shooting experience will help you determine how much to shoot, the kinds of cutaways you'll need, and the most useful angles. But editing experience confers the ability to *see the footage with fresh eyes when you begin editing*, and to disengage from whatever you thought you captured on film when you were shooting.

If you're buying a camera, do your research and buy one that not only fits you ergonomically but also has more than one input for external microphones and for a headphone. Buy a short directional (hyper-cardioid) microphone that you can attach to your camera so that you'll record the sounds of what your lens captures and not those to the side or behind you. Also buy at least one lavalier-type wireless mic (or arrange to borrow one regularly). Buy headphones to wear while you're shooting. Then practice until you're completely comfortable handling the gear and satisfied with the quality of your footage.

Put aside that epic exposé you've wanted to make about the tar sands in Alberta, Canada, and find a character-based story or another logistically manageable story that's located within driving distance. A low-budget or no-budget project means also choosing a subject that can be made into a strong film without archival footage, aerial shots, extensive travel, or music. *Turn these limitations into strengths*. If you have the patience and your story is relatively contained, DIY filmmaking is ideal for following characters over time or through specific challenges.

Plan as much as you can, but hone your abilities to respond to the unpredictable. The intimacy afforded by being a one-person crew plays to your advantage when you're able to get right next to someone during a crucial moment, or to arrive quickly and start shooting when you've gotten word that something's about to happen.

There will be situations where you wish you had better sound. Sometimes even DIY filmmakers recruit sound recordists if they know in advance that a critical scene will need more complex sound work than they can do with their mounted camera mic. But for certain kinds of films, this light-footprint approach is worth the trade-off.

You'll probably be alternating between shooting and editing at first—and you should be—but at some point there's no more shooting to do and you have to face the editing room, or as Michael says, "go into the cave." As director, you intended what you shot to convey certain things. As editor, you need to assess what the scenes can actually convey.

There's something to be said for making a DIY film quickly. If you're working completely alone, you can sour on a project by editing it for too long. The biggest challenge throughout editing is to maintain critical distance from your own footage.

No matter how much you want your film to be beautiful, remember that what's most important is the story. It's fine if you linger on breathtaking images, but once viewers start paying more attention to the scenery than to your story, you've lost them. Don't let aesthetics take over. Recognize which scenes will be essential, then work to add material that supports those essential scenes.

As with any film, rough-cut screenings for other people are critical. We like to show our works-in-progress to filmmakers as well as nonfilmmakers. You might prefer, as Michael does, to invite writers rather than filmmakers—he finds that writers focus more on the story.

When you've managed to get your film to a rough-cut stage, you might consider fundraising. Additional funds are always welcome—especially if you plan to show your film in more discriminating venues than YouTube. While it is difficult to get development or production funds for an observational DIY film, when you have a decent rough cut or, even better, a sample reel that distills the best of your rough cut, consider applying for finishing funds.

## CONCLUSION

While equipment and technology have made it feasible for anyone with basic computer skills to be a filmmaker, there remain numerous critical aspects of the craft that can be learned only by experience. It's important to be realistic about your abilities and what's best for the film you want to make, so that you can make wise decisions about when to do it yourself and when to find someone—or a team of people—to help you.

Most filmmaking is a team effort. It's never too early to start creating strategic alliances with like-minded people. Filmmaking is demanding physically, emotionally, and intellectually. Knowing when and how to get help from the right people can make all the difference for you and your film.

## Chapter 10

# Directing Documentaries

Reality is unpredictable. Not knowing how someone will respond or how things will turn out is precisely what makes the experience of making—and watching—documentaries so compelling. For the nonfiction filmmaker, it can also be exceedingly aggravating—especially for the filmmaker following an ongoing situation as it unfolds (the styles we've described as *observational*, *direct cinema*, or *cinéma vérité*). This uncertainty may partially explain why so many successful documentaries take as their subjects events that have already occurred: knowing the outcome, one can make informed decisions about how to build an effective narrative. It's also generally much easier to schedule and budget for films about the past than it is for ongoing stories with unpredictable outcomes. But whichever style you're working in—observational or historical—it's important to be prepared as well as open to the unexpected.

When Rob started making what would become *The Times of Harvey Milk*, Milk was still alive. The film began as an examination of a grassroots movement then forming to fight a California state initiative that would have allowed school districts to discriminate against gay teachers. Harvey Milk was a key activist in that debate, but the film was not yet about him. Clearly, it would have been a very different film had Harvey Milk and Mayor George Moscone not been assassinated while the project was being developed.

Just as directors of fiction films benefit from unexpected spontaneous emotions or chemistry between characters in a scripted scene, observational filmmakers are always hoping for dramatic, unpredictable magic to happen.

Rob Epstein and Harvey Milk at the "No on 6" victory celebration, 1978. (Courtesy of Rob Epstein)

The irony is that this often puts the documentarian—presumably someone who wants to make the world better by documenting it—in the uncomfortable position of benefiting from the misfortunes of others.

Great social issue filmmaking can happen when a filmmaker accepts this contradiction as an obligation of honor: to convey the truth of a given situation as skillfully as possible. By *skillfully*, we mean emotionally affecting, intellectually stimulating, honest, and effective.

Of course not all unexpected events are tragic. *Where Are We?* had a number of humorous scenes along with others that were bittersweet. With only five encounters scheduled in advance, the film depended on serendipity, continually requiring us as directors to make spontaneous creative decisions large and small. It was exhausting, but having just completed *Common Threads*, for which every detail was painstakingly planned, the experience was also exhilarating.

Skillful directing means recognizing significant events as they arise and knowing how to capture and convey them to an audience. Whether you're filming observational scenes or interviews, the goal is to create the conditions where fortuitous accidents can occur—then to recognize them and stay out of the way.

James Franco, Jeffrey Friedman, and Rob Epstein on the set of *Howl*. Photo by JoJo Whilden. (Property of Radiant Cool, LLC)

## DIRECTING OBSERVATIONAL SCENES

The conceit in observational scenes is that we are witnessing something that would have happened with or without the presence of the filmmakers. This is the ideal "fly-on-the-wall" approach—unobtrusively observing and not interfering.

Such an approach is obviously a fiction. Anyone who has been in a situation with a camera crew knows that the presence of the crew has *some* effect on how people behave. Reminiscent of the Heisenberg "uncertainty principle" in quantum physics, the observer alters the observed by the very act of observing.

On the other hand, the proliferation of portable video recorders—camcorders and mobile phones, as well as surveillance cameras and so-called reality shows—has made people more accustomed to having their actions and words observed and recorded. We have found that even in the most uncomfortable situations, people will soon forget their self-consciousness in front of the camera and focus on things more important to them in the moment.

In emotionally fraught situations, this phenomenon can be even more pronounced. When we were directing *Crime & Punishment*, part of our job was to observe victims of horrific crimes as they prepared to testify. It was

## Two Directors

While most films have one director, filmmakers occasionally share the role. This is what we've done since we began working together. It's not as difficult as you might think. We alternate directing roles, whether we're shooting observational or interview scenes. While one of us is directing and focused specifically on what's being filmed, the other is observing the entire process, wearing a headset to know what's being said, and taking notes. We then confer and trade off. This process has gone just as smoothly for us on dramatic films. One of us might be working with actors while the other works with the crew, then we switch off. One of us stands at the monitor, to watch what the camera is capturing, while the other stays closer to the action. It has never presented a problem to the people we've worked with over the years. Production crews, documentary subjects, storytellers, and actors have all seen us as a filmmaking unit as well as individuals. We attribute this to our overlapping sensibilities and to extensive preparation. We have also figured out how to resolve our differences in ways that benefit the film.

awkward at best, asking people to invite us—and our video crew—into their lives at heartrending moments. But once we started filming, we saw that these people had far more important things to think about than how they would appear on camera. Very soon they seemed to forget all about us.

To help encourage this, we try to build in at least a little time for people to get to know us before we start filming them. This can be a brief visit before the shoot or, when that's not possible, just a few moments before filming to introduce ourselves and the crew.

We also work with the smallest possible crew—usually only a camera person and a sound person in the immediate environment—and keep everyone else out of sight and so out of the minds of the people we're filming. The crews we work with are experienced at making themselves unobtrusive and putting people at ease. The best of them manage to achieve a friendly, benign presence, with hardly any direct interaction with the people we're filming. The goal eventually is for the film crew to seem like nothing more than a comfortable element of the environment—like furniture or family members—and thus create the possibility for real, intimate moments to emerge.

When directing observational scenes, we try to disappear. In these situations the role of the director is to identify what the scene is and then let the cinematographer take over. If we see something happening that the camera person hasn't noticed, we communicate to him silently and subtly with

## Director's Eyes and Ears

On vérité shoots, we like to wear wireless headphones with a feed from the sound recordist's equipment. This allows us to hear the quality of the sound being recorded and to follow conversations without imposing ourselves into the scene. We carry a small pocket pad to make notes of questions that need clarifying or potentially interesting leads to follow up.

a tap or a nod in the direction of the action to which we want him to direct his attention.

Just as the camera operator and sound recordist must improvise delicate choreography to capture a scene without intruding on it (see chapter 9), the director must silently conduct the choreography with his body language. Also like the camera and sound crew, the director must develop a highly refined sense of how human action unfolds and be able to predict how situations might develop. His job is to guide the crew to where the action is—or to where it is likely to occur.

A related skill is choosing situations that are most likely to further the story line. In *Crime & Punishment*, we often had to decide between following a lawyer back to her office or staying with the family of the witnesses. Which was more likely to lead us to a scene that would be useful in constructing a compelling, lucid story? There's no formula for this—it's a sixth sense that develops over time.

## CASE STUDY: UNEXPECTED OBSERVATIONAL SCENES IN *PARAGRAPH 175*

For *Paragraph 175*—our first film shot outside of the United States, when each shoot meant flying several people to Europe—we were especially careful in planning. We were on the train station platform in Berlin with our German film crew as our historian-guide Klaus Müller spoke on a payphone to the man we were on our way to interview, Karl Gorath. Klaus indicated to us that Karl had had a change of heart and wanted to cancel his interview. We had to quickly devise a plan B. We directed Klaus to keep talking as the crew filmed his conversation.

We decided to take the train anyway and traveled from Berlin to Hannover, where Karl lived. Until then we hadn't intended to use Klaus on camera in the film, but in response to Karl's cancellation we chose to make Klaus part of the story by asking him questions on the train.

Outside Karl's building we put a radio mic on Klaus and sent him inside. We sat in a van with our translator and crew listening on headphones as Klaus convinced Karl to invite our cameraman and sound recordist inside. When they got there and started filming, Klaus asked Karl to show him his photo album to try to get him to talk. Klaus was surprised to see that many of the photos had been torn out of the album, and asked Karl why. "Oh, I've already talked so much about the concentration camps," he answered. "You know, it's more than fifty years ago. There have been so many other, better memories."

When it came time to edit we found a way to include all of those scenes in the film—the train ride, the phone call, Karl and Klaus looking at photos in Karl's apartment. Karl filled the role of the "reluctant witness" who didn't want to talk about "those uncomfortable memories."[1]

Karl's reluctance also set the stage stylistically for another reluctant witness, Pierre Seel. Pierre's dramatic eruptions before and during his interview made vivid his conflicting desires to speak and to remain silent about his memories. He was particularly galled to be telling his story to Klaus, a German. His still palpable anger gave his scenes an intense energy. Our role as directors in this case was to sit in an adjoining room on headphones and follow the interview as best as we could with the help of a translator, coaching and encouraging Klaus through the earpiece he was wearing, to help him get through the difficult interview.

## THE ART OF FILM INTERVIEWING

As we discussed earlier (in chapter 3), "talking heads" work best when viewers feel that they are being spoken to directly or that they are privileged witnesses to a compelling private conversation. Sometimes the heads that are talking are not especially dynamic personalities. When they work, however, they can be very powerful.

## THE SETUP AND STYLISTIC CHOICES

The secret to effective interviews is creating a sense of intimacy. Because interviews often involve elaborate setups, lights, sound equipment, and at least a handful of crew members, this intimacy is often a carefully constructed illusion. The director's job is to create a safe, comfortable atmosphere that will allow for moments of spontaneity and emotional vulnerability or intellectual passion—moments that feel *real*.

First decide where the interview will take place. In the subject's apartment? In a café? On a soundstage? If possible, the location should be scouted with your cinematographer and sound recordist, who will help you design the frame and ensure that ambient noise will not be a problem. Think about whether you want a specific look that will be consistent throughout the film and perhaps thematically related to your subject (such as the stylized variations on a soundstage that we used as the background for our interviews in *The Celluloid Closet*).

Whatever location we choose, we avoid positioning interview subjects immediately in front of a wall or other flat surface if at all possible. Adding even moderate distance between the interviewee and the background looks more pleasing and helps keep viewers engaged with the image and focused on the interviewee. Since formal interviews are essentially static, it's worth taking time to design the frame carefully. The trick is to make the frame as interesting as possible without being distracting.

We generally don't try to control what people wear, other than to ask that they not wear white or stripes, both of which can create problems in video.

The director and DP typically discuss shooting style and logistics before the interview. How wide should the frame be? Will the frame size change during the interview? If so, will these changes in framing be hidden by cuts (in which case they will be changed quickly between the end of one answer and the beginning of the next), or will they will be included in the design of the film, as zooms in or out at appropriate moments? If we decide there will be slow zooms during some answers, we work out a system of unobtrusive signals for a camera move to start, and we agree in advance as to how much latitude the DP will have to make these decisions on her own. It's helpful to have a small monitor that the director can refer to easily—without turning his attention from the person he's interviewing—and discreetly, so the subject doesn't see her image and get self-conscious or distracted.

We try to rigorously control the environment so that the interview subject's attention will be focused solely on the interviewer and not distracted by other crew members. If lights are required, we try to do as much setup before the interview subject sits down, so we'll have time to make minor adjustments without having to worry about keeping him relaxed. The producer or AP is usually in charge of making this happen smoothly, while also getting the on-camera release signed. A good associate producer can also help by hanging out and making small talk with an interview subject while the crew is setting up—as long as they don't discuss anything substantively related to your interview questions.

In one particularly noisy situation, our sound recordist constructed soft walls around the interview area, using sound blankets hung from light stands. This created a cozy little tunnel that forced a focused and intimate line of attention between interviewer and interviewee. It worked so well, in fact, that we have asked crews to re-create this environment in other situations, even when it wasn't necessary for sound quality.

After the camera and sound person have been introduced to the interview subject, we let them effectively disappear behind their equipment. Once the interview begins, no one except the interviewer makes eye contact with the subject.

We position the questioner next to the camera as close to the lens as possible, so that the subject's eye line is almost directly to the camera. Some directors prefer more stylized angles. We've found that the more direct eye line heightens the connection between the interview subject and the viewer, creating a sense of intimacy.

Before filming, you should have a clear idea of how much, if at all, your voice will be included in the film. Will the questions be included in the final cut or will the answers stand alone as complete statements? If you plan to keep your voice out of the film, you will have to instruct your interviewee to respond in complete sentences, by including the subject of the question in her answer. This is most easily done with an example, such as "If I ask you when you came to New York, instead of just saying '1968,' say something like 'I came to New York in 1968.' "[2]

Occasionally your voice might end up on the sound track despite your initial intentions. In *Paragraph 175*, when Albrecht Becker revealed that he volunteered to enter the German Army after having been imprisoned by the Nazis for homosexuality, Rob couldn't help expressing surprise. Albrecht then proceeded to explain that he joined the army because that's where the men were. Though we could have cut out Rob's response, the tone of incomprehension in his voice added to the immediacy and drama of Albrecht's revelation, and we hoped Rob's voice would provide a surrogate for the incredulity we expected the viewer would be feeling.

## PREPARATION AND SPONTANEITY

When preparing for an interview, whether it's a personal account or expert analysis, we try to learn as much as possible about the story we will be trying to draw out in conversation. We prepare a list of questions, making sure we cover all the important points we need to touch on. If we can conceive the story as broken down into acts, then we try to devise questions for each of the acts. For *Common Threads*, a typical act 1 question would be: "Tell me about the first moment you became aware of this new disease." Act 2 questions would address the problems and challenges of dealing with the illness, and act 3 about grieving the loss of the loved one and how their lives have progressed since.

How you phrase a question is also important. In the example above, we didn't ask, "When did you first learn about HIV/AIDS?" More often than not, this formulation would produce an answer like "I think it was 1982." This is minimally informative, but not that interesting; it also requires that your question be included to make sense. You can encourage your subjects to answer in full sentences by the way you phrase your questions. It's hard to give a one-word answer to questions that begin with "how" or "why." Better yet is "Tell me about ..." The goal is to coax your subjects back into reliving their memories—and to take you with them—by telling a story. The best interview subjects—including experts—are good storytellers.

Usually we start with a few easy questions about who the interviewee is and what she does. Mostly these are to put the subject at ease, but occasionally the answers are useful. We often add several general questions that relate thematically to the subject, which we try to ask everyone. Sometimes this gives us interesting contrasts in perspective that are useful in constructing the film—or they can lead us in an entirely unexpected direction. Also, asking several people to describe the same event can provide material to construct a larger and more nuanced story during editing. Parts of answers can be cut together to develop a sense of forward motion. A consensus or a divergence of viewpoints can cumulatively create a more fully dimensional understanding of the subject for an audience.

In *The Celluloid Closet*, we had come up with questions for each interviewee about specific films they were involved with. In addition, we had a list of questions that we asked everyone, such as "What was the first gay or lesbian character you remember seeing in a movie?" Sometimes these yielded predictable answers; more often, none at all. Occasionally we hit pay dirt. Tom Hanks recalled seeing an obscure 1971 film, *Vanishing Point*, with a group of other adolescent boys, and hooting and jeering with reflexive homophobia at the appearance of some stereotypically bitchy gay characters in one scene, which he recalled and reenacted in vivid detail. We had never heard of *Vanishing Point* (though we subsequently learned that it was a cult favorite), but we tracked it down and were able to build a strong sequence out of that scene and Hanks's story.

Your list of questions should serve as a checklist, to ensure that you've covered all the points you need to. It's a good idea to have a second person listening and making notes about things that aren't clear or sentences that weren't cleanly recorded, so that you can ask them again before you wrap up. It's also important not to be too slavish about getting through your list of questions. Again, *welcome the unexpected.*

When we interviewed Susan Sarandon for *The Celluloid Closet*, we were prepared to ask her about *The Rocky Horror Picture Show* and *The Hunger*. Susan didn't have much to say about *Rocky Horror*; she did provide some unforgettable moments as she fondly recalled her love scene with Catherine Deneuve in *The Hunger*. But she surprised us by insisting on discussing *Thelma and Louise*, which we had never considered, since neither of its two main characters was presented as lesbian. Susan convinced us with her analysis of the last kiss between Thelma and Louise at the end of the film—and her comparison of that scene with the parallel ending of *Butch Cassidy and the Sundance Kid*, in which the characters also came to a sad end but went down shooting their guns rather than kissing. This digression helped us find a way into a subject that was discussed in the book and that we were eager to include: the difference in attitudes about male and female same-sex affection as reflected in the movies. Thankfully, we had the presence of mind to ask what would have happened if Butch and Sundance had kissed before leaping to their deaths, which led her to some memorable musing on guys and their guns. Though we were not prepared to discuss *Thelma and Louise*, our overall preparation and understanding of the themes Vito raised helped us to respond as we did.

If an interesting tangent arises, be prepared to follow it to see where it leads. Interviews will almost always be more animated if you ask genuinely curious follow-up questions. At the same time, be diligent about not letting the interview get out of control, and when appropriate, make a smooth transition back to your next intended question.

Avoid reading questions from a list. Refer to the list, then look at the person you are talking to as you ask a question. *Maintain eye contact while he answers.* A good interviewer is a good listener. As frequent subjects of interviews ourselves, we can attest that the least satisfying interviews are those in which the interviewer reads a question, then immediately looks down at his notes for the next question as soon as we start to answer. When this happens the speaker feels abandoned and becomes acutely aware of the need to perform rather than relating spontaneously to the questioner. The result is usually a stilted interview. If you must refer to your notes, maintain eye contact while your subject speaks, acknowledge her response when she finishes with a smile or nod, and *then* look down at your list of questions.

The most satisfying interviews are those in which there is a real connection, in the moment, between the interviewer and interviewee. The viewer can

## Tips for Interviews

Make sure your associate producer keeps track of subjects' screen direction. That is, did the interview subject sit camera left with an eye line to camera right, or vice versa? That way, you'll be able to alternate the left/right positions of your interview subjects, facilitating cutting between interviewees and generally making for more interesting viewing.

You can probably expect to do additional interviews later if your film covers an ongoing story or situation. Even if you're making a largely historical film and your interviewees are mostly experts, save one or two to be filmed after you've begun editing, if possible. A rough assembly edit will reveal unexpected "holes" in analysis or stories that need to be filled. Experts can often further be divided into generalists or specialists, so you might save a generalist to be filmed later in case the holes span several different areas of expertise.

A great interview will be little more than an exercise in frustration if you don't have it transcribed. Whether an eager intern gets the assignment or you use a transcription service, transcripts are critical—and the sooner the better. Some transcription services also do time-code spotting—adding the timed numbers from your source material at intervals to the transcript to facilitate locating interview bites during editing. But it's usually better if a member of your team—usually an associate producer—does this, so that time codes will be logged to your specifications and those of your editor.

Finally, if you rearrange the furniture wherever you're shooting—a hotel, a university library, a restaurant—put it back when you're finished. Otherwise you may not only annoy or alienate your subject but also cause the location to be made off-limits to other filmmakers in the future.

sense from the intensity in the eyes of the person speaking on screen that he is fully engaged.

As interviewer, you should communicate that you are hearing what the other person is saying. However, you will want to avoid verbal tics (like "uh-huh" and "really!"), which will clutter up your sound track and drive your editor crazy. Instead, communicate your attention nonverbally. You can even encourage someone to elaborate a point without saying a word but giving a simple quizzical look instead. Sometimes an interview subject will start to answer a question before you're finished asking it. As frustrating as it is to be interrupted, it's better to shut up as quickly as possible. Your sound editor will be thankful.

You may encounter interview subjects who get so excited that they mix up names or other details. Having done extensive research, you're in the position to catch the error. Diplomatically point it out when they're finished speaking. For example, "Excuse me, but you said Bora Tora instead of Tora Bora." Most subjects will be appreciative because they want to be accurate and tell a good story. If you're confident you will have images to cut away to, you don't need to ask them to repeat the entire story.

At some point, you'll have to ask your subject to repeat what he just said, because of an airplane flying over, a siren wailing in the street below, or some other undesirable distraction. Usually your sound recordist will signal if the outside sound is unacceptable. You need to decide whether to interrupt your subject or let him complete his thought and then ask him to repeat it. Some people will be able to repeat themselves with the same intensity or wit, but others will not. Often, if they've been telling a complicated or detailed story, they'll condense it in the second telling—which might be an advantage or might not. As you become a more experienced interviewer, you'll know while you're shooting which sections of an interview are likely to be in the film and will require clean background sound, as well as which sections will never see the light of day and needn't be repeated, no matter how noisy the ambient sound.

There are aspects of interviews—and any kind of shot—that fail to register as significant when you're shooting but become key moments once you're in the editing room. In *Paragraph 175*, the elderly Heinz Dormer spoke with lengthy pauses between words. Sometimes it took him so long to finish a sentence that we'd forgotten how he'd started it. We were also getting simultaneous translations from German, which made understanding him almost impossible. We left Germany convinced his interview was unusable. Yet Dormer's halting description of "the singing forest," a form of torture the Nazis used on Jewish prisoners, was one of the film's more haunting stories.

And an interview shoot is never just the interview. Bernd Meiners, our DP on *Paragraph 175*, shot a number of close-ups in Heinz Dormer's room: clocks on tables and on the wall, faded photos, even Dormer's hand quietly shaking. These shots would allow editor Dawn Logsdon to establish the pace and tone for Dormer's interview and give his pauses an element of drama and the weight of history instead of simply feeling interminable.

One of the most difficult things to learn is not to assume the answer is over just because someone stops talking. Often the most telling moments in interviews occur after what seems like the end of an answer. Sometimes the speaker appears to be reflecting on what she has just said. Sometimes it takes a few moments of silence for the really important stuff to come out. The interview subject will let you know, by a shift in attitude or posture, when it's time to move on to the next question.

Similarly, don't assume the interview is over when you've reached the end of your questions. Often the interviewee sighs, relaxes, and then suddenly thinks about something important to add. Talk casually with her for a bit, don't let the crew start breaking down the equipment, and see what she says unprompted. Alternately, you can ask if there's anything she'd like to add that hasn't been brought up yet. Frequently, your film will be better for it.

## KNOWING WHEN TO CALL "CUT"

Whatever you're shooting, whether observational or interview, it's important for directors to know when to say "cut." In the days of shooting film, directors were aware of every second the camera was running, because it cost so much to process and print each foot of film, and you could literally hear the film running through the camera. In the digital age, filmmakers tend to be much more cavalier about shooting indiscriminately. The idea seems to be that with enough material, there's bound to be a story in there somewhere.

But this approach is often counterproductive. "Overshooting" can wear out your subjects (you don't want to overstay your welcome), it can wear out your crew, and it can certainly wear out your editor. It's also a formula for burning through your budget long before the film is finished. On the other hand, you need enough material to make a scene with a beginning, middle, and end. Remind yourself that a big part of filmmaking—and certainly directing—is making choices. It takes instinct and experience, and for this reason, directors and cinematographers with experience in editing have the advantage of knowing how much material is enough to make a scene work in the cutting room. Generally, this decision follows a brief conference between director and camera person, where they agree, "I think we've got it."

## CONCLUSION

The look and feel of the finished film reflects all the decisions—large and small—that the director makes throughout production. These decisions will define the director's "vision." Conversely, the more clearly you're able to imagine your film before you make it, the easier it will be to make these defining choices: what to shoot, how to shoot it, whom to talk to, what to ask them. It can be helpful in preproduction to watch films whose themes or storytelling style feel akin to the film you want to make. Be prepared, plan carefully—and then be open to the unexpected.

The director's job in production is to gather enough material to construct a story. Knowing this comes from experience—or from a good editor, who can assess the potential of raw footage. The true test is in the editing room.

# Part Four

# Postproduction

_____ *Chapter 11* _____

# Editing

The editing room is where the documentary film takes form and comes to life. You can think of the editor as writing the story, using the footage as a writer uses words. One editor colleague compares his work to sculpting—chipping away the excess until the bare bones of the story emerge. While it's clearly a process that inspires metaphor, it's also one that requires a willingness to sit in a small, dark room for months on end. Editing also requires organization, perseverance, ruthlessness, diplomacy, a sense of structure and pacing, and the ability to link individual shots and sequences to create a whole that's greater than the sum of its parts.

In years past, given the time-consuming processes associated with flatbed film editing benches or traditional video editing systems, it was not unusual to spend many months, perhaps a year or more, editing a documentary. Some documentaries are still completed according to their needs—in other words, as long as it takes. With the advent of digital editing technology, however, many funders and broadcast partners have concluded that three or four months maximum is sufficient time to edit a documentary.

The steps described below apply to all editing, regardless of how much or little time your budget has allotted for postproduction. Editing is what will make your raw footage into a film. Finding the film takes time. Don't short-change the process.

## LEARNING TO EDIT

Jeffrey: When I was an assistant editor on documentaries and features in New York, I had no idea what I was learning. I was always good at organizing, so that wasn't something new for me. I assumed I was learning the most by watching how the editor solved problems (an opportunity unfortunately not available to most assistant editors today), but what really made me an editor involved the fact that we were editing actual celluloid film. If the editor was working on a sequence, I would pull certain shots and have them ready to hand over when she asked for them. I didn't realize it at the time, but by learning to anticipate which shots she would want, I was learning to think as an editor.

## TEACHING EDITING

Rob: I think the hardest leap for students is to go from the production mind-set to the editorial mind-set. In production, you have an idea in your mind of what you hope you've captured with the camera, and you already have specific expectations for how you'll edit. But in editing, it's all raw material, it's all pliable, and nothing's sacred. Many students do one pass of editing, trying to make the material fit their preconceived notions, and think they're finished. They don't realize that they've just begun to edit, that they have to see the footage for what it really is and then make a film based on that.

## THE EDITING PROCESS

Before you can start making the creative choices that will bring the film to life, you need to assess what you've got to work with.

As soon as you've got some material to edit, start experimenting with it. You don't have to wait till you've finished shooting. In fact, you're better off not waiting. You'll never really know how your story is working until you begin to string it together. And this way you can see if there are parts of the story that still need to be sharpened or clarified with additional footage before you've used up all your budgeted shooting days.

## SCREENING DAILIES, MAKING SELECTS

The first thing to do is to look at all the footage. It should start to become clear that some scenes are more compelling than others. Moments will jump out as emotionally potent, others as tedious. Look for those moments that have potential to build to emotional high points, as well as those smaller moments that reveal something distinctive or intriguing about a character. The more you edit, the more you'll be able to view footage with an editorial eye. Instead of simply looking for information, look for moments that are visual, emotional, informational, and ideally all three at once. These are the moments around which you will be able to build scenes.

Don't count on remembering everything—take careful notes, highlighting anything that you think will be useful. Inevitably, repeated viewing will dull the impact of the material; it's important to try to recall *your first reaction* when you screened it. This is not to be confused with your reaction to that particular moment as you were filming it. A real-life event may or may not retain the emotional resonance you remember by the time it becomes a moment of shot footage.

During this part of the process you can start winnowing the footage down to a manageable quantity. You can set aside scenes or characters that aren't working, and focus on those that are stronger. If your shooting ratio is 30:1 or 60:1—that is, if you shoot 30 or 60 times as much footage as will be in the finished film—now is the time to narrow it down. *Selects* (shots, or parts of shots, selected as possibly useful) might be 5 or 10 times longer than the target length for the film—still a lot of material, but an amount humanly possible to wrap one's mind around.

If your film has interviews, part of identifying selects is marking your transcripts. If there are many interviews or they're long or wide-ranging, as tends to be the case with historical films relying on experts, it helps to make two printed sets of interview selects: one organized by the interviewee and the other by common themes or subjects that arose in the interviews. If, for example, you're making a film about the Spanish American War, in which the United States drove Spain out of Cuba and then occupied the Philippines, your selects categories could include William McKinley, Theodore Roosevelt, the Anti-Imperialist League, the USS *Maine*, Cuban Concentration Camps, and U.S. Atrocities in the Philippines.

Copy and paste the selected portions of the transcripts of all of your interviewees about a particular category together, for each category that all or most of them comment on. If someone talks about more than one subject within the same sentence or related sentences, copy and paste that select to all applicable categories. To continue from the example above, an interview bite might be repeated in three subject categories: Theodore Roosevelt, the USS *Maine*, Cuban Concentration Camps. For this kind of content-heavy film, you'll find that you will refer to the thematically organized transcripts more often than the set organized by interviewee. Doing this process yourself, instead of delegating it, allows you to become very familiar with your interviews, so that replacement bites will come to mind when something doesn't work as well as you hoped.

Be sure to include time-code references in any excerpts you extract from the transcript. This may be the only way to locate the footage it refers to later on.

## THE OUTLINE OR "PAPER CUT"

Some filmmakers use transcripts to cut and paste paper cuts to guide the editor before she begins the first assembly. Some directors physically cut out selected sections of transcripts and move them around on a bulletin board or even create a paper-cut script. This can be helpful, especially in films that depend heavily on interviews. You can be fairly confident that if the story works on paper, there's at least a chance that the overall structure—if not the specific order of selects in every case—will work as a film. The reverse is also true: if it doesn't work on paper, it will not work in the cutting room.

Another advantage is that the meter on the editor's time clock is not ticking yet, though the editor might be organizing footage into bins or doing other preliminary prep work to familiarize herself with the footage. Be aware, however, that a paper cut can also be misleading, since words in a transcript never fully convey the feeling of a moment of filmed reality. In observational films, paper cuts are significantly less useful—though outlines still come in handy for any kind of film.

We find it helpful—indispensable, in fact—to jot summaries of scenes or sequences on index cards or sticky notes that we can then juggle on a board. We develop elaborate color-coded systems—for example, white for interviews, green for archival, blue for observational, pink for thematic points, and so on. This enables us to construct a visual representation of the narrative that can be quite revealing. (Too much white in act 1? Let's find some blue to mix in with it.)

Use whatever method works for you—a storyboard of index cards on a bulletin board, a paper cut, or a simple outline. (For simplicity, we'll refer to this in whatever form from now on as the "outline.")

By defining and classifying the structural elements in this way, you can start to see major plot points emerging—as well as gaps in the story that you will have to fill in.

## FIRST ASSEMBLY

Once the footage is narrowed down to a manageable quantity, some editors will string out the selects in story order. Following the outline, if there is one, and her own narrative instincts, the editor will organize her selected shots into scenes, then place the related scenes into sequences in story order and finally string them all into one large narrative arc.

This *first assembly* could be anywhere from two to six hours for a feature documentary or over an hour for a short film. However long it is, it's critical to view the whole thing in a single sitting. The first assembly will almost always be a mess, but don't be discouraged. Use the assembly to gain a deeper understanding of the strengths and weaknesses in scenes, in characters, and in story. Start to sense the rhythms of the story unfolding. You will see moments and scenes that are already working, others that have the potential to work, and some that simply don't work at all and never will. You can begin to see where the emotional high points might be. As new story lines emerge, revise your outline accordingly. (Colored dot stickers can be useful at this stage—be creative!)

This raw iteration of the film is strictly for in-house use, perhaps primarily for the editor's own benefit. Most people—including many directors and most producers—don't know how to look at material in this form and assess its potential. We certainly would avoid showing the film at this stage to funders or broadcasters. It's a messy process of gathering all the useful bits and putting them roughly in the order that seems to make sense.

The next step is to refine each scene and the overall structure so that they work together as a narrative. This first draft of the film becomes the *rough cut*.

## ROUGH CUT

The rough cut is what it sounds like: rough and ragged around the edges, probably containing far more material than the eventual film can possibly hold, but approximating how the story will be told. Getting from first assembly to rough cut is the heavy-lifting stage for the editor, when major structural challenges are addressed and the ability of characters to carry story elements forward is confirmed or disproved.

Rough cuts often include "temp" material—that is, temporary visual placeholders for material that has yet to be secured. Stills can act as good stand-ins for archival footage that you're not quite positive you need.[1] *The Celluloid Closet* was constructed around clips from Hollywood movies. The rough cut was created entirely of temp material—clips we had scavenged from video stores, recorded from TV, or borrowed from collectors—until we had a clear sense of how we wanted to tell the story. At that point we started replacing the temp material with licensed footage when we could get it, or recutting sequences when we couldn't get the footage we wanted.

The rough cut stage is also the time to evaluate and keep or eliminate experiments you tried while in production. During the research stage of *Paragraph 175*, we were given access to the Shoah Foundation's videotaped oral histories of those Nazi concentration camp survivors whose memories included any encounters with gay or lesbian concentration camp inmates.[2] There were a few compelling stories about "the men with the pink triangle," as they were called. We considered interviewing one of these elderly individuals ourselves, to give the film more legitimacy by including other concentration camp inmates' perspectives, but the best storyteller was in Australia and in poor health. As an alternative, we came up with a plan to use the actual Shoah Foundation footage, which presented its own challenges. Shot flatly and almost severely, without lighting or attention to background, these interviews were historical records, not carefully framed, artful scenes. We couldn't intercut them with our own interviews because they looked so different and would be distracting. Instead, we came up with the idea of presenting the Shoah tapes as artifacts in a scene with our on-camera historian, Klaus Müller. We set up several monitors with one Shoah Foundation tape running on each monitor, and we had Klaus reference individual stories as a transition into each of the interviews. During the rough-cut phase, we eliminated this scene entirely. It had become clear that the scene did not fit into the stylistic approach that was emerging.

### DEFINING THE STYLE

During the editing process, besides writing the story, we write the laws of our filmic universe—that is, we set guidelines for how we're going to tell the story and see if we can stick to them. Will there be a narrator? What role will he play? Will information be conveyed with text? What kinds of information and how much? Will music be used? What kind of music, and where will it be effective? Throughout this process, we're always also responding to the footage. Rather than imposing a particular style or approach, we use the rhythms of our characters and our story to create the rhythm of the film.

The rough cut is the time to experiment with all these elements. We scavenge for music, using whatever seems tonally appropriate—music from other films, classical or pop music we've collected—to get a sense of how music might support the story and to find the tone that makes the most sense. We do this knowing that we will have to replace all of this music—or get the rights to it—before we exhibit the film. Stylistic elements such as graphics and on-screen text cards can be easily approximated with digital editing systems.

We start editing almost every project with the intention not to use narration. The first experience many people have with documentaries is one of those eat-your-spinach educational films, which inevitably includes an omniscient narrator dispensing information for your own good. We've all nodded off at some point while listening to that familiar voice drone on. Who would want to perpetuate that? Luckily, there are alternative and much more imaginative ways to use narration, if you find it's desirable or necessary. If we realize that there are points we need to make that are too cumbersome to communicate with text cards, or that the interviews don't express exactly the information we want to convey, then we consider narration. But we don't employ it merely to convey information. We make it a character, as in *The Times of Harvey Milk* and *The Celluloid Closet*, or we give it a stylistic function, as in *Paragraph 175*.

## THE ART OF NARRATION

Narration's bad reputation comes from overuse and lack of imagination. But there are certain functions narration can accomplish more efficiently, seamlessly, and even sometimes more gracefully than just about any other filmic element at your disposal: introducing themes, providing crucial background information, clarifying or amplifying interview remarks, foreshadowing, setting up flashbacks, and making transitions or segues. The artful transition may be one of narration's most valuable contributions to your film.

Writing narration is different from any other kind of writing you'll do. As in poetry, each word counts. In fact, you might find it helpful to reacquaint yourself with your favorite poems before you set out to write narration. While you read, pay attention to the weight and meaning given to each word. Ideally, you will aim to achieve that level of precision and concision. But these concerns arise during your final narration polish. First you have to figure out what needs to be communicated.

We begin simply writing what we want to say as concisely as we can, sometimes referring to the original treatments or proposals for language we've already worked out. We record it in the editing room, using the best voice available, and then cut it into the rough cut.

If you're using index cards, as we do, you might first sit with your editor and writer and mark the spots that need narration, agreeing generally on what should be said or where narration—its exact content yet to be determined—would help bridge two sequences. In some instances narration can take as long as it needs to, though it should never be verbose. More often, owing to shot length or an edit that is working visually, narration must be written to fit the available time.

Once you have a sense of what narration needs to accomplish in each spot, then you can figure out how best to say it. You're not writing an essay, so ask yourself what's the bare minimum you need to communicate, drop the rest, and figure out how to gracefully phrase what remains. If you find yourself writing long convoluted sentences, you're most likely trying to say too much. Either eliminate information or split your sentences in two.

When a straightforward declarative sentence won't do the job, one technique that allows you to tie seemingly disparate things together or summarize several important bits of information briefly is to turn them into a list. In English, a spoken list of three of anything has a certain rhythm that people respond to. In one scene of *Super Chief*, a documentary about Supreme Court Chief Justice Earl Warren, Sharon was writing narration to cover the 1952 Republican Convention where Warren was a presidential candidate. She was stumped as to how to explain a complicated series of backroom deals that led to World War II hero Dwight (Ike) Eisenhower promising Earl Warren a seat on the Supreme Court if Warren supported his presidential bid. Sharon's solution was to first identify what information she absolutely had to convey and eliminate the fascinating but ultimately unimportant details that were bogging her down. Then rather than explain the process, she made it into a list of three. The on-camera interviewees who followed the narration would reveal how controversial the deal was better than narration could have.

> NARRATION: But America's favorite war hero, Dwight Eisenhower, decided that he wanted to be president. They met on the convention floor. There was a hard-fought battle, a private meeting, a crucial vote, and suddenly Ike had a new supporter.[3]

The items in the list needn't be all of a kind. In Jon Else's masterful *The Day after Trinity: J. Robert Oppenheimer & the Atomic Bomb*, a list in one spot does more than summarize—it becomes a transition, almost invisibly. At one point, narration introduces the rise of Hitler, noting that Oppenheimer was Jewish. Having already established that he was a brilliant physicist, interview bites describe Oppenheimer's growing political awareness in the wake of Nazi attacks on German Jews. Then narration resumes.

> NARRATION: The late 1930s. While America endured a great depression, fascism seethed in Germany, a civil war raged in Spain, and Oppenheimer moved further to the left.[4]

The narration succinctly sums up several national political and economic crises, then turns back to the individual protagonist, with the last phrase not only making Oppenheimer's actions part of a larger political ferment

## Sharon's Basic Narration Dos and Don'ts

Learn to be concise without being terse. Every word counts. Buy and use a real dictionary and thesaurus—don't be lazy and rely on the ones in your word-processing software program.

Use adjectives sparingly. Your words will be spoken, so count on your narrator's delivery to provide emphasis.

Use the active, not the passive form of verbs. One of the few exceptions is when you use narration to introduce a person, event, or idea and the sentence needs to end with whatever or whoever you're introducing. For example, instead of writing, "Only Henry could solve the problem," write, "The problem could only be solved by Henry," then cut to a shot of him.

Ideally, narration should not overtly tell viewers what to think or how to feel. If you have strong views, find like-minded interviewees to make those points in their own words.

*But* is your friend; *and* is not. Overuse of the word *and* will make your narration drone on, boring viewers. *But* connotes a break or change, which gets viewers' attention.

Avoid "see-say": don't simply describe what people are seeing. If you must write about the image, use narration to add something of value so that viewers will see the image in a new way. However, don't err in the other direction—using shots as mere wallpaper to fill the space while you make your point.

Rhetorical questions can help guide the audience, but they should be used sparingly and only if they fit the tone you've established.

Read what you write aloud. If you can't say it easily, neither can your narrator. Listen to temp narration being read aloud to catch unintended repeated words and other mistakes, as well as to evaluate pacing and tone.

but also functioning as a transition back to his personal story. The trick, as with any narration tool, is to use the lists of three judiciously and sparingly.

Both of the examples above employ a traditional approach in which narration functions in dialogue with on-camera storytellers, often supplementing or serving as a bridge between their observations. In our own films, we define the role of the narrator narrowly. We might decide the narration will only convey historical facts and never comment on the characters or tell their personal stories. Or the narration might be omniscient, commenting on characters and context as needed—the default approach to narration. Start thinking about what kind of voice you would want: Male or female? Intimate or authoritative? It's helpful to think of the narrator as a character, someone who will be leading viewers through the story. How much of an obvious point of view will the narrator express? Will the voice be argumentative and ironic, or will it aspire to objectivity? The important thing is to make these stylistic decisions and stick to them. Then try them out for viewers at screenings and see how they respond.

It was viewer response at screenings that convinced us to put ourselves on camera and to supply first-person narration in our road movie *Where Are We?* Throughout production of this observational film, we had coordinated with DP Jean de Segonzac deliberately to shoot in such a way that we could be included as characters in the film or not—leaving the decision to be made during editing.

The conceit of the filmmaker guide has a venerable pedigree. Ross McElwee, Agnès Varda, Michael Moore, Morgan Spurlock, and others have successfully made themselves on-screen characters or guides in their own documentaries in recent years.[5] Clearly, some people are comfortable in front of the camera and feel they have the requisite charisma. Not us. The sequences of ourselves on camera and the voice-over autobiographical narration we wrote, however minimal, still make both of us squirm whenever we see the film. But screenings with colleagues whose opinions we trusted convinced us to make our presence part of the film.

As a road movie, the film was by definition episodic and needed some form of continuity or at least thematic bookends to hold it together, and our personal stories served that function. In brief voice-over musings we established the film's premise and why we were making it, created transitions between chapters, set the tone, and provided a conclusion. More important, because we were by most measures more worldly and cosmopolitan than many of the people we interacted with, we risked coming off as elitists having a laugh at their expense. It's true that we found some of them entertaining, but we certainly didn't intend to mock them. Some told quite poignant stories. By placing ourselves within the picture, especially in ways that made us uncomfortable, we hoped to position ourselves on a more equal footing with the people we were observing. We, too, were being observed—though this was admittedly a conceit, since we were choosing the images.

First-person narration almost by definition requires a point of view. If you decide that a first-person narrator is best for your film, think about having fun with it: the first-person voice needn't be yours. Ellen Spiro's 1996 film *Roam Sweet Home* was about a road trip through the American Southwest that she took with her aging dog, Sam, in an Airstream trailer, encountering many retirees and other travelers along the way. It's Sam the dog who narrates, and his observations are witty and insightful—which may not be surprising since the narration was written by novelist Allan Gurganus.[6]

### Narration Case Study: *Paragraph 175*

In *Paragraph 175*, we already had an on-camera interviewer/narrator: historian Klaus Müller. However, the background he provided was about the individuals we'd be meeting—not the larger historical narrative. So we decided that our "omniscient" voice-over narration would never refer directly to the characters or their personal stories. Instead it would stick to the larger story. As a result, viewers could let the intensely personal and emotional stories told by our characters sink in while the larger story was advanced.

It was appropriate that our narrator be male. Though the film included an interesting and moving story of a lesbian who fled Hitler's Germany, the Nazis specifically targeted homosexual men. Because all the characters were elderly, we wanted a younger narrator, whose voice would more closely reflect the age of our characters when they'd been persecuted. We also wanted an actor who publicly self-identified as gay, which even today is more difficult to find than one might expect. These criteria led us to the actor Rupert Everett, whose British accent obliquely underscored that the story we were telling was European. Since the historical narrative and the personal stories were already disturbing and shocking, we chose to make the tone of the narration direct and understated—both in the writing and in Rupert's performance.

We did, however, allow this narration to be more lyrical in a few places. One such passage is the introduction, which needed to draw viewers into a film on what was, after all, a horrendous subject:

> The Berlin Wall is only a memory now. The wartime generation is fading away, and the country seems determined to create a shining vision of the future. But a culture is also constructed of memories. Some loom large, others are hidden.[7]

This narration established a geographic and historic context. It also introduced our parallel themes of national history and personal memory.

*Paragraph 175* also used text, for which we made rules as well. We decided to use text exclusively for quotes by historical figures such as Hitler and Himmler. Hearing their words read as voice-over would have been laughable. (German accent? Harshly shouted or calmly spoken?) Presenting their words as on-screen text for viewers to read in conjunction with music and pictures was chilling.

Audiences appreciate these kinds of rules even if they are not aware of them, because they imply meaning and intentionality in the filmmaker's choices. When viewers start to feel that structural or stylistic choices are random, their confidence in the filmmaker may be undermined. Trusting they are in the hands of a capable storyteller, viewers can relax and experience the film in its totality.

Narration usually continues being refined until the very end, sometimes even being tweaked in the recording session, though this isn't ideal. Below are three chronological versions of a narrated section in *Paragraph 175* that describes a key turning point in the larger story of Hitler's rise in the 1930s. The first version was primarily an effort to convey information and to explain political cartoons that showed the Nazis as homosexuals. The second draft represented a brief flirtation with using present-tense narration—a fairly common practice with historical documentaries. Filmmakers often hope that using the present tense will give dusty historical events a you-are-there kind of immediacy. But we weren't there, and creating a false sense of familiarity about historical events and individuals can sometimes impede understanding rather than enhance it. By the final version, individual words had been honed. (*Threat*, a stronger word, replaced *liability*, for example.) Finally, this narration segment no longer ended by simply completing its description of the event. It also set up a transition that introduced the next step the Nazis would take, while ramping up the suspense.

*Early Version*

1934. Hitler consolidated his power with help from Ernst Roehm's Storm Troopers. But Roehm's own ambition—to head the German Army—had become a liability. Hitler ordered Roehm and 300 others murdered. The massacre became known as "The Night of the Long Knives." A week later, Hitler announced that the killings were justified because of Roehm's homosexuality.

On hearing the news, the opposition had a field day. They began using Roehm's homosexuality as a propaganda tool to demonize the Nazis. At the same time, the Nazis were busy demonizing homosexuals.

*Second Version*

1934. Hitler consolidates his power with help from Ernst Roehm's Storm Troopers. But Roehm's own ambition—to head the German Army—has become a liability. Hitler orders Roehm and 300 others murdered. The massacre is called "The Night of the Long Knives." A week later, he announces that the killings are justified because of Roehm's homosexuality.

On hearing the news, the opposition has a field day. They begin using Roehm's homosexuality as a propaganda tool to demonize all Nazis. At the same time, the Nazis are busy demonizing all homosexuals.

*Final Version*

By 1934, Hitler had forged powerful alliances with industry and the military. Ernst Roehm's ambition—to further strengthen the S.A. at the expense of the Army—had become a threat. On June 28th, Hitler ordered the execution of Roehm and 300 suspected enemies of the Reich.

This massacre, the Nazis' first, would be called "The Night of the Long Knives." One week later, Hitler cited Roehm's homosexuality as further justification for his murder, and vowed to cleanse the entire Nazi Party of homosexuals.

The German opposition once again branded the Nazis as homosexual. The Nazis did more than denounce homosexuals: they stepped up persecution. Gestapo Headquarters established a special department for the crime of homosexuality.[8]

### Narration Case Study: *The Celluloid Closet*

*The Celluloid Closet* presented unusual narration challenges. We knew early on that Lily Tomlin, who had championed the film from the beginning, would narrate, but we also knew that given the subject, the narrator's tone couldn't be blandly impartial. Who was Lily supposed to be speaking for? We had already realized it wouldn't work to include the voice of Vito Russo, the book's author, which was witty, political, and uniquely his. We wanted narration to be authoritative, with at least hint of gay sensibility: an omniscient voice with attitude.

Unlike *Paragraph 175*, *The Celluloid Closet* narration flowed into and out of the interview bites as well as dialogue from the movie clips. While writing narration, you should always be aware of the shots immediately preceding and following the shot the narration will accompany. But you can also go one step further. If you want to create a sense of an ongoing conversation among multiple speakers, which was our goal in *The Celluloid Closet*, one technique is to play off what has just been said or, alternately, to set up what's about to be said. It's important not to overdo this because it can lead to a lazy kind of self-referential narration writing. Also, your narration can refer only to the shot immediately preceding or following it. Viewers, unlike readers, can't turn back a few pages to reflect on what was said earlier. Instead, viewers are following the forward movement of the film—which narration should assist, not hamper.

As a critique of gay and lesbian stereotypes in the movies, *The Celluloid Closet* offered a unique opportunity to "write to picture." But writing to picture is not the same as simply describing what viewers are seeing, which would be superfluous. To do it successfully, first analyze the shots you'll be writing for. Look for emotional, thematic, or metaphorical qualities in the images, then see if you can find words that subtly reference or build on those qualities to give the image greater resonance, as in the following example.

A clip from *The Gay Divorcee* (1934) featured perennial Hollywood sissy Edward Everett Horton looking ridiculous in shorts, surrounded by a line of dancing women on one side and dancing men on the other. Our narration called attention to the beginning of a new section of the film by making a familiar theatrical and movie phrase into a short declarative statement: "Enter the Sissy: Hollywood's first gay stock character." While Horton's comic efforts to join either dancing line kept getting rebuffed, the narration continued: "The Sissy made everyone feel more manly or more womanly by occupying the space in between," making what was visually evident—a flustered Horton in the middle of the dance floor—into a metaphor.

In a clip from *Call Her Savage* (1932), two gay waiters with aprons, feather dusters, and frilly chambermaid caps wound their way through a restaurant, singing a risqué song, and passing a table where a group of mannish-looking women sat together. "In one movie," went the narration, "you could even find sissies table-hopping in Hollywood's first peek at a gay bar." (It wasn't necessary to name the film because we'd established a convention of identifying film titles along with their release dates in text on the screen.) We could have said "look" or "view," but "peek," with its hint of voyeurism and lasciviousness, was stronger. The word doesn't call attention to itself but does help shade the viewer's impression of the scene. If this seems like a lot of work over a few words, it is. But attention to details like this in every aspect of postproduction will make your film exponentially better.

## SCREENING THE ROUGH CUT

In the rough-cut stage, we don't spend a lot of time trying to make every cut work. Instead we focus on making the sequences play and defining the story elements. The film is still probably 30 to 50 percent longer than its final running time. To continue the sculpting metaphor, the subject of the sculpture is now recognizable but the features are still rough and unrefined.

It's important to screen the entire film from time to time, without stopping, to see how the overall structure is working. Otherwise it's easy to get lost in the details and lose sight of the big picture. Once we feel the film is starting to come together, we usually screen it for a few trusted colleagues. Simply watching the film with other people who are unfamiliar with it can be instructive: we become more sensitized to parts that are working and parts that drag on too long. Then we ask for their "brutally honest" feedback.

We might have one or more additional rough-cut screenings, where we ask viewers to home in on specific areas of concern.

Use these screenings to help assess the results of your work. Do we care about the characters? Do we have the information we need in order to get invested and understand their story? You should have a pretty good idea at this stage if any additional shooting will be needed.

It's important to pick your test audience carefully. Whether you choose other filmmakers, scholars, friends, or a combination of viewers, you want people whose opinions you trust and who will give completely frank reactions. Then the director's job is to listen. This might seem self-evident, but it's remarkable how often filmmakers ask for feedback and then respond to criticism with defensiveness and self-justification. A more useful approach is to hold one's tongue and take careful notes, then look at them later and try to analyze what the problems really are.

Your viewers can identify the elements, characters, and scenes that contribute to the film and those that are distractions—what works for them and what doesn't—and they may be able to articulate why. But even very specific feedback might reveal an altogether different problem. A sequence or a

## Take a Break

If you possibly can, take a break during editing, particularly if energy and creativity are flagging and funds are running low. Returning to the material refreshed almost always enables you to solve problems that you thought were insurmountable. During the editing of *HOWL* we had an enforced hiatus while final animation was being done. When we resumed editing, we were able to see problems and solutions we hadn't before. Even though the film was scripted, we moved many elements around, calibrating and juggling according to their relative impact. While the final structure generally followed the script, we made many small but significant changes. For example, we intercut the various elements (courtroom drama, Ginsberg interview, live reading of "Howl," memory flashbacks, poem animation) much more than we had anticipated. There were also more documentary elements early in the editing process, including interviews with some of Ginsberg's fellow poets. While we kept a few of the documentary elements, such as footage of New York's West Village, scenes of dancing, and headlines, we dropped all the interviews, which became one element too many. And shots of elderly men reflecting on their youth didn't mesh with the reality we were creating, which was making their youth come alive again.

character just doesn't seem right for one reason or another, and it's up to you and the editor to find a solution. You know the strengths and weaknesses of your footage better than first-time viewers of a rough cut. Rely on feedback to identify problems rather than to find solutions.

## FINE CUT

By now we have a good idea of what's working and what's not. Fine-cutting is a process of smoothing rough edges, making difficult decisions about problem scenes, and generally making the film flow as a seamless narrative. This is usually a shorter process than the rough-cutting, and it can be the most satisfying. This is the stage at which you can find ways to make the film *sing*.

The film should now be very close to its final length. Watching the film all the way through, you should be carried from moment to moment on a journey that feels inevitable in its trajectory—all the toiling and patching and

### Using a Tease to Set Up the Film's Structure

*The Times of Harvey Milk* opens with Dianne Feinstein, then a San Francisco city supervisor, stoically announcing to a spontaneous press gathering in City Hall that Supervisor Harvey Milk and Mayor George Moscone had been shot and killed. There follows a brief explanation by narrator Harvey Fierstein to orient the viewer, then a short sequence over which we hear an audiotaped message Milk had actually recorded in case he was murdered. In retrospect this seems an obvious opening, but it didn't appear that way immediately.

When the filming was done, Rob started working on an outline with colored index cards. With all the scenes laid out before him, it became clear that the Feinstein announcement—her tortured face, the shouts of disbelief and shock from the crowd of reporters—made for some of the most powerful, immediate, and gripping footage he had ever seen. His first instinct was to save this moment for a dramatic high point, probably at the end of act 2 after the assassinations (where it does reappear in the film, from a different angle).

At the time, Harvey Milk was not well known outside of San Francisco. There was no reason to believe a general audience would seek out this story. Harvey needed to be situated in a historical context with a dramatic event to draw viewers in. The Feinstein announcement proved to be a key dramatic hook. The audience was engaged by the intense emotion and intrigued about these assassinations of public figures—one of whom had apparently expected to be killed. As a result, the questions that arose for the audience were less about *what happened*, but rather *Who was Harvey Milk?* and *Why was he murdered?*

elisions are invisible—until at the end, you feel you've arrived at some place different from where you started.

Often the last thing we do is figure out how the film begins. It sometimes takes getting to this final stage of the storytelling process to know enough about the dynamic of the film to be able to edit an opening sequence. In television, this is usually a brief opening sequence called a *tease*. A TV tease has a very specific mandate: to grab viewers' attention so they won't change the channel. Theatrical feature documentaries, on the other hand, assume the luxury of a somewhat captive audience—or at least an audience that has already chosen to watch the film. Openings of feature documentaries can thus be less sensational, more mysterious, more "filmic."

Whether short and punchy or long and lyrical, the opening is critical: it sets the tone of your film, visually, musically, and through spoken or written language. Usually the tease introduces the film's theme or premise as well as key characters. It also begins to establish the rules of your film's universe, a process that continues into the first scenes of your film.

## FINAL MUSIC AND NARRATION

If the film calls for an original score, the fine-cut stage is a good time to start working with a composer.

The use of music in documentaries requires a delicate touch. It's clearly a directorial comment on the action, but you don't want the viewers to feel you're using music to manipulate them. The power of emotional scenes in particular can be undermined by a heavy-handed score. As a rule we try not to use music at all in scenes that are already emotionally potent. Sometimes music may lead the editing—in montage sequences, for instance—but in general we don't want the audience to be aware of the music. It should be experienced as an integral part of the texture of the film.

Some composers will want to see a cut of the film with the temp music you've chosen, to give them a sense of what you're looking for. Most composers we've worked with prefer to watch the film without any music, so as not to color their own musical responses.

It's helpful for the director, editor, and composer watch the film together, stopping and starting at places to discuss where music might be helpful. This is known as a *spotting session*—choosing the spots where the music will start and end. Since you're still editing, the composer might encourage you to open up sequences and let them breathe more, allowing space for music. Or she might suggest that sound effects in a certain scene would be more effective than music.

Then the composer goes off to work, creating rough sketches, usually digitally generated, for you to try out. Your editor should cut these sketches into the film as they come in, replacing the temp music whenever possible. This will give you the chance to see how the music is working and discuss any problem areas with the composer. The final score will be composed and recorded once picture editing is finalized and the picture is locked—that is, when editing is complete and no more changes will be made.

Our composer for *Paragraph 175* was Tibor Szemzö, who lives in Budapest. Communication was difficult, but we managed. Tibor responded to the sequences we sent him and sent back recordings he composed and produced. His music was haunting and beautiful—but in some cases we felt it didn't fit the mood of the scenes as we saw them. So we tried moving the music cues around,[9] even experimenting with music in places where we hadn't intended to have it. We sent the sequences with his repurposed music back to Tibor for his approval. This was 1999, and we were sending tapes back and forth via international post. Today, file-sharing technology would make that kind of long-distance collaboration much easier. Usually we work with composers closer to home.

For *The Celluloid Closet*—a movie about the history of the movies—we wanted an appropriately big Hollywood-type score. As temp music, we were using a score that Carter Burwell had composed for another film. When it came time to hire a composer, we decided to approach Carter. But when we showed him how we had used his temp score, he seemed perplexed—the music he had written for a completely unrelated film made no sense to him with our picture. So he asked us to describe what we felt the music was accomplishing. We used adjectives like *nostalgic, romantic,* and *wistful,* and Carter composed and conducted a ravishingly romantic, nostalgic, wistful score for the film, with a lush orchestral arrangement.

We expected he would do something similar with *HOWL.* Instead, he convinced us that an orchestra would be too much for the story and that a chamber piece would work much better with a film about the spoken word. (It also fit more comfortably into our budget.) Carter composed beautiful themes around the voice of James Franco as Ginsberg reading the poem. In effect, the voice became the lead instrument.

One pitfall of using temp music is that it can work so well you fall in love with it. On *Where Are We?* our editor Ned Bastille had been using "The Carnival of the Animals" by Saint-Saëns as a temp theme. Its dreamy quality worked well with the reflective road-trip movie he was constructing from our footage. We began working with a composer to come up with a variation on the Saint-Saëns piece, but eventually we realized it was futile—we couldn't match the quality of the original. "The Carnival of the Animals" is in the public domain, so we had to pay only for a master recording license[10] for a less expensive but perfectly fine recording of the piece Ned had been using all along. We were lucky. Sometimes people fall in love with their temp music, then discover they can't afford it.

On *The Times of Harvey Milk*, Rob chose to use the theme from *The Battle Algiers*,[11] a film that partly inspired the making of *Harvey Milk*. The theme music worked so well in constructing the candlelight march scene that editor Debbie Hoffmann feared the sequence wouldn't work without it. But composer Mark Isham's original score, with his haunting trumpet solo, helped to make that sequence an iconic one. Rob's direction to Mark was a single adjective: elegiac.

If we're using narration, we usually record the final version just *before* locking picture. That way we know how long each piece of narration needs to be, and in cases where it doesn't quite fit, we still have the opportunity to make small timing adjustments of the shots as needed. We time each bit of narration before the recording session, noting on our copies of the script where timing is tight. While it's helpful to have a copy of the film handy to reference, we don't find it necessary to record to picture. If you have a celebrity narrator, you will most likely have to record him in a sound studio in a location convenient for him. No matter how famous your narrator is, it's important to get at least two takes of everything. Bring along your producer or editor if possible so that you'll have two pairs of ears evaluating the reading.

## LOCKING PICTURE AND FINAL TOUCHES

When we feel the film is getting close to completion, we like to screen it again, this time for a larger audience. If the film is meant for the big screen, we rent a screening room and project the fine cut for an audience of 20 to 50 guests. We try to include a combination of film and nonfilm people in order to get a wider sampling of responses. Generally, we ask people to fill out a short questionnaire afterward, stay for a discussion, or both. These screenings are always helpful in determining if the film is working and in locating those places where it still needs more tweaking.

After making changes in response to our final screening, we view the cut one or two last times, making any little necessary adjustments. Many editors make one final pass to adjust pacing, opening up or lengthening certain shots or scenes to let their impact sink in, tightening others to make them stronger. If your film already has a broadcast home, you will also be trimming it (somehow documentary filmmakers rarely need to add material) to meet the precise required length.

When everything is working as well as it can work, and nothing we try in the way of improving it actually makes it any better, then we know it's time to lock picture.

The last stages of postproduction are generally an intense, compressed period of detailed technical work. The final music and voice-over are recorded and built into the sound track so that they start and stop at exactly the right places. If you're working with a sound editor, this is usually when his work begins. The director and editor go through the film with the sound editor, spotting sound effects in a process similar to spotting music with the composer—stopping and starting, identifying problem areas and places where the sound could be enhanced or improved. The sound editor then goes to work, preparing the sound tracks for the final sound mix.[12] With digital sound-editing tools such as ProTools, the sound editor can create a final mixed sound track in the editing suite. For a film intended for the big screen, though, it's always better to mix on a professional mixing stage.

Meanwhile, the picture gets its final touches. If the film was edited in low resolution to save digital memory space, all the shots will be replaced with the same shots at high resolution (the *online edit*). This is also when the temporary graphics and titles are replaced with the final versions. Lastly, the picture is *color corrected*—the contrast, saturation, and color temperatures of each shot are meticulously adjusted. Each of these stages calls for special expertise. Professional sound mixers, online editors, and colorists will add polish to your film if you can afford them.

## EDITING CASE STUDY: *COMMON THREADS*

### First Assembly

We had determined the basic structure in writing the treatment. The film was conceived as five duets, each comprising a storyteller and someone he or she loved who had died of AIDS. We had outlined our three-act structure in various treatments and proposals (see chapter 4).

Our first step was to look at all the footage and find the best parts of each person's story. Then we organized each character's anecdotes and memories into an order that made sense and that fit into each of the three acts. Finally, we integrated the five stories with one another. To plan and keep track of our structure, we "outlined" the story using index cards for each of the story beats, with a different color for each storyteller.[13]

NAMES Project AIDS Memorial Quilt in Washington, DC—Common Threads: Stories from the Quilt, 1987. (Courtesy of Telling Pictures)

The stories all began with an early relationship anecdote that would give a sense of both the storytellers and their partners.

Sara Lewinstein told a story about playing tennis with Tom Waddell, and how their mutual competitiveness created a bond between them. So we made a blue card that said:

| |
|---|
| SARAH<br>Tennis—competitive |

Vito told a story about first seeing Jeffrey Sevchik in San Francisco, up on a ladder changing the letters on the Castro movie theater marquee. Thus an orange card:

| |
|---|
| VITO<br>Meeting Jeffrey—Castro marquee |

And so on, for each of the five storytellers.

We assembled the footage following this index card outline, selecting shots for each character in story order. We made adjustments as needed to make the individual stories flow more smoothly, but we didn't try to make them play as scenes; we just strung them together in an order that seemed to make sense. We experimented with different orderings and kept moving the cards until we felt there was a logical and emotional progression through each character's story.

### Rough Cut

We then began weaving together the five stories, still following our index card template.

To illustrate the personal stories and to cover awkward jump cuts, we started experimenting with whatever visual material we had: home movies, family photos, appearances on local news, as well as the original images we had filmed for each of the characters. These images included gardens designed by landscape architect David Campbell, Commander Tracy Torrey's lover; the hospital room where Sallie Perryman's husband, Rob, spent his last days; and the toy collection of David and Suzi Mandel's young son, David. Blurring the line between archival and re-created material is ethically and journalistically problematic,[14] so we had taken care to film these sequences in a distinctively stylized manner. We didn't want anyone mistaking these shots for actual archival material—or giving the impression that we were trying to pass it off as such.

We wrestled with the material for months. Along with trying to establish a context of the growing awareness of the epidemic and its increasing toll, we tried to work as much humor into the first act as we could, since we knew that the film was going to get emotionally intense rather quickly. Audiences like to be moved, but they don't like to be drowned in emotion. We wanted to draw people into the stories and make them want to spend time with the storytellers. We knew that the empathy created in the first act would intensify the emotional response to the later parts of the story.

We structured the second act so that it built to an emotional climax. Although not all the deaths had occurred at the same time, dramatically it made sense to group most of these stories together. We decided that the precise year of each death and the order in which they occurred were less important than the common emotional experience of losing a loved one.

The film ended on the Quilt in Washington, DC, when most of our storytellers inhabited the same physical space for the first and only time, visually signaling their shared experience.

When you are editing a documentary without a clear narrative line, it's sometimes best to start at the end and work backward, or to start in the middle and work outward. This applies to editing scenes as well as the overall film. In this case, the last sequence, our act 3 finale, was actually the first sequence we edited. And the last sequence we edited was the opening. We created a montage of images from Quilt panels—moody, evocative, abstract—with dreamy music and voice-over of actors reading from letters that had been sent in to the NAMES Project along with completed Quilt panels. These were the letters we had used in our research to find our stories, and we felt their raw eloquence would make a powerful opening.

When we believed we had a structure that was working, we invited a few dozen people to a screening room to watch the film.

### Fine Cut

We analyzed the feedback and identified some common themes. The consensus was that the film was strong, even emotionally wrenching—and that it was oppressively claustrophobic. The ending in Washington seemed to work, but the opening letter montage didn't.

As we thought about this and discussed the comments, we concluded that the opening didn't work because it just wasn't compelling to hear random excerpts from anonymous letters about people we hadn't met. We had simultaneously submitted the rough cut to HBO—perhaps prematurely, but we needed the payment that this would trigger. The head of the network also commented on the "lack of a ticking clock," which was a particularly helpful observation.

To mitigate the feeling of claustrophobia, we began to open up the film with other footage than that of our characters, creating sequences that conveyed the toll AIDS was taking in the larger world—the disease's historical context.

Debbie Hoffmann had coedited *The Times of Harvey Milk* with Rob. A key element of that film was raw news footage shaped into narrative sequences that played dramatically. Debbie came on board to edit sections composed of news reports about AIDS and other archival footage. Aside from supplying important information, these "context sequences," as we began to think of them, provided narrative momentum, served as punctuation, and gave the film breathing room.

To evoke the ticking clock, we integrated on-screen text indicating dates and statistics of the growing epidemic. In fact, we had included these kinds of statistics in our original treatment, but they hadn't made it into the rough cut.

Using the AIDS Quilt as a visual motif was an obvious choice, since it was the Quilt that inspired the project and the Quilt itself makes such a strong visual statement. We chose to film it in several distinct ways. First, we filmed it observationally, as it was displayed on the Capitol Mall, getting as many angles as we could using a crane, a Steadicam, and a forklift in addition to three handheld cameras. During the editing process we took a number of Quilt panels into a studio, rigged and lit them, and shot them using a dolly and crane. Finally, we created a graphic photomontage of the Quilt and filmed animated moves into and out from the Quilt panels that related directly to our characters.

Each of these shooting styles produced a different effect, and in the course of editing we developed a strict set of rules as to how they would be used. We used the graphic animation in the first act to introduce each of our five storytelling pairs (our "duets" of storytellers and their loved ones). Each story was introduced by a shot that began wide, showing many Quilt panels, then zeroed in to the panel of the person whose story we were telling. We saved all the observational shots of the Quilt in DC for the third act, when the Quilt would finally be introduced as a story element. This made logical and emotional sense to us, as two of the Quilt's main functions were to memorialize and serve as a focus for grieving. It also made thematic sense, by allowing us to expand the visual scope to encompass a growing community. After two acts of intense storytelling, this new, expansive visual style gave variation to the film—and allowed the viewer a break from intense storytelling. Finally, we used the studio shots as a visual element in the interstitial "context sequences," which served as de facto chapter markers.

In these context sequences we gave ourselves permission to break free of the constraint of using only those Quilt panels that were directly related to the individual stories we were telling. When possible we began each of these sequences with a news report featuring a prominent AIDS activist who had died, then segued to his or her Quilt panel. We then chose certain panels that placed us in a certain year and others that were emotionally expressive. We used superimposed text on screen to convey the growing number of AIDS deaths from year to year, with narration to convey some of the more complicated factual information.

So now we had developed our set of aesthetic rules. Here's a summary:

> *Personal stories*: Our storytellers would talk about themselves, as well as their relationships to their loved one who had died and to the society around them. Quilt element: animation (linking the stories to their Quilt panels).

Other visual elements: photos, home movies, archival footage, original footage (the evocative environmental footage we had shot).

*Context*: The narration would tell the larger story, using information that did not refer personally to any of our characters. Rather, it would cover the history of the epidemic and the responses (or lack thereof) of both the government and the most affected communities. Archival news footage would advance the historical narrative and reflect changing attitudes about the disease. On-screen text would be used only to convey mounting statistics over time. Quilt element: stylized studio footage of the Quilt, linking people who appeared in news footage to a Quilt panel when possible, and using dates of deaths to indicate the passage of time.

*The Unfolding*: The Quilt became an active story element in the third act, when we used observational footage of its ritualized unfolding in Washington, DC, visually conveying the magnitude of the epidemic. If we had any footage of our storytellers on the Quilt, we used those shots here.

Now the film was more or less working, but we still had to figure out the opening. We knew what the film was trying to say, so we knew what themes we wanted to introduce up front. It was also impressed upon us, by our co-producer Bill Couturié and our HBO executives, that we needed something snappier than our "letters to the Quilt" montage to hook viewers from the outset: a way to universalize the story for a broad audience very quickly.

We reconceived the opening (the tease) as a kind of miniature version of the film. We begin with a series of photomontages showing concise life stories of people with AIDS, tracing their trajectories from childhood to young adult-hood to illness, accompanied by Bobby McFerrin's haunting score. The last of these life stories segues from photos to newspaper headlines to video news reports that reveal that this last "life story" is that of Rock Hudson. At this point we introduce the voice of our narrator, Dustin Hoffman, telling how it wasn't until Rock Hudson's death that most people became aware of the disease, and introducing Hudson's memorial panel as the most famous in the Quilt. We segued from Hudson's Quilt panel, pulling back to a grand crane shot revealing the Quilt unfolded on the Capitol Mall before the White House. Then we cut to the title. The structure of the tease began intimately with the personal life stories, then expanded through the news reports to the wider cultural context and broadened yet again—this time visually—with the panoramic Quilt display, representing the community's response.

We had initially resisted the idea of using "celebrity Quilt panels" like Hudson's—it felt predictable and sensational. Further, we wanted to avoid using Hudson's celebrity to make the epidemic relevant, as the news media had done. We ended up with a solution that allowed us to have it both ways. We did focus on Rock Hudson, but we used the reference to make our point—that it took the death of a pop-culture celebrity to bring AIDS into the consciousness of most Americans. It was a hook.

Throughout the rough cuts and fine cuts we had been using temp music by Mark Isham (who had scored *The Times of Harvey Milk* as well as a number of major Hollywood movies) and, oddly, a Carly Simon song from the Mike Nichols comedy *Working Girl*. As incongruous as this sounds, there was something stirring in the choral arrangement of "Let the River Run" that worked when played against images of the Quilt unfolding—it seemed to evoke a chorus of voices emanating from the Quilt, and the effect was powerful. At some point while we were editing the film, we had lunch at a restaurant where we spotted singer-composer Bobby McFerrin at a nearby table, and the idea came to us that he would be an interesting choice to compose the music. We restrained ourselves from approaching him at lunch, but wrote him a letter that week through his manager, introducing ourselves, describing the project, and explaining why we thought his vocal music would be right for it. He responded within days. He was in the process of assembling a chorus of voices that he wanted to use as a collaborative ensemble—he called it Voicestra.

This was an unusual and exciting collaboration. Bobby composed by improvising while watching scenes. As exciting as this was, it also promised to be pricey if we had to pay recording studio time while waiting for inspiration to strike. To make things go more smoothly, we hired composer Todd Boekelheide to produce the music at his home studio. Todd managed the technical and creative logistics of recording Bobby's improvisational riffs and synching them to the film. Watching the scenes with the temp score allowed us to discuss and adjust the mood and placement of the music cues. When everyone was satisfied, we went into a professional recording studio with Bobby and his ensemble and recorded the cues one by one, synchronized with picture. Bobby had invented distinct but musically related themes for each of the five characters. As the stories progressed, he was able to modulate each of the themes to resonate with the changing emotional tone of the stories.

One of the last elements we produced was the Quilt animation introducing our main characters. We had chosen which story would introduce each of the storytellers, but we lacked a device to link the stories visually through the Quilt. We met with Drew Takahashi, a San Francisco animation producer, who put a team at his company at our disposal to design and execute a series of short animated graphics. The animators began by cutting and pasting together photos of large sections of the Quilt, so that each shot could begin wide, the frame filled with tiny, colorful Quilt panels. Then, through animation, the camera was made to swoop and twist and zoom in to the individual panel memorializing one of our subjects. This graphic treatment of the Quilt panels was so pleasing that we eventually adapted it for the movie poster.

## CONCLUSION

The process of editing a documentary, during which the film seems to come to life, comprises a prosaic series of steps: screening of dailies, first assembly, rough cut, fine cut, picture lock. The dividing line between some of these steps can get fuzzy, but the process is always the same, allowing you to base your work on progressive milestones as the film takes shape. And payment schedules—whether the project is funded by a broadcaster, a granting organization, or another financing entity—are often based upon delivery and approval of these stages.

The final processes after the picture is locked—sound editing, sound mixing, color correction, and online editing—generally take a month or so at the end of a film project. There is also a significant amount of finishing work for your producer or associate producer at this stage, such as music cue sheets (logs with timings of music used for licensing calculations), archival footage usage reports and payments, securing E&O insurance, and registering copyright. The details of all of these steps are beyond the scope of this book.

While the color correction and sound mixing require specialized technical skills, they also require creative sensitivity to achieve a smoothly polished presentation. With these last steps, the creative work on the film is finally done and it's time to send the film out into the world.

*Chapter 12*

# Launch Your Film

Films need audiences—not just to justify their existence but indeed to pay for their creation. After a century of movie making, some basic patterns of distribution have become established: filmmakers create a product, which is then packaged by distributors and disseminated to exhibitors that offer viewings to paying customers in theaters and on home video or via Internet streaming.[1] Revenues are passed back down the chain, from consumer to exhibitor (or broadcaster) to distributor (or studio), and then—if there is anything left after deducting distribution costs—occasionally back to the filmmaker.

Just as the medium has been transformed by digital technologies, so has the means of distribution. A few years ago, film festivals were the only venues where many documentaries had a chance of attracting attention. Festivals continue to offer a mechanism to highlight those films that the festival programmers deem worthy. Festivals also serve as markets, where a small number of films get bought for television broadcast and an even smaller number get picked up for theatrical distribution. But they are no longer the only game in town.

The Internet, with its insatiable hunger for content, has started to usurp television's role. This offers new promise for filmmakers hoping to get their films seen by large audiences. It also creates new challenges as filmmakers and content providers negotiate a business model that will allow artists to profit from their work.

The model that seems to be taking shape at this writing (2012) is similar to a television licensing arrangement—broadcast networks are being replaced by *content aggregators* that license streaming and download rights from distributors. As always, the challenge for filmmakers will be to carve out some of this revenue stream for themselves.

The biggest challenge in the shifting marketplace is to get noticed. Use all the qualities you dreamed up when pitching the idea for your film that make your film uniquely attractive—from its topical urgency to its celebrity narrator—to make it stand out from the crowd.

## FILM FESTIVALS

Film festivals, with their submission fees and insistence on exclusive premieres, can look like a confusing, expensive racket to first-time filmmakers. There are ways to make the festival experience a positive one for both you and your film, and ideally even jump-start your next film.

External deadlines can help you make that final push to the end, but don't let festival application dates unduly affect your fine cut. It's yet one more balancing act to master: to finish your film to your satisfaction *and* submit to the appropriate festivals in time. Filmmaker service organizations such as IDA (the International Documentary Association) post festival deadlines on their websites throughout the year. There are other websites that list festivals worldwide, as well as documentary listserv groups such as Doculink and the D-Word (http://www.doculink.org and http://www.d-word.com) that you can join. These websites regularly feature lively discussions critiquing various festivals, including filmmakers' accounts of their experiences and offers to share venue rentals or meet up at the festivals.

There are reasons to show your film at festivals beyond the prestige and the undeniable pleasure of watching your film with a film-loving audience. If you have no distributor or broadcast venue, a festival is where you might find either or both, or perhaps a sales agent. At the very least, you'll gain experience in presenting your work and responding to audience questions, as well as in networking. A number of festivals are held in conjunction with film markets, which are great networking opportunities. You will inevitably meet funders, broadcasters, distributors, and other filmmakers who will become part of your professional network. Even if nothing comes of these meetings immediately, they can lead to future opportunities in filmmaking and exhibition—and survival in a tough professional field.

While it may be every filmmaker's dream to have a film premiere at Sundance, it's wise to have a backup plan for getting your film launched and subsequently distributed.

## Case Study: What Worked and What Didn't with
*The Times of Harvey Milk*

In the summer of 1984, as Rob and his team were in the final post-production phase, producer Richard Schmiechen began showing *Harvey Milk* to potential distributors. The film was partially funded by PBS (through a program of WNET in New York called *Non-Fiction Television*, which sadly no longer exists), so a scheduled airdate for fall 1985 was already set. Richard and Rob had previously negotiated with PBS for the right to a festival and theatrical release before the broadcast—that is, a *theatrical window*.

The theatrical window in this case was relatively short, so their strategy was to secure a distributor before their festival launch, enabling the potential distributor to immediately begin booking the film into theaters. But the plan backfired: every distributor but one turned down *The Times of Harvey Milk*. Back then, documentaries almost never played in theaters; in addition, the film was deemed too risky because of its subject. Also, the potential distributors viewed the film on VHS videotape rather than on the big screen with an audience, thereby degrading the entire experience and initial impression of the film. Since then we've learned it's always better to get distributors to see your movie on the big screen, with an audience, which is why festival screenings are so valuable.

In retrospect, Rob and Richard hadn't chosen the best strategy, but the film's launch did have a happy ending. They signed with Teleculture, a small distributor that had made an attractive offer after viewing a video transfer of the fine cut of the film. In September 1984, the film had its world premiere at the Telluride Film Festival to great acclaim, and then things began to snowball. A headline in *USA Today* named *The Times of Harvey Milk* the "hit of the festival." The film was invited to the New York Film Festival at Lincoln Center, then to the very first Sundance Film Festival, where it won a special jury citation. A few weeks after that, it was named Best Non-Fiction Film of the year by the New York Film Critics Circle, then screened at the Berlin Film Festival. In the midst of the Berlin excitement, the film received an Academy Award nomination, and then it went on to win the Oscar—all within six months!

Although Teleculture was able to capitalize on the critical response to the film, it was still a small company and in fact would soon go bankrupt. Nonetheless the film took on a life of its own, and by the time it won the Oscar, it was playing in theaters all over the United States. In retrospect, it would have been better to gamble that a larger, more established distributor would come on board during festival screenings. Fortunately, after

Rob Epstein, director, and Richard Schmiechen, producer—*The Times of Harvey Milk*, 1985. (Courtesy of The Academy of Motion Picture Arts and Sciences)

Teleculture went under, Rob was eventually able to reclaim the rights to the film (but not without substantial legal fees), and it continues to have a long life, most recently as part of the Criterion Collection.

### Sundance and Beyond

If you do find yourself lucky enough to have your film premiere at Sundance, go armed with well-designed publicity materials such as a press kit, production stills, and a temporary poster (temporary, because if you sell your film to a distributor, its marketing department will create new artwork). For Sundance, it is also worth putting together a team—specifically a publicist and a sales agent to negotiate with potential distributors if your film does well. Even if you cannot afford a professional publicist to represent your film at the festival, try to work with a publicist to produce your press kit.

If your film isn't invited to Sundance, don't turn your back on all festivals. Festivals are a wonderful way to get your work seen and discussed, to meet other filmmakers, and to expand your professional network. As wonderful as Sundance may be to launch a film, there are plenty of other festivals out there such as Full Frame, True/False, SXSW, Hot Docs, and Silverdocs, just to name a few. Some of the smaller or newer festivals will give much more attention to a film that would otherwise get lost in a big, established festival. If your documentary addresses a particular issue (and what documentary doesn't address an issue one way or another?), track down the festivals organized around that issue. It's not an exaggeration to say that there's a festival somewhere for just about any issue, identity, or special interest. There are also regional festivals that give priority to local filmmakers.

If your film thematically relates to an academic discipline, there are large annual meetings for each of these. For example, the American Historical Association (AHA) and the Organization of American Historians (OAH) both hold yearly meetings with large numbers of attendees and corresponding film festivals with cash prizes. There are also more specialized annual meetings of scholars, such as the Middle East Studies Association (MESA).

Most festivals don't pay for transportation and lodging. Of course your film can screen at festivals without your attendance, but since nonfiction filmmaking may be the ultimate deferred-gratification art form, treat yourself to at least one festival appearance if you possibly can. Ideally, you will chart a one- or two-year festival schedule. Come up with first, second, and third choices for your world premiere, then identify the appropriate theme-based and regional festivals to which you may want to apply later. If your film will be broadcast, there are also some television-oriented festivals to consider when you have a broadcast date, such as INPUT, a huge international conference and festival for public television producers, held in a different country each year. Be aware that once your film has screened at a particular festival, your chance of being accepted there with your next film—or at least being seriously considered—can increase. Also keep in mind that most of the major festivals require exclusive premieres, so it's important to aim for the festival that best suits the needs of your film.

The marketplace for nonfiction work is forever shifting, but it's always good to learn from the films and filmmakers who came before you. Consider doing a case study of a film you admire and believe to be similar to yours—but be realistic in choosing your comparison. Research how that film was launched and released. Try getting feedback from friends, colleagues, and festival veterans about the chances for your film at any particular festival.

If you think your documentary has theatrical potential as either a feature or short, you may also want to look into the rules for Academy Awards consideration (http://www.oscars.org). The rules for documentary qualification can change from year to year, so make sure you are current. There is also a category for student Academy Awards, which can be found on the same website.

## EDUCATIONAL DISTRIBUTION

During the height of an earlier documentary renaissance that began in the 1970s, many filmmakers were able to fund their next films with proceeds from institutional sales (schools, universities, libraries) of their previous films via educational distributors. Institutional sale prices, because they assume multiple viewings by large numbers of people, are traditionally much higher than individual home-use sale prices. Today, a combination of technology, politics, and economics has made it difficult, if not impossible, to start new films with distribution proceeds from prior work. Between video on demand, YouTube, Bit Torrent, and other legal and illegal Internet portals for media exchange on one hand and slashed school and library budgets on the other, educational distribution has not been a reliable or substantial resource for filmmakers for some time. But you made your film to have it seen, not left on a shelf, and there are still a number of valiant educational distributors and even filmmaker cooperatives such as New Day Films (http://www.newday.com).

Research which distributors handle films similar to yours. If one offers to distribute your film, confer with filmmakers already working with that distributor about percentages of profit, frequency of sale reports, reliability of payments, and general transparency. The most important quality to look for in a distributor is honesty.

Some filmmakers also choose to distribute their films themselves. If you find this daunting, you're not alone. The entire field of distribution, both educational and home use, is in flux, as is the medium of transmission. DVDs are being replaced by streaming and downloads, eliminating any consistency of sale and rental price. As with any other aspect of nonfiction filmmaking, do your research, choose people and organizations you believe you can trust, and protect yourself with a written agreement in advance about how to resolve differences.

## THE SMALL—AND SMALLER—SCREEN

So-called free television offers few venues for airing nonfiction films. Most of those venues reside on public television, including such series as *POV*, *Independent Lens*, and to a lesser extent, *American Masters, American Experience*, and very occasionally *Frontline*.[2]

HBO and Showtime both purchase finished feature and short-form nonfiction films. As of 2012, Netflix and Google are getting into the production business. More and more documentaries are finding audiences on computer screens, tablets, and even mobile phones—not ideal venues, perhaps, but virtual venues all the same. The only predictable aspect of broadcast, cable, and Internet venues today is that they will continue to evolve rapidly over the next several years. This will inevitably make the market increasingly difficult to navigate—and it will also open up unforeseen possibilities.

## CONCLUSION

Be both optimistic and realistic about your film's prospects out in the world. Screening your film is the ultimate goal, and if you've done all the work to make a film, you owe it to yourself and your film to make sure it's seen. And then start making your next film.

Oscar night: Rob Epstein, Bill Couturié, and Jeffrey Friedman—*Common Threads: Stories from the Quilt*, 1990. (Courtesy of The Academy of Motion Picture Arts and Sciences)

As trite as it sounds, we've always believed that *if there's a will, there's a way*. It's up to you to manifest the requisite level of passion and dedication—with full knowledge going in that it will be a long, tough road. But if that commitment is there, with perseverance, blind faith, commitment to craft, and direct, honest storytelling, you can make your dream a reality. Whether your film changes the world or touches a few hearts, the results can be more than you ever imagined.

_Appendix 1_

# Sample On-Camera Release
(your production company name and address here)

General Release

Date:

    For good and valuable consideration, receipt of which is hereby acknowledged, I, the undersigned, do hereby grant to YOUR PRODUCTION COMPANY, INC. and its affiliated companies and their respective successors ("Producer"), assigns and licensees, the irrevocable right and license to use my name, voice, likeness and biographical material concerning me, and the right to exhibit, distribute, transmit, display, exploit, project, perform, reproduce, edit, alter and modify any video tape, motion picture and/or still photographs made by Producer of my likeness, poses, acts and appearances, and any sound recordings made by Producer of my voice in any such video tape and/or motion picture (as well as any quotes I may give), without additional compensation to me, in any manner or medium, whether now known or hereafter developed, throughout the world, in perpetuity. I, the undersigned, further release Producer and its respective partners, officers, directors, employees, agents, successors, assigns and licensees from any and all claims that I have or might have by virtue of or arising out of the production, exhibition, distribution, promotion and/or advertising of "TITLE" [working title] (the "Program"), including without limitation, any claim for defamation, slander or invasion of privacy or infringement of rights of publicity. The results and proceeds of such taping, filming, photography and/or recording shall be deemed a "work made for hire," as such term is defined under the copyright laws of the United States, with Producer as the author and exclusive owner thereof.

The foregoing permission and release is given for Producers' benefit and for the benefit of each of its successors, licensees and assigns, and any persons, firms or corporations which shall have the right to promote, distribute and/or exhibit such taping, filming, photography and/or recording, as set forth herein.

I hereby acknowledge that the foregoing consent and release was given for good and valuable consideration, the receipt and sufficiency of which I hereby acknowledge, and that Producer is proceeding with the Program in reliance hereon.

Dated: _____          Signature: _____
                                Name (Printed): _____
                                Address: _____
                                Telephone: _____
                                E-mail: _____

ACCEPTED AND AGREED: YOUR PRODUCTION COMPANY, INC.
By:_____
Name:
Title:

*Note*: Courtesy of Telling Pictures, Inc. Offered as an example only. Please consult with an attorney before entering into any legal agreement.

# _Appendix 2_

# Sample Deal Memo

To:

Re: [title of film]

Dear _____,

This letter confirms our agreement regarding your services for _production company name_ ("Producer") in connection with the film or video production named above (the "Film").

1. Beginning as of _date_, you agree to provide the following services, equipment and/or materials in the production of the Film:

2. Producer agrees to pay you for such services, equipment and/or materials as follows:

3. Provided you fulfill your obligations outlined above, Producer agrees to provide a credit on the completed film as follows:

4. If you do not satisfy your obligations as defined above, your compensation will be reduced proportionately, and your screen credit may be re-determined.

5. Your work as described herein shall be deemed a "work made for hire," as such term is defined under the copyright laws of the United States. As between you and Producer, Producer, its successors and assigns shall be the sole and exclusive owner of all materials produced under this agreement, for any and all purposes whatsoever.

6. You agree to render services as an independent contractor and payment to you will be made without any deductions. You will be responsible for all withholding taxes, other taxes, contributions to Social Security and any other deductions and contributions which may be required by law or by any union. You shall

hold Producer harmless from and indemnify Producer against any claims made against Producer by your failure to adhere to the provisions of this paragraph.

7. Additional terms: _____.

Please indicate your agreement to and acceptance of the foregoing by signing below where indicated.

AGREED TO AND ACCEPTED:

By_____ Date: _____

Address: _____

Phone: _____ E-mail: _____

Social Security or Federal Tax ID #: _____

*Note*: Courtesy of Telling Pictures, Inc. Offered as an example only. Consult with an attorney before entering into any legal agreement.

*Appendix 3*

# The Pink Triangle

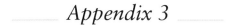

(excerpt of treatment for what would become *Paragraph 175*, based on original research and archival sources)

Thematic questions:

1. The post–World War II gay rights movement adopted the pink triangle as the symbol of gay resistance to homophobic oppression. What is the real story of the people who originally wore that symbol, those who survived and those who did not? Was there a gay Holocaust? If not, how should Nazi treatment of homosexuals be understood?
2. What are the similarities and differences between Nazi treatment of homosexual and of Jews?
3. How could a society in which the first gay rights movement and a significant gay and lesbian subculture emerged turn so quickly to demonizing homosexuals?
4. Given that the Nazi regime was the only one in history that set out to eradicate homosexuality if not homosexuals (one scholar calls Nazi policy "systematic persecution"), what are we to make of the historic and still current assumptions linking Nazism with homosexuality?

**PROLOGUE or TEASE**
VISUAL: *We see a succession of mug shots of gay German men from the 1930s, as we hear a letter being read.*

(ACTOR V/O) "Berlin, West, 12 June 1935. Reverend Reich Bishop! May God grant that this letter comes directly into your hands. May God grant that you . . . do everything in your power to put an end to the horror ... In the last half-year, in Berlin and throughout the Reich, round-ups have been made of homosexuals or people suspected of being homosexual ... For fear of revenge (I have my grounds!) I cannot tell you my name, Reverend Reich Bishop. Heil Hitler!

*VISUAL: Archival footage of Himmler is superimposed over a pan down of a document with Himmler's signature, as we hear an excerpt of Himmler's 1937 Bad Tölz speech to the SS.*

> HIMMLER (ACTOR V/O): "18 February 1937.... We must be clear that if we continue to have this vice in Germany without being able to combat it, then it is all up with Germany and the Germanic world. Unfortunately it is not as easy for us as it was for our forebears.... The homosexual ... was lowered into the marshes ... This was not a punishment but simply the snuffing out of an abnormal life."

*VISUAL: Cut from archival footage of Gestapo arrests to expressionistic shots of dark, deserted streets and alleys.*

> (ACTOR V/O) "One of the first to be arrested was my friend, with whom I had had a relationship since I was 23 ... After four weeks my friend was released ... the effects of his arrest were terrifying. Hair shorn off, totally confused, he was no longer what he was before ... I had to break off all relations with my friend ... We lived like animals in a wild game park, always sensing the hunters."

*VISUAL: HEINZ F. sits at a table in a sunny room. He talks haltingly to his interviewer, whose question we hear.*

**HEINZ F.:** "I could not talk to anybody. Yes, I have never talked to anybody about this. (Q: Would you have liked to talk to somebody?) Perhaps, perhaps to one person. (F. starts crying) You shouldn't have asked that."

*VISUAL: Cut to a close up of PIERRE SEEL who speaks with urgency.*

**PIERRE SEEL:** "If I continue to speak about this, I'll end up hating you. I will not be able to tolerate it. Do you understand that? I won't be able to control myself. Isn't that terrible? Because the hatred that I suffered, that my little body suffered, that my love suffered, that my little Jo suffered, that hatred can transform itself into hate in me. I don't want that. I'm afraid of that. Because if I become a man of hatred, I'm worthless. There is no more love. Only love gives me worth. Hate gives me nothing."

*VISUAL: Interior of the Holocaust Museum in Washington, D.C. where a Pink Triangle is on display.*

## TITLE APPEARS: THE PINK TRIANGLE

### ACT ONE

We join Holocaust scholar KLAUS MÜLLER on a train, en route to a survivor's home. A man with a mission, Müller has sought out homosexual concentration camp survivors and encouraged them to talk about their experiences. He observes that only a few are still alive. He commends the remaining survivors' courage in testifying, and describes their fragile psychological states and general health.

We first meet graduate students STEFAN MICHELER and MORITZ TERFLOTH at the Hamburg Archives, doing research on World War II-era homosexual arrest records. Cut to the picturesque messiness of the room these two young historians share. They speak excitedly about the implications of the material they're uncovering. Both engaged and engaging, they assert that the history of gays before, during, and after the Nazi era is still being discovered. There are no typical victims or simple conclusions, they assure us.

We return to KLAUS MÜLLER, and follow him walking up a flight of stairs. He tells us we're approaching the apartment of "Heinz Heger," the man who saved the only existing Pink Triangle and produced the first memoir of a homosexual concentration camp survivor. Though Heger died some years ago, his lover, who encouraged him to tell his story, has agreed to talk. Müller knocks on an apartment door and greets WALTER KRÖPFEL. Not fully "out," KRÖPFEL is hesitant about cooperating yet committed to telling his lover's story to the world.

*VISUAL: Photos of 1930s Vienna and family photos of the young Heinz Heger.*

On-camera and in voice-over WALTER KRÖPFEL tells how Heger, a middle class Viennese university student, met and fell in love with "Fred," the son of a Nazi official, shortly after Germany annexed Austria in 1938. Heger looked forward to enjoying the rest of his school years and a good career afterwards, and planned to spend his adult life with "Fred."

Cut to GAD BECK (b. 1923) on camera, intercut with photos of himself as a child, his family, and his school. A German Jew and Berliner who would lead a Jewish resistance group during the war, Gad tells how he fell in love with his sports teacher when he was 12 years old. He was showering with the teacher at school, and Gad made the first move. He describe running home and exclaiming, "Mummy, today I had my first man!" After their initial surprise, his family responded positively, and invited him to bring male friends home.

WALTER SCHWARZE was more of a late bloomer, and received no support from his family. He sits in the kitchen of his family home in Leipzig, in the former German Democratic Republic. It is the house in which he was born in 1914. His on-camera account is punctuated with family and archival photos.

WALTER SCHWARZE: "I did not think of sex, I only thought about the psyche, I thought about the man, his development, his anatomy, I admired a man like I admired a beautiful woman. But when somebody had asked me at the time who do you feel drawn to, I could not have answered. To me a woman was something beautiful and a man was perhaps a little more beautiful.

Until one day, I went to the Pavillion at Augustusplatz. It was the most noble pub and I was wearing a snow-white suit, looking very spruce. And there was a young man sitting there, and we looked at each other and somehow looking at each other was a fascination. It was like a magical link that attracted me. And this is what it turned into: there grew, very, very slowly love toward a man, but such a love that when I got home nobody could get through to me. Sometimes both of us were so aroused, that we did not even reach full satisfaction. But as I have said before, love meant more to me than just sexuality."

SCHWARZE describes receiving an engraved silver candlestick from his lover for Christmas, and his father's angry reaction when he discovered the engraved message.

WALTER SCHWARZE: "He said, 'I'll give him a piece of my mind! You have been born a normal person. He seduced you. I'll file a charge against him!' And I said, 'If you do that, you have to file a charge against me as well. Because I want to see him.' "

We meet ANNETTE EICK (b. 1909) at a country inn near her home in the English countryside. She tells us her story on-camera and voice-over.

*VISUAL: Photos of late 1920s lesbian night life in Berlin from the "Eldorado" exhibit, supplemented with Annette's own photo collection.*

At the age of 19, Annette, the daughter of a middle class Jewish family in Berlin, set off to visit her first lesbian nightclub. That night she met and was seduced by a woman named Ditt, who reminded her of Marlene Dietrich. Years later, it was Ditt who would send Annette immigration papers from abroad, enabling her to escape Nazi Germany. But first, Annette immersed herself in Berlin's vibrant lesbian social and literary scene.

**ANNETTE EICK:** "I discovered a bar near Gleisdreieck, the Dorian Gray, and behind the bar was a club, the Monbijou. It was totally pleasant and friendly. There was a piano in the back room and you could dance and chat. I met several writers there . . . and became friends with young girls my age. One of them had a boat. We would go out on the lakes and sleep outside in tents. It was a wonderful life."

*VISUAL: Photos of gay men's bars, parties and events from early 30s Germany.*

On-camera and voice-over HEINZ F. (b. 1905) describes the social world he discovered in Weimar Berlin during his years as a law student.

**HEINZ F.:** The El Dorado, that was a well-known homosexual bar in Berlin. I have only been there once and I did not like it at all. I preferred more stable things, for example dancing. They were fun, at mostly large halls with a bum-bum band, and then hell broke loose and the men danced with each other. I think the largest dance bar for men was at Alexanderplatz. That's where people met and apart from that, oh my God, I also got to know people in the street. You simply let everything take its course.

*VISUAL: Archival stills show the popular look among young gay French men in the late 1930s.*

PIERRE SEEL (b. 1923) begins to tell his story, supplemented with quotes from his book. A native of Alsace, Pierre describes adopting the dandyish "Zazou" style of hair and clothes popular in 1930s France after realizing he was gay when he reached his teens. Robbed of a family heirloom watch by another man, he reported the theft to the local police. Instead of simply recording his complaint, the police grilled him about the site of the theft, a gay bar, and added his name to a "pink list" of known homosexuals.

NARRATOR:   Though upset by his treatment, Pierre was not overly concerned
              about the list. Homosexuality was not illegal in France.

VISUAL: *Scenes from the film "Anders als die Anderen" showing the black-
mail attempt.*

NARRATOR:   But male homosexuality had been illegal in Germany since
              the country united under Kaiser Wilhelm I in 1871. The law
              in question was Paragraph 175. Though not vigorously
              enforced, it offered numerous possibilities for blackmail,
              and blighted the lives of many men.

Filmed in a neutral studio setting, historian CLAUDIA SCHOPPMAN
notes that patriarchal Germany was untroubled by any potential challenges
to the established order lesbians might represent. Though many individual
lesbians would face persecution in the years to come, the state would not target them as a group.

VISUAL: *More archival stills of late 20s–early 30s Berlin lesbians, including
photos of Annette and Francis.*

ANNETTE EICK tells of beginning a relationship with an American woman
named Francis. She adds that Francis was getting counseling at Magnus
Hirschfeld's Institute, and describes the world famous sex research institute.

HEINZ F. recalls meeting Hirschfeld, gives his personal impression of him,
and tells how important he was to the burgeoning gay community in
Germany's large cities.

VISUAL: *Photos of Magnus Hirschfeld or possibly footage of him at the end
of "Anders als die Anderen"*

NARRATOR:   A physician, a sexologist, a homosexual, and a Jew, Magnus
              Hirschfeld was an heroic pioneer for gay rights. At the time,
              homosexuality was increasingly considered an infectious
              disease and form of degeneracy. Hirschfeld popularized the
              idea of homosexuality as a "third sex"—innate, therefore
              both permanent and normal.

Shot in studio, medical historian GÜNTER GRAU voices admiration for
Hirschfeld's courage and achievements, but observes that some of his
research and public speaking on homosexuality were later twisted by Nazi
propagandists and used against gay men.

NARRATOR:   Hirschfeld's theories of homosexuality were not the only
              ones being developed in Weimar Germany.

*Note*: Courtesy of Telling Pictures, Inc.

*Appendix 4*

# *HOWL* Treatment and Script Excerpts

Openings are critical both in treatments and in films. Below is the opening of our documentary treatment, followed by that of the final script from *HOWL*. Notice that while you may be compiling huge amounts of information when you're doing research, by the time you write a treatment (or a script), the task becomes a two-step process of structuring that mass of information into a filmic shape with compelling characters, then paring down and clarifying.

## DOCUMENTARY TREATMENT

### Opening

The film will open on Allen Ginsberg as he reads the still-startling first lines of the poem:

> *I saw the best minds of my generation destroyed by madness, starving, hysterical, naked,*
> *dragging themselves through the negro streets at dawn looking for an angry fix,*

As Ginsberg reads on and the viewer is drawn into the poem's almost hypnotic power, interviews with individuals remembering their first encounters with the poem are interpolated between Ginsberg's own words. Young and old, Ginsberg's friends and readers, the famous and the unknown convey the powerful visceral impact of *Howl*, the result of Ginsberg's ability to make great art out of an uncanny mixture of deeply personal revelation and engaged social criticism. The poem, a personal and professional breakthrough in his life, is the culmination and record of a twelve-year odyssey leading to personal and poetic self-discovery.

**Expelled for Crazy:**

Images of New York in the mid-forties cascade across the screen, its massive buildings and raucous street life, a city at once home to corporate chieftains, jazz musicians, criminals and aimless souls. These give way to scenes of a serene Columbia University campus as underneath we hear Ginsberg's subversive description of his student years:

*who passed through universities with radiant cool eyes hallucinating*
*Arkansas and Blake-light tragedy among the scholars of war*
*who were expelled from the academies for crazy & publishing obscene*
*odes on the windows of the skull . . .*

As the documentary traces Allen Ginsberg's troubled, searching years of poetic apprenticeship, charting his path toward the creation of *Howl*, the New York of Ginsberg's youth will be recreated through vintage black and white archival footage of postwar New York jarringly cut to portray this period of Ginsberg's "dark night of the soul."

Ginsberg was a kind of brilliant social misfit and rebel, a talented young man who was nevertheless at odds with the world around him. Recognized for his intellect by illustrious members of the English faculty such as Lionel Trilling and Mark Van Doren, he was, at the same time, suspended for writing obscenities on his dorm room windows. Just seventeen when he entered Columbia, the still-naïve Ginsberg was a quick mind in search of worldly experience. His father a poet, his mother suffering from insanity, Ginsberg was early on a romantic spirit, plagued with a dark sensibility.

In meeting fellow student and aesthete Lucien Carr, Ginsberg would find the doors to a new world opening before him. Through Carr he would meet his future Beat colleagues, Jack Kerouac, William Burroughs and Neal Cassady and his real education would begin. Misfits and dreamers like Ginsberg himself, they were in search of what they called a "New Vision" for literature, a radically different mode of writing that would buck established literary traditions and conventional social morality.

\* \* \*

**FINAL SHOOTING SCRIPT FOR HOWL**

INT. SIX GALLERY, 1955 - 35MM B&W - NIGHT

A funky experimental art gallery in San Francisco. CLOSE ON ALLEN GINSBERG, 29, entering frame. He squints, puts on his coke-bottle black-framed eye glasses, looks out at an unseen audience, and looks down at several pages of typewritten text. He takes a breath, and begins, reading publicly for the first time:

ALLEN

Howl for Carl Solomon.
I saw the best minds of my generation destroyed by madness, starving hysterical naked,

SUPERIMPOSED TITLE CARD:
1955
San Francisco

ALLEN (CONT'D)
dragging themselves through the negro
streets at dawn looking for an
angry fix,
angelheaded hipsters
burning for the ancient heavenly
connection to the starry dynamo in
the machinery of night,
who poverty and tatters and hollow-eyed
and high sat up smoking in the
supernatural darkness of cold-water
flats floating across the tops of
cities contemplating jazz,

OPENING TITLE SEQUENCE, INTO

TITLE:
In 1955, an unpublished 29-year-old poet
presented his vision to the world as a poem in four parts.
He called it . . .

TITLE:
Howl

TITLE:
The poet was Allen Ginsberg.

TITLE ON BLACK SCREEN:
Composed from interviews,
records of the obscenity trial and HOWL by Allen Ginsberg.

INT. ALLEN'S EAST VILLAGE APARTMENT, SEPTEMBER 1957 -
35MM COLOR - DAY

SUPERIMPOSED TITLE –
1957
NEW YORK CITY

ALLEN, 31, scruffy, sporting a week's growth of beard and rumpled
clothes, sits on a funky couch. His apartment consists of a couch, an overstuffed
chair and a coffee table, a sleeping area with a double bed, a writing table
with an old typewriter, and a kitchen area with a small table. He lights a
cigarette.

ALLEN

Sometimes I feel in command when I'm writing. When I'm in the heat of some
truthful tears, yes. Other times, most of the time, not. Just diddling around,
woodcarving, finding a pretty shape; like most of my poetry. There's only a
few times when I reached a state of complete control. Probably a piece of
"Howl," and one or two moments in other poems.

A tape rolls across a 50's-era reel-to-reel tape recorder. He puts out the
cigarette.

ALLEN (CONT'D)

The beginning of the fear for me was what would my father think of something
that I would write. At the time, writing Howl, I assumed when writing it, it
would not be something that would be published. Because I wouldn't want
my daddy to see what was in there. So, I assumed it wouldn't be published,
therefore I could write anything that I wanted to.

INT. ALLEN'S SAN FRANCISCO APARTMENT, AUGUST, 1955 -
35MM B&W - NIGHT

ALLEN GINSBERG, 29, in a white t-shirt, sits at a desk in a modest San
Francisco apartment. An unmade bed, lots of books, and lights of San
Francisco out the window.

SUPERIMPOSED TITLE:
TWO YEARS EARLIER

WE SEE the blank page, as Allen begins typing with two fingers.
ON THE TYPEWRITER we SEE the words being typed:

I saw the best minds of my generation destroyed by
madness

COLOR ANIMATION SEQUENCE 1.A
MUSIC segues to animation score, as we HEAR ALLEN'S VOICE.

ALLEN (V.O.)
I saw the best minds of my
generation destroyed by madness,
starving hysterical naked,

dragging themselves through the
negro streets at dawn looking for
an angry fix,

angelheaded hipsters
burning for the ancient heavenly
connection to the starry dynamo in
the machinery of night,

who poverty and tatters and hollow
eyed and high sat up smoking in the
supernatural darkness of cold-water
flats floating across the tops of
cities contemplating jazz,

who passed through universities
with radiant cool eyes
hallucinating Arkansas and Blake-
light tragedy among the scholars of
war,

who were expelled from the
academies for crazy & publishing
obscene odes on the windows of the
skull,

who cowered in unshaven rooms in
underwear, burning their money in
wastebaskets and listening to the
Terror through the wall,

who got busted in their pubic
beards returning through Laredo
with a belt of marijuana for New
York,

who ate fire in paint hotels or
drank turpentine in Paradise Alley,
death, or purgatoried their torsos
night after night

with dreams,
with drugs, with waking nightmares,
alcohol and cock and endless balls,

INT. 1950'S COURTROOM - 35MM COLOR - DAY
TITLE CARD:
1957
San Francisco

MOVE DOWN to the face of RALPH McINTOSH's, 60's, a career civil ser-
vant in Eisenhower era attire, seeming a bit out of his depth as he addresses
the court:

MCINTOSH
What I wanted to read into the
record, your Honor, is not very
much, but it is pertinent to our
case.

(NOTE: this description applies to all courtroom scenes.)
The small sunny courtroom is packed with SPECTATORS, standing
room only, all ages, mostly white, but a few black faces. A COURT
STENOGRAPHER is seated before JUDGE CLAYTON HORN, 60's, stern
and no-nonsense. LAWRENCE FERLINGHETTI, late 30's, sits at the
defense table next to JAKE EHRLICH, 50's, a tough civil liberties lawyer,
snappy dresser.

INT. ALLEN'S EAST VILLAGE APARTMENT
Allen being interviewed, as before by an off-screen Reporter.

REPORTER (O.S.)
Why aren't you in San Francisco, at the trial?

ALLEN

The trial's not about me. As much as I have to thank them completely for
my fame. It's the publisher, Lawrence Ferlinghetti . . .

*Note:* Courtesy of Telling Pictures, Inc.

# Filmography

The website of Telling Pictures: http://tellingpictures.com

## NONFICTION FEATURE FILMS

*The Times of Harvey Milk*, written and directed by Rob Epstein, produced by Richard Schmiechen, cinematography by Frances Reid, edited by Deborah Hoffmann and Rob Epstein (1984, New York: The Criterion Collection, 2011), DVD.

*Word Is Out*, directed by Peter Adair, Nancy Adair, Andrew Brown, Rob Epstein, Lucy Massie Phenix, and Veronica Selver, produced by Peter Adair (1977, New York: Oscilloscope Laboratories, 2011), DVD.

*HOWL*, produced, directed, and written by Rob Epstein and Jeffrey Friedman, cinematography by Ed Lachman, ACS, edited by Jake Pushinsky (New York: Oscilloscope Pictures, 2010), DVD.

*Paragraph 175*, produced and directed by Rob Epstein and Jeffrey Friedman, produced by Michael Ehrenzweig and Janet Cole, director of photography Bernd Meiners, edited by Dawn Logsdon, written by Sharon Wood (New York: New Yorker Films, 2000), DVD.

*The Celluloid Closet*, produced and directed by Rob Epstein and Jeffrey Friedman, director of photography Nancy Schreiber, story by Rob Epstein, Jeffrey Friedman, and Sharon Wood based on book by Vito Russo, narration written by Armistead Maupin, edited by Jeffrey Friedman and Arnold Glassman (New York: Sony Pictures Classics, Columbia TriStar Home Video, 1996), DVD.

*Where Are We?*, directed and produced by Jeffrey Friedman and Rob Epstein, cinematography by Jean de Segonzac, edited by Ned Bastille (New York: New Yorker Video, 1991), DVD.

*Common Threads: Stories from the Quilt*, directed and edited by Rob Epstein and Jeffrey Friedman, produced by Bill Couturié, Rob Epstein, and Jeffrey Friedman, written by Rob Epstein, Jeffrey Friedman, and Cindy Ruskin, cinematography by Jean de Segonzac and Dyanna Taylor (New York: HBO Home Video, 1989), DVD.

## TELEVISION PROGRAMS

*Sex in '69: The Sexual Revolution in America*, executive produced by Rob Epstein and Jeffrey Friedman, produced and written by Mark Page, edited by Bill Weber (New York: A&E Television Networks, 2009), DVD.

"The Gold Rush," *Ten Days That Unexpectedly Changed America*, season 1, episode 6, directed by Rob Epstein and Jeffrey Friedman, aired April 11, 2006 (New York: The History Channel, 2006), DVD.

*Crime and Punishment*, seasons 1 and 2, 7 episodes, directed by Rob Epstein and Jeffrey Friedman (Los Angeles: NBC, 2002), VHS, http://www.tv.com/shows/crime-punishment-2002/episodes/.

*Xtreme: Sports to Die For*, directed by Rob Epstein and Jeffrey Friedman, cinematography by John Chater and Robert Elfstrom, edited by Michael Chandler (New York: Home Box Office, 1999), DVD.

# Notes

## INTRODUCTION

1. The medium continues to evolve—from celluloid to video to, at this writing, digital. Throughout this book we use *film* generically, regardless of the medium: a narrative composed of moving images and sounds lasting anywhere from a few minutes to several hours.
2. These are offered only as examples. You should consult with a lawyer before entering into any legal agreement.

## CHAPTER 1

1. *Tarnation*, DVD, produced, written, directed, cinematography, edited by and starring Jonathan Caouette, coeditor Brian A. Kates (2003; New York: Wellspring Media, 2005).
2. *Sherman's March*, DVD, written, directed, cinematography, and edited by Ross McElwee (New York: First Run Features Home Video, 1986); *Nobody's Business*, VHS, produced, directed, and edited by Alan Berliner, cinematography by Phil Abraham, Alan Berliner, and David W. Leitner (1996; Harrington Park, NJ: Milestone Film and Video, 2002); *Complaints of a Dutiful Daughter*, VHS, produced, directed, and written by Deborah Hoffmann, cinematography by Frances Reid, edited by Jennifer Chinlund and Deborah Hoffmann (1994; New York: Women Make Movies, 1994); *Always a Bridesmaid*, VHS, produced, directed, written, cinematography, and edited by Nina Davenport (2000, New York: New Video, 2001).
3. *If a Tree Falls: A Story of the Earth Liberation Front*, DVD, produced and directed by Marshall Curry and Sam Cullman, cinematography by Sam Cullman, written and edited by Matthew Hamachek and Marshall Curry

(2011: New York: Oscilloscope Films, 2011); *Better This World*, DVD, produced and directed by Kelly Duane and Katie Galloway, cinematography by
David Layton, edited by Greg O'Toole (2011; San Francisco: Loteria Films,
2011).

4. Note that hyphenated words count as one word, which matters when you're
trying to boil down your film to 25 words or less.

5. *Pumping Iron*, DVD, directed by George Butler and Robert Fiore, written by
George Butler, cinematography by Robert Fiore, edited by Geof Bartz and
Lawrence Silk (1977; New York: HBO Video, 2003); *Spellbound*, DVD, pro-
duced, directed, and cinematography by Jeffrey Blitz, edited by Yana
Gorskaya (2002; Culver City, CA: Columbia TriStar Home Entertainment,
2003); *Wordplay*, DVD, produced and written by Patrick Creadon and
Christine O'Malley, directed and cinematography by Patrick Creadon, edited
by Douglas Blush. (2006; Santa Monica, CA: IFC Films, distributed by
Genius Products, 2006); *Mad Hot Ballroom*, DVD, produced and directed by
Marilyn Agrelo, written by Amy Sewell, cinematography by Claudia Raschke,
edited by Sabine Krayenbühl (2005; Hollywood, CA: Paramount Pictures,
2005).

6. *Paris Is Burning*, DVD, produced and directed by Jennie Livingston, cinematography by Paul Gibson, edited by Jonathan Oppenheim (1990; Burbank,
CA: Miramax Home Entertainment, 2005).

7. *Hoop Dreams*, DVD, produced by Peter Gilbert, Steve James, and Frederick
Marx, written by Steve James and Frederick Marx, directed by Steve James,
cinematography by Peter Gilbert, edited by William Haugse, Steve James, and
Frederick Marx (1994; Irvington, NY: Criterion Collection, 2005).

8. *Streetwise*, VHS, produced and written by Cheryl McCall, directed and cinematography by Martin Bell, edited by Nancy Baker and Jonathan Oppenheim
(1984; New York: Orion Home Video, 1994).

9. *Dark Days*, DVD, produced, directed and cinematography by Marc Singer,
edited by Melissa Niedich (2000; New York: Palm Pictures, 2001).

10. *Salesman*, DVD, produced by Albert and David Maysles, directed by Albert
and David Maysles and Charlotte Zwerin, cinematography by Albert
Maysles, edited by David Maysles and Charlotte Zwerin (1968; Chicago:
Home Vision Entertainment, 2001); *Welfare*, DVD, produced, directed, and
edited by Frederick Wiseman, cinematography by William Brayne (1975;
Cambridge, MA: Zipporah Films, 1975).

11. Literally "truth film," cinéma vérité requires patience, persistence, flexibility,
the willingness to follow your story wherever it goes, and discipline to refrain
from interfering in the course of the story.

12. In television, nonfiction directors are often referred to as "producers." Don't
ask us why.

13. *Seven Up*, DVD, directed by Paul Almond (1964; New York: First Run
Features, 2004); *7 Plus Seven, 21 Up, 28 Up, 35 Up, 42 Up, 49 Up*, DVD,
directed by Michael Apted (1970; New York: First Run Features, 2004).

14. *An American Family*, DVD, produced by Jacqueline Donnet and Craig Gilbert,
directed by Craig Gilbert, cinematography by Alan Raymond, edited by Ken
Werner (1973; Arlington, VA: PBS Home Video, 2011). See the original series,

which was broadcast on public television. Then see its dramatized HBO reconstruction, *Cinema Verite*. *Cinema Verite*, DVD, directed by Shari Springer Berman and Robert Pulcini (2011; United States: HBO Home Video, 2011).

15. The treatment is the written narrative of your film, the documentary equivalent of a script, written before production. It helps you raise production funds but also gives you an opportunity to develop a structure for your film. See chapter 4 for a detailed discussion of treatments.


## CHAPTER 2

1. *Company: Original Cast Album*, DVD, directed and cinematography by D. A. Pennebaker, cinematography by Richard Leacock (1970; New York: New Video Group, 2000); *Fahrenheit 911*, DVD, produced, directed and written by Michael Moore, edited by Kurt Enghehr, T. Woody Richman, Christopher Seward (2004; Culver City, CA: Columbia TriStar Home Entertainment, 2004).

2. A university library will have more recent research books. Most sell yearly library cards to nonstudents. If no universities are nearby, you can request interlibrary loans from your friendly neighborhood public library—if you live in a community that still has public libraries.

3. See chapter 8, "Legal Headaches: Releases, Rights, and Licenses."

4. Occasionally experts will be both consultant and interviewee, in which case they should be paid. Some writers or independent scholars, i.e., those without tenured positioned in universities, will understandably insist on being paid, though some tenured experts will as well. It may help to remind them that you'll be listing the title of their latest book when they're identified on-camera in the film.

5. See, however, *A Film Unfinished* for a cautionary tale about careless use of propaganda films as archival footage. *A Film Unfinished*, DVD, produced by Itai Ken-Tor and Noemi Schory, directed by Yael Hersonski, cinematography by Itai Neeman, edited by Joelle Alexis (2010; New York: Oscilloscope, 2011).

6. Though we did not use that interview in *The Celluloid Closet*, parts of it did find its way into another film: the 2011 documentary *Vito*, produced and directed by Jeffrey Schwarz, who had served as assistant editor on *The Celluloid Closet*.

7. The *option fee* is the amount paid to a rights holder for the option to license material he controls, in this case for the purposes of making a motion picture. The terms of the option are detailed in the *option agreement*, which specifies the period of time within which you may exercise your option to license the material for an agreed-upon fee. This agreement should be drafted by an attorney.

8. Fourteen years after the film was released, the deferrals were paid in full.


## CHAPTER 3

1. For more on classic three-act structure in fiction film, see Syd Field, *Screenplay: The Foundations of Screenwriting* (New York: Dell, 1994).

2. *Blacks & Jews*, DVD, produced by Alan Snitow, Deborah Kaufman, and Bari Scott, directed by Alan Snitow and Deborah Kaufman, edited by Veronica Selver (1997; San Francisco: California Newsreel, 1997).

3. *Sans Soleil*, DVD, directed, shot, written, and edited by Chris Marker (1983; Irvington, NY: Criterion Collection, 2007); *The Last Bolshevik*, DVD, directed, shot, written, and edited by Chris Marker (1993; Brooklyn, NY: Icarus Films, 1998).

4. *Tokyo Waka*, theatrical release, produced, directed, shot, and edited by John Haptas and Kris Samuelson (Palo Alto, CA: Stylo Films, 2011).

5. *The Five Obstructions*, DVD, directed by Jørgen Leth and Lars von Trier (2003; Port Washington, NY: KOCH Vision, 2004).

6. *The Sorrow and the Pity*, DVD, directed and cowritten by Marcel Ophuls, cowritten and produced by André Harris, produced by Alain de Sedouy, cinematography by Andre Gazut and Jurgen Thieme, edited by Claude Vajda (1969; Harrington Park, NJ: Milestone Film & Video; Chatsworth, CA: Distributed by Image Entertainment, 2001).

7. *Story beats* are plot events that drive the narrative forward.

8. *The Civil War,* DVD, produced and directed by Ken Burns, coproduced by Ric Burns, written by Geoffrey C. Ward, Ric Burns and Ken Burns, cinematography by Ken Burns, Allen Moore, Buddy Squires, edited by Paul Barnes, Bruce Shaw, Tricia Reidy (1990; Boston, MA: PBS Home Video, 1990).

9. DP is director of photography, used here to refer to the camera operator, whatever the format (film, video, or digital).

10. "A Hero Ain't Nothin' but a Sandwich," by Steven Watson, ARTFORUM International, September 1, 2010.

11. The German government changed its position in 2000. As reported by the Associated Press (March 22, 2000), "The number of surviving gay Nazi victims is unknown, but their plight has gained attention since the release this year of a U.S.-made documentary, 'Paragraph 175,' which won awards at the Sundance and Berlin film festivals."

12. *Pink Triangle: Proposal for a One-Hour Documentary*, unpublished, written by Sharon Wood for Telling Pictures and courtesy of Telling Pictures.

13. *Planes, Trains, and Buses*, unpublished proposal written by Rob Epstein and Jeffrey Friedman, and courtesy of Telling Pictures.

## CHAPTER 4

1. Presenting treatments to potential interviewees is a judgment call, and not always appropriate or necessary. In some cases, the proposal may be a better calling card, or with busy experts for instance, a brief written description in an introductory letter may be preferable. If you are making an observational film with people about some aspect of their lives, offering a face-to-face explanation of the film followed by a request to participate may be most effective.

2. Scripts are almost never necessary for documentaries. Treatments, which are not as detailed as scripts for feature films nor bound by scripting format conventions, nonetheless perform similar storytelling functions.

3. Public television requires time for funder credits and, if the program is part of a series, additional time for series intros. In commercial broadcasting, usually less than 75 percent of the program's time slot is actually allocated to content, and the rest for commercials. Often the credits for the film itself are limited to a minute or less.

4. While the Academy of Motion Picture Arts and Science defines a feature film as 40 minutes or longer (http://www.oscars.org/awards/academyawards/rules/index.html), most feature documentaries intended for theatrical release are between 70 and 120 minutes.

5. vo: voice-over

6. *Common Threads* treatment, 1988, written by Rob Epstein, Jeffrey Friedman, and Cindy Ruskin, and courtesy of Telling Pictures.

7. *The Celluloid Closet* treatment, 1993, written by Sharon Wood for Telling Pictures, and courtesy of Telling Pictures.

8. *The Pink Triangle* treatment, 1996, written by Sharon Wood for Telling Pictures, and courtesy of Telling Pictures.

9. © Telling Pictures.

10. © Telling Pictures.

11. NEH awards grants for planning, scripting, and production.

12. Script and screenplay mean essentially the same thing and are interchangeable.

## CHAPTER 5

1. *Company: Original Cast Album*, DVD, directed and cinematography by D. A. Pennebaker, cinematography by Richard Leacock (1970; New York: New Video Group, 2000).

2. *Pumping Iron*, DVD, directed by George Butler and Robert Fiore, written by George Butler, cinematography by Robert Fiore, edited by Geof Bartz and Lawrence Silk (1977; New York: HBO Video, 2003); *Paris Is Burning*, DVD, produced and directed by Jennie Livingston, cinematography by Paul Gibson, edited by Jonathan Oppenheim (1990; Burbank, CA: Miramax Home Entertainment, 2005); *Wordplay*, DVD, produced and written by Patrick Creadon and Christine O'Malley, directed and cinematography by Patrick Creadon, edited by Douglas Blush (2006; Santa Monica, CA: IFC Films, distributed by Genius Products, 2006); *Spellbound*, DVD, produced, directed, and cinematography by Jeffrey Blitz, edited by Yana Gorskaya (2002; Culver City, CA: Columbia TriStar Home Entertainment, 2003).

3. *Harlan County U.S.A.*, DVD, directed and produced by Barbara Kopple, cinematography by Kevin Keating and Hart Perry, edited by Nancy Baker, Mirra Bank, Lora Nays, and Mary Lampson (1973; Irving, NY: Criterion Collection, 2006).

4. *American Dream*, DVD, produced and directed by Barbara Kopple, cinematography by Tom Hurwitz, Mathieu Roberts, and Nesya Shapiro, codirected and edited by Cathy Caplan, Tom Haneke, and Lawrence Silk (1990; Burbank, CA: Miramax Home Entertainment, distributed by Buena Vista Home Entertainment, 1992).

5. Columns are identified with letters (in this case A–G) and rows by numbers (1–121). A cell is identified by referencing a letter and a number. In the sample

budget, for example, the total number of months of the project is indicated in cell A2 (eight months). Don't confuse *row numbers* with *account numbers*: the account number for Director is indicated in column A, row 13, that is, cell A13.

6. High definition (HD) is technically superior to standard definition because it has upwards of five times as many pixels—bits of video information—as standard def. HD's crisper image with much more detail is easily discernable to the naked eye. However, wrinkles and physical imperfections are also significantly more visible.

7. *Sample reel* is a film term, but we're using it here to refer to any short edited presentation, whether on film, video, digital movie file, whatever.

8. While funders will not donate money to write proposals, they do sometimes support the making of sample reels.

9. If you have a particular funder in mind, see what its guidelines say about sample reels. Some state that they watch only a certain number of minutes. Even if your sample reel is longer, you'll know you need to make those first few minutes really count.

## CHAPTER 6

1. *License* is used here to mean an agreement between filmmaker and broadcaster, defining the broadcaster's right to broadcast the film for a limited number of times, in a defined territory and form of transmission (e.g., *7-year domestic cable*; or *10-year German television*). When the license expires the rights generally revert to the filmmaker, who can then try to resell them.

2. While the executive producers of these series most often prefer producers they've worked with before, occasionally new filmmakers are invited into the fold. If the project you're starting fits the guidelines of one of these series, pitch it but first make sure you've secured exclusive rights to your story or cooperation from key characters. After winning numerous festival awards, Gail Dolgin and Vicente Franco's independent documentary *Daughter from Danang* was aired on the PBS series *American Experience*. *Daughter from Danang*, DVD, produced and directed by Gail Dolgin, directed and cinematography by Vicente Franco, edited by Kim Roberts (2002: Waltham, MA: Balcony Releasing, 2002). Gail Dolgin later produced a commissioned episode for *American Experience* on San Francisco's Haight Ashbury neighborhood in the 1960s.

3. http://www.itvs.org/funding.

4. Cutdowns are shorter versions of films made to fit specific television time slots, and may include creating breaks for commercials. Sometimes the filmmaker does the cutdown; other times the broadcaster does, with the filmmaker retaining the right of approval.

5. Everywhere but in the United States, *commissioning editor* refers to a broadcast executive who makes programming decisions.

6. *Super Chief: The Life and Legacy of Earl Warren*, VHS, produced by Bill Jersey and Judith Leonard, directed and cinematography by Bill Jersey, edited by Gary

Weimberg, written by Sharon Wood, Bill Jersey, Judith Leonard, and Gary Weimberg (1989; Berkeley: University of California Extension Center for Media and Independent Learning, 1989). *Super Chief* and *Common Threads* were both nominated for Oscars that year.

## CHAPTER 7

1. *A Midwife's Tale*, DVD, produced and written by Laurie Kahn-Leavitt, directed by Richard P. Rogers, cinematography by Steven Poster and Peter Stein, edited by William A. Anderson and Susan Korda (1997; Boston: American Experience, distributed by PBS Video).
2. This also applies to politicians, famous scientists, writers, athletes, and other public figures.
3. For a fascinating examination of this complex relationship, see Janet Malcolm, *The Journalist and the Murderer* (New York: Knopf, 1990).

## CHAPTER 8

1. See appendix 1 for a sample release—but consult with your own lawyer before using it!
2. See chapter 2, "Researching a Historical Film: *Paragraph 175*," n. 4.
3. With some exceptions, copyright in the United States extends 70 years after the death of the composer. In France, however, copyright extends 70 years plus 8 years to cover composers' presumed lost income during the two world wars. Copyright can be complicated and inconsistent and should be thoroughly researched if you plan to use prerecorded music.
4. See http://fairuse.stanford.edu/Copyright_and_Fair_Use_Overview/chapter9/9-b.html and http://www.centerforsocialmedia.org for more detailed discussions of fair use. In *Color Adjustment*, filmmaker Marlon Riggs's 1992 examination of television portrayals of African Americans, he successfully claimed fair use for the television clips he used. *Color Adjustment*, DVD, produced by Marlon Riggs and Vivian Kleiman, directed and written by Marlon Riggs, cinematography by Rick Butler, edited by Deborah Hoffmann (1991; San Francisco: California Newsreel, 1991).
5. See chapter 2, "Research and Evaluate Your Subject."
6. See chapter 7, "Casting the Nonfiction Film."

## CHAPTER 9

1. Occasionally, someone's credit may be revisited because she has done exemplary work above and beyond the call of duty.
2. The "line" in line producer derives from budget jargon, as in "line item." The line producer is usually responsible for the budget.

3. In cases when the producer also performs the role of the director, he is credited as such. Some television documentaries list producer only, with no director credit.

4. *Pull My Daisy*, VHS, directed and edited by Robert Frank and Alfred Leslie, additional editing by Leon Prochnik, written by Jack Kerouac, starring Allen Ginsberg, Gregory Corso and Larry Rivers. 1959 (2001, New York, Museum of Modern Art Kultur Video, 2001).

5. The terms *coverage* and *cutaway* are cinematic terms that emerged from traditional Hollywood movie making. *B-roll* is a related term that migrated from TV news and refers to all footage other than interviews, reflecting—perhaps unconsciously—the relative insignificance of footage of the news event itself in relation to the on-camera correspondent or talking heads.

6. Often on two-person camera-sound crews who work together regularly, the sound recordist assists with setting up lighting.

7. Before the advent of nonlinear editing, assistant editors worked closely with the editor throughout postproduction. Now assistant editors often work at night or even in a remote location downloading new material or doing other support work the editor needs, with little direct contact. Sadly, this efficiency all but eliminates the possibility for a meaningful mentoring relationship between editor and assistant.

8. *The Waiting Room*, produced by Peter Nicks, William Hirsch, and Linda Davis, directed by Peter Nicks, edited by Lawrence Lerew (web-based social media project: http://www.whatruwaitingfor.com; Oakland, CA, 2011).


## CHAPTER 10

1. *Paragraph 175*, DVD, directed by Rob Epstein and Jeffrey Friedman, produced by Rob Epstein, Jeffrey Friedman, Michael Ehrenzweig, and Janet Cole, written by Sharon Wood, cinematography by Bernd Meiners, edited by Dawn Logsdon (2000; New York: New Yorker Video, 2000).

2. But don't force the "whole sentence" rule at the expense of spontaneity. Some people are incapable of disciplining themselves to answer in full sentences. Others get carried away by the emotional content. If this happens, go with the strong emotion, and figure out how to deal with the incomplete sentences later.


## CHAPTER 11

1. Archive houses generally charge fees for "screeners," the low-resolution material you use while editing, in addition to the footage use fee, which is on a per-second basis and totaled when your film is locked.

2. The Shoah Foundation is a nonprofit foundation established by Steven Spielberg to record oral histories of Jewish survivors of the Holocaust.

3. *Super Chief: The Life and Legacy of Earl Warren*, VHS, produced by Bill Jersey and Judith Leonard, directed and cinematography by Bill Jersey, edited by Gary Weimberg, written by Sharon Wood, Bill Jersey, Judith Leonard, and Gary

Weimberg (1989; Berkeley: University of California Extension Center for Media and Independent Learning, 1989).

4. *The Day after Trinity: J. Robert Oppenheimer & the Atomic Bomb*, DVD, produced, directed, and cinematography by Jon Else, written by Jon Else, David Webb Peoples, and Janet Peoples, edited by David Webb Peoples and Ralph Wikke (1980; Chatsworth, CA: Image Entertainment, 2002).

5. *Sherman's March*, DVD, written, directed, cinematography, and edited by Ross McElwee (New York: First Run Features Home Video, 1986). A longtime filmmaker and member of the French New Wave, Agnès Varda has recently turned to autobiographical films, *The Gleaners & I* (2002) and *The Beaches of Agnes* (2008). Michael Moore and Morgan Spurlock both appeared in their first feature films, *Roger & Me* (1989) and *Super Size Me* (2004) respectively, and have continued to feature prominently in their subsequent films. *The Gleaners & I*, DVD, produced, directed, written, cinematography, and edited by and starring Agnès Varda (2000; New York: Zeitgeist Films, 2000); *The Beaches of Agnès*, DVD, produced, directed, written, and cinematography by and starring Agnès Varda, edited by Baptiste Filloux and Jean-Baptiste Morin (2008; New York: Cinema Guild, Inc., 2008); *Roger & Me*, DVD, produced, directed, written by, and starring Michael Moore, cinematography by Chris Beaver, John Prusak, Kevin Rafferty, and Bruce Schermer, edited by Jennifer Berman and Wendey Stanzler (1989; New York: Warner Bros., 1989); *Super Size Me*, DVD, produced, directed, written by and starring Morgan Spurlock, cinematography by Scott Ambrozy, edited by Stela Georgieva and Julie Bob Lombardi (2004: Los Angeles, Samuel Goldwyn Films, 2004).

6. *Roam Sweet Home*, DVD, produced, directed, and cinematography by Ellen Spiro, written by Allan Gurganus (1996; Austin, TX: Mobilus Media, 1996).

7. *Paragraph 175* (see chap. 10, n. 1).

8. All drafts of *Paragraph 175* narration written by Sharon Wood for the film, and courtesy of Telling Pictures.

9. A *music cue* is a continuous piece of musical score, of whatever length.

10. See the section Music Rights in chapter 8.

11. *The Battle of Algiers*, DVD, directed and written by Gillo Pontecorvo, cowritten by Franco Solinas, music by Ennio Morricone and Gillo Pontecorvo (2004; New York: The Criterion Collection, 2004).

12. The *sound mix* is the process of combining all the edited sound effects, dialogue, and music into one harmonious soundtrack.

13. The use of index cards began for us both early in our careers: for Rob on *Word Is Out*, the first film he worked on, and for Jeffrey in New York editing rooms where he worked as an assistant editor. We both continue to find it useful, no matter how "old school" it may seem.

14. *Mighty Times: The Children's March*, DVD, produced by Robert Hudson, directed by Robert Houston, cinematography by Geoffrey George, edited by Mark Brewer and Sean P. Keenan (2004; Montgomery, AL: Teaching Tolerance, 2005). This film became controversial for failing to distinguish between archival footage and reenactments. More recently, two films directed by James Marsh also made extensive use of reenactments but raised fewer hackles because the reenactments were easier to distinguish from archival

footage; *Man on Wire*, DVD, directed by James Marsh, produced by Simon Chinn, written by and starring Philippe Petit, cinematography by Igor Martinovic, edited by Jinx Godfrey (2008; New York: Magnolia Home Entertainment, 2008); *Project Nim*, theatrical release, directed by James Marsh, produced by Simon Chinn, cinematography by Michael Simmonds, edited by Jinx Godfrey (London: Red Box Films, Passion Pictures, and BBC Films, 2011). See also chapter 2, n. 5.

## CHAPTER 12

1. The commercial broadcast model is a bit more complicated: the broadcaster creates or buys programming, then recoups its investment by selling commercial time to advertisers based on the show's number of viewers, measured by *ratings*. This model makes commercial television less adventurous than other venues and generally not inviting to independent documentaries. Subscriber supported cable networks tend to be more adventurous.
2. Though *Frontline* has a certain stylistic formula that it usually adheres to and most often airs its own in-house productions, in 2012 it broadcast an independent feature documentary, *The Interrupters*. Produced by Steve James and Alex Kotlowitz, directed and cinematography by Steve James, edited by Steve James and Aaron Wickenden (DVD; Boston: PBS Online, 2011)

# Index

# About the Authors

Jeffrey Friedman and Rob Epstein have been making films together since 1987, starting with *Common Threads: Stories from the Quilt*, which won the Oscar for Best Documentary Feature (1989). This was Epstein's second Oscar, having previously won for *The Times of Harvey Milk* (1984). Their other collaborations include *The Celluloid Closet* (directing Emmy, 1996), *Paragraph 175* (Sundance directing award, 2000), *HOWL* (2010), and *Lovelace* (2012).

Epstein is the recipient of the Pioneer Award from the International Documentary Association. He has taught in the graduate film program at NYU's Tisch School for the Arts and is a professor in the Film Program at California College of the Arts (CCA). Friedman has taught in the graduate documentary program at Stanford University and at CCA. They are members of the Directors Guild of America and the Academy of Motion Picture Arts and Sciences, where Epstein has served on the Board of Governors representing the documentary branch. They are partners in Telling Pictures, an international film and television production company based in San Francisco.

Sharon Wood's writing credits include the Academy Award-nominated feature documentaries *Tell the Truth and Run: George Seldes and the American Press* and *Super Chief: The Life and Legacy of Earl Warren*, as well as *Isamu Noguchi: Stones and Paper*. Wood collaborated with Epstein and Friedman on *The Celluloid Closet* and *Paragraph 175*. In recent years, she has written and produced a number of historical documentaries for Lucasfilm, culminating in 2011 with *Manifest Destiny*, a three-part series on U.S. foreign policy.